Oracle Cloud Infrastructure for Solutions Architects

A practical guide to effectively designing
enterprise-grade solutions with OCI services

Prasenjit Sarkar

BIRMINGHAM—MUMBAI

Oracle Cloud Infrastructure for Solutions Architects

Copyright © 2021 Packt Publishing

Group Product Manager: Vijin Boricha
Publishing Product Manager: Vijin Boricha
Senior Editor: Arun Nadar
Content Development Editor: Romy Dias
Technical Editor: Sarvesh Jaywant
Copy Editor: Safis Editing
Project Coordinator: Ajesh Devavaram
Proofreader: Safis Editing
Indexer: Subalakshmi Govindhan
Production Designer: Nilesh Mohite

First published: August 2021
Production reference: 1170821

Published by Packt Publishing Ltd.
Livery Place
35 Livery Street
Birmingham
B3 2PB, UK.

ISBN 978-1-80056-646-0
www.packt.com

Foreword

Cloud computing and related technologies such as Kubernetes, serverless, and microservices have changed the way we communicate and live. Today, we are immersed in a software-defined world, where every company (no matter what their size is) needs to have a well-defined software strategy if they want to survive in a competitive landscape with more agile and adaptive competitors.

With the cloud, we've seen a shift in the business model, where companies have more flexibility and unlimited opportunities to grow their business at scale. Not having to invest in infrastructure – you can consume resources in a pay-as-you-go or subscription-based model – allows you to invest in other areas that help fast time to market at an affordable cost. You can always get into the entrepreneur mindset and build your own start-up with a few bucks. Today, it's much easier than 10 years back. I took that journey a few years ago and built my own start-up with a couple of good friends. We were all passionate about building and fixing things. Today, it's a $2M start-up and growing.

As you can see, the cloud has democratized the industry and has created huge opportunities for businesses across multiple industries. However, we are still at the beginning of this digital revolution. Think of Oracle as an example. For many years, we've been a database company and we are currently in the transition of becoming a platform/service company. We've rebuilt our entire product line to run in the cloud, and that's just the beginning. The future is moving toward cognitive services, and that's where we want to be. I must admit that it's exciting redefining 43 years of history and seeing how progress is coming faster than expected.

Over the last few years, I've spent more time than I recall answering the questions *What is Oracle Cloud Infrastructure (OCI) and why should I care about it?* Until now, we have shared our own experience, the lessons learned, presentations, podcasts, whitepapers, and blogs that provide an overall view of OCI. There is no doubt that with every new technology, there are challenges. That is why books such as this one are so valuable. Prasenjit has charted a course to the cloud-native world in an easy way.

This book is extremely approachable for anyone interested in cloud computing, including undergraduate and graduate students, IT engineers, managers, and curious learners. You will begin with the fundamentals of OCI and as you dive into the chapters, you will advance through more sophisticated cloud-native features. You will discover all the components that are part of developing, deploying, and managing highly secure applications using modern DevOps approaches. With this book, you now have a comprehensive resource on OCI that will help you build and deploy applications in the cloud…and who knows, maybe you'll end up being the next unicorn in the industry.

But let's stop talking and get hands-on…it's time to learn!

Guillermo Ruiz

Head of DevRel, Oracle

P.S. I've known Prasenjit for more than half a decade, and even before knowing him, I was already using some of the technologies he patented. If you come from the early days when VMware became the default technology in data centers, I'm sure you have used vSAN. That's one of the 12 patents that Prasenjit has co-authored.

It was no surprise when he told me he was writing a book about Oracle Cloud, but it really was a surprise when he asked me to write the *Foreword*. I hope you find the book useful.

To the doctors, nurses, public health officials, and first responders who are protecting us from COVID-19.

Contributors

About the author

Prasenjit Sarkar is a Director of Product Management at Cisco for their Emerging Technologies and Incubation venture. His primary focus is on cloud-native application networking and security. He is a seasoned product leader in the cloud-native space. He has vast knowledge of Kubernetes, containers, container and Kubernetes networking, Service Mesh, API management, and serverless computing, among other things.

He is also an author of the virtualization blog Kube-Mesh and has authored six industry-leading books on virtualization, SDN, physical compute, and the cloud, among other topics.

He has 12 granted patents in the US and has authored numerous research articles.

I want to thank my wonderful wife, Debarati, and my super supportive son, Reyan, for giving me the space and support I've needed to write this book. I'd also like to thank the entire Oracle team for encouraging me and giving me the time to complete this journey. The whole Packt editing team has helped this journey immensely, but I'd like to give special thanks to Romy Dias, who edited most of my work, and Vaidehi, for always being on top of the schedule.

About the reviewer

Neetika Jain is a cloud enthusiast with 11 years of experience with various cloud and integration technologies. She is passionate about building useful impactful products. She is an Oracle Cloud certified professional and is currently working as a Principal Product Manager – SaaS Integrations at Oracle-NetSuite. Prior to her current role, she worked as a cloud architect and consultant at various IT firms, including Oracle, IBM, and Wipro. You can reach out to her at LinkedIn.

I would like to thank my family and friends for always supporting me and helping me to achieve my dreams; you are all my motivation.

Table of Contents

3

Designing a Network on Oracle Cloud Infrastructure

4

Compute Choices on Oracle Cloud Infrastructure

5

Understanding Oracle Cloud Infrastructure Storage Options

Section 2: Understanding the Additional Layers of Oracle Cloud Infrastructure

6

Understanding Database Choices on Oracle Cloud Infrastructure

7

Building a Cloud-Native Application on Oracle Cloud Infrastructure

8

Running a Serverless Application on Oracle Cloud Infrastructure

9

Managing Infrastructure as Code on Oracle Cloud Infrastructure

10

Interacting with Oracle Cloud Infrastructure Using the CLI/API/SDK

11

Building a Hybrid Cloud on Oracle Cloud Infrastructure using Oracle Cloud VMware Solution

Other Books You May Enjoy

Index

Preface

With enterprises looking at more agile ways of delivering applications, cloud computing has become the standard way of delivering enterprise applications. Cloud computing, especially the public cloud, is a convenient way to access on-demand infrastructure, platforms, and software, at web scale. This is more convenient for enterprise companies because of their cost modeling as well. With the surge in cloud computing adoption, enterprise companies are cutting down on their capital investment, streamlining service desk operations, scaling up their business, and pushing the security and flexibility to a much higher level so that they can help their customers in different ways and achieve much higher business growth in this ever-changing global market.

When an enterprise deploys its application on a public cloud, predominantly, the public cloud provider owns the whole infrastructure, that is, the hardware, the software that manages the public cloud, and other supporting infrastructure. Enterprise companies access these exclusively over the internet.

Within cloud computing, **Infrastructure as a Service (IaaS)** is the building block of cloud-based IT. IaaS replaces the traditional IT infrastructure that is hosted in customers' on-premises environments. Traditionally, you will find that customers have physical servers that run both traditional operating systems and hypervisor, storage, and network infrastructures.

Oracle Cloud Infrastructure (OCI) is a set of complementary cloud services that enables you to build and run a wide range of applications and services in a highly available hosted environment. OCI offers high-performance compute capabilities (as physical hardware instances) and storage capacity in a flexible overlay virtual network that is securely accessible from your on-premises network.

In this book, you will find step-by-step explanations of key OCI concepts along with practical examples that demonstrate the key use cases of OCI's IaaS model. It follows a hands-on approach where each OCI service is followed by the steps you'd follow to implement it in your infrastructure. By the end of this book, you will have a solid understanding of OCI implementation and use cases.

Who this book is for

This book is for solution developers/architects and cloud engineers who want to learn about building, governing, and managing IaaS using OCI.

What this book covers

Chapter 1, Introduction to Oracle Cloud Infrastructure, introduces OCI and the fundamentals of OCI as second-generation cloud computing to prepare you for a technical deep dive in the forthcoming chapters.

Chapter 2, Understanding Identity and Access Management, includes a technical walkthrough of governing and managing OCI's IAM principles. It will explain how to manage access to your cloud resources.

Chapter 3, Designing a Network on Oracle Cloud Infrastructure, educates you about the setup process of **virtual cloud network** (**VCN**) resources. You will learn about the VCN components and typical scenarios of VCN deployment. This chapter describes various methods of connecting to your OCI instances and configuring network access between on-premises infrastructure and the OCI data center.

Chapter 4, Compute Choices on Oracle Cloud Infrastructure, covers different options of computing nodes. This chapter describes various choices of compute within OCI and how to operate them as per your application's requirements.

Chapter 5, Understanding Oracle Cloud Infrastructure Storage Options, introduces the vast storage options to choose from for your various different storage needs. You will learn how to pick and choose which storage option is best for your application.

Chapter 6, Understanding Database Choices on Oracle Cloud Infrastructure, discusses OCI database operations and how to manage Autonomous Database.

Chapter 7, Building a Cloud-Native Application on Oracle Cloud Infrastructure, discusses modern application development on OCI using OCIR, Cloud Shell, and OKE. You will learn how to create an OCIR repository to store your application container images, how to create a Kubernetes cluster and operate it, how to use Cloud Shell for zero local dependency setup, among other things.

Chapter 8, Running a Serverless Application on Oracle Cloud Infrastructure, demonstrates the use of Oracle Functions as standalone serverless computing as well as integration with OCI Events as event-driven code execution.

Chapter 9, Managing Infrastructure as Code on Oracle Cloud Infrastructure, discusses how to use **Object-Relational Mapping** (**ORM**) to create infrastructure blocks using Terraform code. You will also see how to integrate ORM with GitLab for version control of those Terraform scripts. You will also run a CI/CD pipeline and learn how ORM can help generate Terraform code from existing OCI resources in an account.

Chapter 10, Interacting with Oracle Cloud Infrastructure Using CLI/API/SDK, discusses how OCI introduced a rich set of tools around REST APIs, such as SDKs and the CLI. You will learn how to use these tools to interact with OCI and perform operations on OCI resources.

Chapter 11, Building a Hybrid Cloud on Oracle Cloud Infrastructure using Oracle Cloud VMware Solution, discusses the modern hybrid cloud solution using VMware on OCI. You will learn how to deploy an **Oracle Cloud VMware Solution** (**OCVS**) solution and its connectivity.

To get the most out of this book

This book uses OCI from the console. You will need an OCI account with sufficient credit to run the infrastructure workloads to complete the tasks. A free account can be created from `https://signup.oraclecloud.com/`. If you have an on-premises server infrastructure lab environment available, that can also be used to complete the scenarios covered.

Software/hardware covered in the book	Operating system requirements
An OCI account	Windows, macOS, or Linux
Visual Studio Code	Windows, macOS, or Linux

If you are using the digital version of this book, we advise you to type the code yourself or access the code via the GitHub repository (link available in the next section). Doing so will help you avoid any potential errors related to the copying and pasting of code. It is recommended to execute all hands-on exercises to get the most out of this book and learn effectively.

Download the example code files

We also have other code bundles from our rich catalog of books and videos available at `https://github.com/PacktPublishing/`. Check them out!

Download the color images

We also provide a PDF file that has color images of the screenshots and diagrams used in this book. You can download it here: http://www.packtpub.com/sites/default/files/downloads/9781800566460_ColorImages.pdf.

Conventions used

There are several text conventions used throughout this book.

`Code in text`: Indicates code words in text.

Here is an example: "Now run the $ `oci os ns get` command to check the object storage namespace of your tenancy."

A block of code is set as follows:

```
import oci
config = oci.config.from_file()
identity = oci.identity.IdentityClient (config)
user = identity.get_user(config["user"]).data
print(user)
```

When we wish to draw your attention to a particular part of a code block, the relevant lines or items are set in bold:

```
{
    "data": "intprasenjits"
}
```

Any command-line input or output is written as follows:

```
oci os bucket delete --bucket-name testbucket
```

Bold: Indicates a new term, an important word, or words that you see onscreen. For example, words in menus or dialog boxes appear in the text like this. Here is an example: "Open the navigation menu, select **Compute**, and then select **Instances**."

Get in touch

Feedback from our readers is always welcome.

General feedback: If you have questions about any aspect of this book, email us at customercare@packtpub.com and mention the book title in the subject of your message.

Errata: Although we have taken every care to ensure the accuracy of our content, mistakes do happen. If you have found a mistake in this book, we would be grateful if you would report this to us. Please visit www.packtpub.com/support/errata and fill in the form.

Piracy: If you come across any illegal copies of our works in any form on the internet, we would be grateful if you would provide us with the location address or website name. Please contact us at copyright@packt.com with a link to the material.

If you are interested in becoming an author: If there is a topic that you have expertise in and you are interested in either writing or contributing to a book, please visit authors.packtpub.com.

Share Your Thoughts

Once you've read *Oracle Cloud Infrastructure for Solutions Architects*, we'd love to hear your thoughts! Scan the QR code below to go straight to the Amazon review page for this book and share your feedback.

https://packt.link/r/1800566468

Your review is important to us and the tech community and will help us make sure we're delivering excellent quality content.

Section 1: Core Concepts of Oracle Cloud Infrastructure

In the first part of this book, you will understand the core architectural components with which **Oracle Cloud Infrastructure (OCI)** Generation 2 is built, including IAM, compute, network, and storage. These are the building blocks of OCI.

The following chapters are in this section:

- *Chapter 1, Introduction to Oracle Cloud Infrastructure*
- *Chapter 2, Understanding Identity and Access Management*
- *Chapter 3, Designing a Network on Oracle Cloud Infrastructure*
- *Chapter 4, Compute Choices in Oracle Cloud Infrastructure*
- *Chapter 5, Understanding the Oracle Cloud Infrastructure Storage Options*

1
Introduction to Oracle Cloud Infrastructure

Oracle Cloud Infrastructure (OCI) is an **Infrastructure-as-a-Service (IaaS)** cloud platform that allows consumers to create resources, such as compute instances, databases, networks, containers, functions, and storage, in order to run their applications and workloads. A number of different parties can interact with the OCI cloud. Some of these are actual users, while others are external systems that OCI services communicate with.

So, what do you need from the cloud? Well, an enterprise always looks for scalable, available, and on-demand solutions when they want to move their workload to the cloud. However, for critical enterprise applications, you need no-compromise security and performance guarantees. Remember, you want to offer the same, or better, **Service-Level Agreements (SLAs)** for your business.

In this chapter, we will cover the following topics:

- Regions and **Availability Domains (ADs)**
- Off-box virtualization
- Fault domains

Regions and ADs

OCI has been built using the concept of **regions**. A region is simply a physical location in the world where OCI hosts data centers. In a nutshell, a region is a localized geographic area. Within a region, OCI hosts one or more physical data centers and calls this an **Availability Domain (AD)**.

In this section, we will look at the main concepts of OCI in more detail, such as regions, ADs, and fault domains. Additionally, we will learn how to subscribe to other regions.

A lot of OCI services are regional; for example, **Virtual Cloud Networks (VCNs)**. If you create a VCN, it will span across the AD. Other services are AD-specific, such as compute resources. You can create a compute instance that has access to a specific AD. Additionally, there is a very strong interconnectivity between the ADs within a region and across regions. Within an AD, interconnected traffic is encrypted as well.

As of August 2020, there are 26 regions and 6 interconnected Azure regions that are live. The following map shows the different regions that are currently live across the globe:

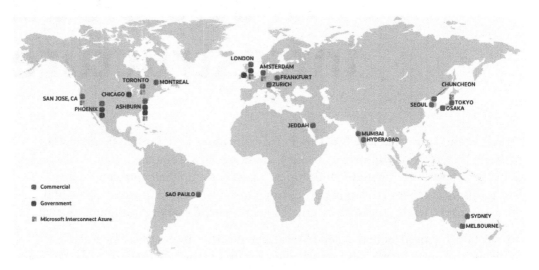

Figure 1.1 – OCI regions

Oracle's strategy is to add new regions around the world in order to give customers local access to its cloud resources. To speed up the process and still provide high availability, OCI has launched one AD region that has three fault domains inside the physical AD. We will discuss fault domains in more detail later in this chapter.

OCI regions are dispersed via vast distances across countries and even continents. When a customer deploys their application, they typically put that application in the region where it is most heavily used. However, there are multiple reasons why someone might choose to put their applications in different regions, such as the following:

- A natural calamity could affect a whole country or continent.
- Data jurisdiction drives data locality requirements.

The following table identifies a region, its identifiers, location, region key, realm key, and the number of ADs within it:

Region Name	Region Identifier	Region Location	Region Key	Realm Key	AD
Australia East (Sydney)	ap-sydney-1	Sydney, Australia	SYD	OC1	1
Australia Southeast (Melbourne)	ap-melbourne-1	Melbourne, Australia	MEL	OC1	1
Brazil East (Sao Paulo)	sa-saopaulo-1	Sãu Paulo, Brazil	GRU	OC1	1
Canada Southeast (Montreal)	ca-montreal-1	Montreal, Canada	YUL	OC1	1
Canada Southeast (Toronto)	ca-toronto-1	Toronto, Canada	YYZ	OC1	1
Germany Central (Frankfurt)	eu-frankfurt-1	Frankfurt, Germany	FRA	OC1	3
India West (Mumbai)	ap-mumbai-1	Mumbai, India	BOM	OC1	1
Japan Central (Osaka)	ap-osaka-1	Osaka, Japan	KIX	OC1	1
Japan East (Tokyo)	ap-tokyo-1	Tokyo, Japan	NRT	OC1	1
Netherlands Northwest (Amsterdam)	eu-amsterdam-1	Amsterdam, Netherlands	AMS	OC1	1
Saudi Arabia West (Jeddah)	me-jeddah-1	Jeddah, Saudi Arabia	JED	OC1	1
South Korea Central (Seoul)	ap-seoul-1	Seoul, South Korea	ICN	OC1	1
Switzerland North (Zurich)	eu-zurich-1	Zurich, Switzerland	ZRH	OC1	
UK South (London)	uk-london-1	London, United Kingdom	LHR	OC1	3
US East (Ashburn)	us-ashburn-1	Ashburn, VA	IAD	OC1	3
US West (Phoenix)	us-phoenix-1	Phoenix, AZ	PHX	OC1	3

> **Important note**
>
> The data in the table is accurate as of August 2020. However, it may not remain accurate as Oracle is rapidly adding new regions and interconnected Azure regions. You can refer to Oracle's public documentation to find the latest information on the available regions at `https://docs.cloud.oracle.com/en-us/iaas/Content/General/Concepts/regions.htm?`.

Managing regions from the OCI console

You can subscribe to any of the commercially available regions from the OCI console. However, doing so requires administrative privileges.

During the sign-up process, OCI will create a **tenancy** and assign a region to you. This is called the **home region**. You cannot change this home region later. However, you can subscribe to other available regions. By doing so, OCI will replicate your identity resources to the new region.

To view the subscribed regions, follow these steps:

1. Log in to the OCI console.
2. Open the **Regions** menu.
3. View the subscribed region(s). Please note that all the region names that appear in the **Regions** menu are the regions that you are subscribed to already.

To subscribe to other regions, perform these steps:

1. Log in to the OCI console.

2.   Open the **Regions** menu, and then click on **Manage Regions**, as highlighted in the following screenshot:

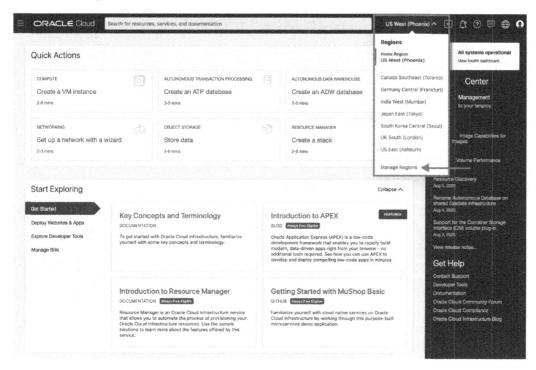

Figure 1.2 – The list of subscribed regions

3. Check which region you want to subscribe to, and then click on **Subscribe**, as shown in the following screenshot:

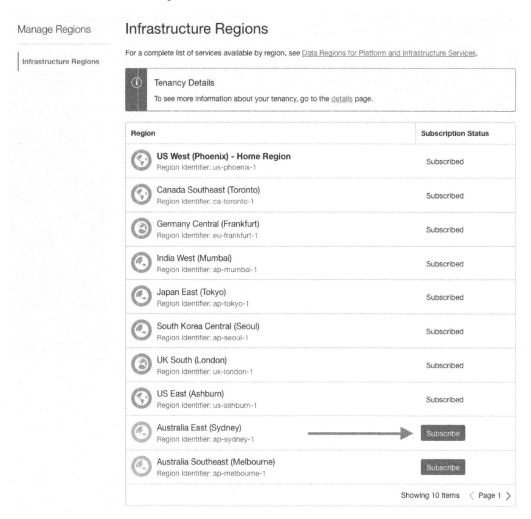

Figure 1.3 – The Infrastructure Regions subscription page

So, you can see how simple it is to subscribe to regions where you want to consume cloud resources.

Logical view of Oracle Cloud Infrastructure components

OCI regions are part of a realm. A **realm** is a logical collection of regions. Realms do not share any data. While regions within a realm can share data via replication, regions in separate realms are completely isolated from each other.

Tenancies

OCI users live in a tenancy, which is a logical grouping for a business customer that contains users, groups, and compartments. A tenancy is based in a home region but can be subscribed to other regions. When a tenancy is subscribed to another region, tenancy data created in the home region is automatically replicated to the subscribed region. Replication of this data is required to call services in that region. Identity data can only be modified in the tenant's home region.

Bootstrapping

A tenancy is created when the accounts service receives a request to create an account entitlement. The account service coordinates with the **Identity and Access Management (IAM)** service to generate several resources, such as the tenancy (root compartment), a default access policy, a user account, and an administrators group to which the user is added.

When the user account is created, a **one-time password (OTP)** is generated. With this password, the user can sign in to the web console and upload the public part of the key pair they generated. Once this is done, the user can start making signed calls to the OCI APIs using **command-line interface (CLI)** tools.

Compartments

Compartments are the logical containers of resources. Compartments typically have a policy attached to them to control access to the resources inside. Compartments can be nested as well. They can span regions, which makes it possible to add, for example, compute instances from different regions to the same compartment and have them guarded by the same policy.

Oracle Cloud Identifiers (OCIDs)

Resources in OCI are identified by unique **Oracle Cloud Identifiers (OCIDs)**. An OCID consists of different parts separated by dots:

```
ocid1.<resource type>.<realm>.[region][.future use].<unique ID>
```

Let's take a look at the various parts that make up the OCID:

- `ocid1`: This indicates the version of the OCID.
- `resource type`: This is the type of resource. For example, a resource can be an instance, a volume, a VCN, a tenancy, a user, or a group.
- `realm`: This indicates which realm the resource is in. For example, all production regions use `ocl`.
- `region`: This indicates where this resource is located.
- `future use`: This is reserved for future use; therefore, you are likely to see a blank space here.
- `unique ID`: This section is the unique portion of the ID. You might notice a different format depending on the type of resource or service.

Here are a couple of examples:

```
ocid1.tenancy.ocl..
aaaaaaaaba3pv6wkcr4jqae5f44n2b2m2yt2j6rx32uzr4h25vqstifsfdsq
ocid1.instance.ocl.phx.
abuw4ljrlsfiqw6vzzxb43vyypt4pkodawglp3wqxjqofakrwvou52gb6s5a
```

OCI's regions are physically divided into ADs, which are named by numbering them (for example, `phx-ad-1`, `phx-ad-2`, and `phx-ad-3`). It is a human tendency to pick the first AD from a given list when it comes to creating a compute instance in an AD. In order to stop you from doing this, OCI gives each tenancy a random set of logical ADs. This is called **AD obfuscation**. Logical AD names look like `SQPR:PHX-AD-1`, and physical AD names look like `phx-ad-1`.

AD, which is nothing but physical data centers, are far away enough that they are completely independent, from a failure perspective, but are close enough to have very low-latency connectivity. Customers get to choose what AD they create resources in, such as compute instances, databases, and more. This selection, however, is randomly mapped to a physical AD to prevent the uneven usage of ADs. In the following screenshot, you can see a logical view of the mapping of ADs in a region and how that maps to a fault domain inside it:

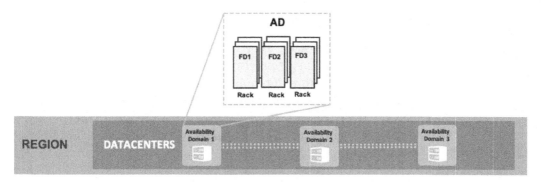

Figure 1.4 – An OCI AD

Inside an AD, OCI runs a highly scalable and high-performance network, which is not oversubscribed. Due to this design of non-oversubscription, there is no noisy neighbor problem. In terms of scalability, this AD can scale up to approximately 1 million ports. Additionally, because of the no noisy neighbors and non-oversubscription network, this AD has predictable low latency and high-speed interconnectivity between hosts that don't traverse more than two hops. In the following logical diagram, you can see a mapping of how the physical network infrastructure connects to the regions:

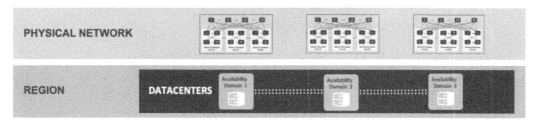

Figure 1.5 – The layout of OCI's physical infrastructure

OCI's first four regions (Phoenix, Ashburn, London, and Frankfurt) consist of three ADs. Each AD is in a physically separate data center.

In these initial regions, Oracle built many foundational services that were specifically tied to a single AD. This is so that there would be no dependencies outside of a single AD. A compute service is the most prominent example of this.

After the first four regions, Oracle shifted their strategy. The majority of customer workloads do not take advantage of ADs for high availability, and, instead, they rely on high availability within an AD and use multiple regions to support disaster recovery. Therefore, OCI adapted to this by launching a larger number of single-AD regions.

Off-box virtualization

If you look at any traditional cloud provider, they are all made up of **Virtual Machines (VMs)** running on top of a hypervisor. A hypervisor's job is to isolate these VMs by sharing the same CPUs, and then capture I/O from each VM to ensure that they are abstracted from the hardware. The VM is, therefore, secure and portable, as it sees only a software-defined network interface card. The hypervisor can inspect all of the packets between the VMs and enable features such as IP whitelists and access control lists. This is depicted in the following diagram:

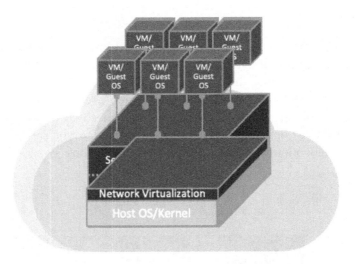

Figure 1.6 – In-kernel network virtualization

In in-kernel virtualization, whenever there is a need to inspect packets to and from a VM, you can put pressure on the host hypervisor by taking away its CPU cycles. This is mainly because this type of hypervisor performs packet switching, encapsulation, and enforces stateful firewall rules. However, this is not the only risk. There is another risk of having noisy neighbors. A noisy neighbor VM monopolizes bandwidth, disk I/O, and CPUs at the expense of its neighbors.

The fundamental purpose of off-box virtualization is that it no longer commits I/O virtualization into the hypervisor but to the network outside of the physical box. You can't reach the control plane that runs the virtual network from the public internet. However, you can create an explicit tunnel to reach the virtual network, which can be monitored, audited, and, in the case of an emergency, switched off as well. This is shown in the following diagram, where you can clearly see that the network I/O virtualization is not being done at the host hypervisor level:

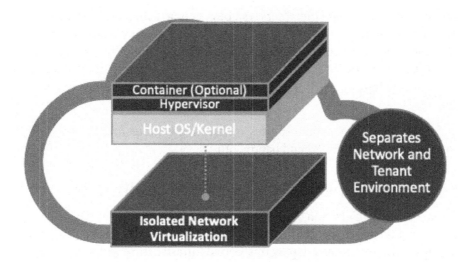

Figure 1.7 – Off-box network virtualization

When you move network virtualization from in-kernel virtualization to off-box virtualization, it results in a dramatic change in performance and improved security posture. This is because you are no longer getting any performance overhead associated with the hypervisor. Another benefit of off-box virtualization is that you retain the flexibility to plug anything into the virtual network. You can perhaps add another bare metal host, an **Non-Volatile Memory Express** (**NVMe**) storage system, a VM, a container, or even an engineered system, such as Exadata. All of them can run on this virtual network and reach each other within two hops. Take a look at the following diagram:

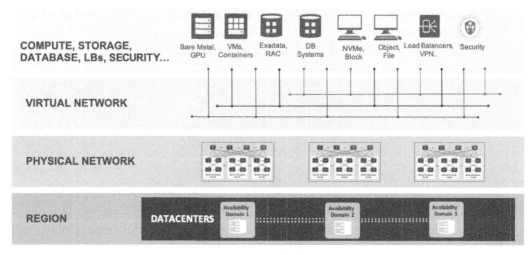

Figure 1.8 – OCI's holistic architecture

OCI's unique offering of bare metal servers doesn't come with a pre-installed operating system or any software. This increases the level of security over traditional virtualization. You can choose any hypervisor that you want to install on top of the OCI bare metal instance and then deploy VMs and install applications on top of that. OCI doesn't offer any access to the memory space of these bare metal instances, allowing complete physical isolation.

As you can see, these bare metal instances are running without any adjacent co-tenants; therefore, they boost both IOPS and bandwidth.

The security benefits of off-box virtualization

Traditional server virtualization comes with an abstraction layer. This layer abstracts the application that is running on the virtualized server from compute resources, storage, and networking hardware. You can deploy this virtual infrastructure without any disruption as it has nothing to do with user experience. You have to virtualize the CPU, main memory, network access, and I/O if you want to take advantage of partitioning, isolation, and hardware independence, which all result from the virtualization process.

Traditional server virtualization in first-generation public cloud infrastructures might come at a cost to the performance overhead and lead to weaker security. The performance overhead is mainly because the hypervisor needs to manage network traffic and I/O for all of the VMs that are running on a host, causing noisy neighbor problems. Additionally, the level of security is inherently weaker because, in traditional virtualization architectures, the hypervisor has complete trust and makes access decisions on behalf of the VM. This means a hostile actor that compromises the hypervisor can easily spread beyond the single hypervisor to other systems in the same cloud. More specifically, the traditional model implies that the attacker of a compromised host/hypervisor can access *any* VCN because the host/hypervisor is trusted to do so. You can see an example of in-kernel network virtualization in the following diagram:

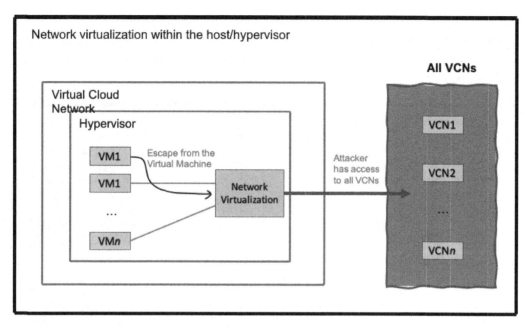

Figure 1.9 – In-kernel virtualization

The security isolation between one customer's compute resources from other customers' compute resources is critical. Fundamentally, OCI designed its security architecture with the assumption that customer-controlled compute resources can be hostile. It has a multi-pronged *defense in-depth* security architecture, which has been designed to minimize the security risks of traditional virtualization.

Oracle's Gen 2 Cloud infrastructure uses a unique approach that eliminates some of the disadvantages of traditional server virtualization. OCI uses off-box network virtualization, which takes network virtualization out of the software stack (hypervisor) and places it in the infrastructure. Oracle uses off-box network virtualization technology in both bare metal instances (for example, physical servers dedicated to a single customer) and VM instances.

Isolated network virtualization limits the attacker surface to *only* a VCN connected to the hypervisor by the control plane. OCI moves the trust from the hypervisor to the isolated network virtualization, which is implemented outside of the hypervisor. In the following diagram, you can see how this is done:

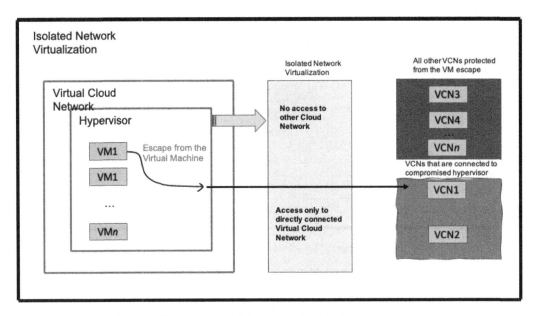

Figure 1.10 – Off-box network virtualization

Bare metal is unique as no hypervisor is needed to run resource virtualization for the network and I/O. Instead, OCI moves network virtualization into the infrastructure, resulting in dramatic performance and security gains. This is because the performance overhead associated with traditional virtualization (in the hypervisor) is eliminated.

OCI effectively uses a coprocessor in the infrastructure, which performs network virtualization, and thus allows the hypervisor to focus on other virtualization tasks. Offloading network virtualization eliminates a number of traditional hypervisor security risks by creating a security boundary between the hypervisor running on one host and the virtual networks of other VMs running on other hosts.

OCI engineered this solution in an attempt to reduce the attack surface and potential damage that an attacker might cause in the case of a compromised hypervisor.

OCI has also implemented additional layers of network isolation, which prevent malicious actors from sending unauthorized network traffic even in the extremely unlikely case of an attacker breaking through the first line of defense that is provided by off-box network virtualization.

For bare metal instances, off-box network virtualization provides a security boundary for the virtual network. This boundary prevents an attacker on a bare metal instance from gaining access to the virtual networks of other bare metal instances and VMs running on other hypervisors.

Fault domains

OCI has achieved high availability by distributing resources to regions and ADs. A region is a geographically distributed area where one or more ADs are placed. During the initial process of OCI deployment, Oracle created multiple ADs inside a single region, such as Ashburn, Phoenix, Frankfurt, and the UK. These ADs are simply physically separated data centers in a single region.

To further segregate one single AD into more physically isolated areas, OCI created fault domains. A fault domain is a group of rack hardware that has been physically isolated within an AD. Each AD contains three fault domains. You can further choose which fault domain to put your cloud resources into, creating a high-availability structure even when you have just one AD within a region. Fault domains provide anti-affinity rules for your cloud resources. The physical hardware in a fault domain also has its own power supplies, which are redundant, to provide a further layer of availability. You can view a high-level logical diagram of the physically separated fault domain structure within a single AD here:

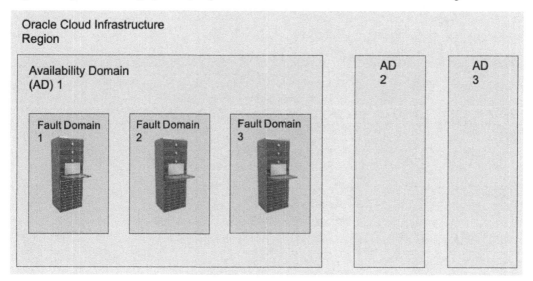

Figure 1.11 – OCI's fault domain

Fault domains are based on the compute racks within an AD. All of the resources that share a rack will also share a fault domain, and resources in different fault domains cannot exist on the same rack. Customers can choose which fault domain they want to create resources in. This selection, similarly to ADs, is randomly mapped to a physical fault domain per tenancy in order to prevent the uneven usage of fault domains.

In *Chapter 4*, *Compute Choices on Oracle Cloud Infrastructure*, we will show you how to choose a fault domain while creating an instance to distribute your workload across physical racks.

Summary

In this chapter, we have learned about the fundamentals of Oracle's second-generation cloud infrastructure and its building blocks, such as regions, ADs, fault domains, and off-box virtualization. These foundational pillars help Oracle to uniquely distinguish itself from other cloud providers in the market.

In the next chapter, we will go through the first and most important block of OCI's foundation, which is IAM. We will examine how OCI creates a logical separation of its resources using compartments, and we will learn how to assign roles and accesses using policy definitions.

2
Understanding Identity and Access Management

The **Oracle Cloud Infrastructure (OCI) Identity and Access Management (IAM)** service gives you full control of your cloud environment, allowing you to decide what type of access you want to give to a group of users. This is done through the unique approach of having an **Oracle Cloud ID (OCID)** assigned to each resource in your cloud environment.

OCI IAM includes its own IAM service, which can be integrated with an existing Microsoft Active Directory configuration using **Active Directory Federation Services (AD FS)**, along with any SAML 2.0-compliant **Identity Provider (IdP)**. OCI also offers integration with the Oracle Identity Cloud Service for those customers who have previously created IAM entities in that service. This integration enables customers to manage their IAM entities within the OCI console, regardless of whether they have been created within OCI or inside the broader Oracle Cloud Identity Service. The concepts and guidance that follow are the same regardless of the approach taken.

IAM uses traditional identity concepts, such as principals, users, groups, and policies, and introduces a new feature, called compartments. IAM Principal is the foundation of OCI IAM; therefore, we will be discussing this first before moving on to other constructs.

In this chapter, we will cover the following topics:

- Principals
- Organizing resources using compartments
- Accessing resources from compartments using policies
- Using instance principals to make a call to the OCI API
- Federating OCI access using a third-party IdP

Principals

Like any other IAM, OCI IAM also has principals. OCI IAM Principal is a method that allows you to interact with OCI resources. There are three types of principals, and we will define each of them next.

The root user

This is the very first user on the OCI account. A root user is persistent in nature and has full administrator access to all of the OCI resources on the account.

IAM users/groups

Users are persistent and can be individual people or applications, whereas a group is a collection of users. You can put the same users into multiple groups. These users enforce the policy of least privilege. Users have no permissions until they are placed in one, or more, groups.

Instance principals

Instance Principals are used when you want to call the OCI API from an instance deployed on top of OCI itself. The main benefit of using an instance principal is that you don't have to store any credentials within the instance to make these API calls. Oracle uses **Dynamic Groups** to implement instance principals and control them by using a policy definition. You can create these dynamic groups based on matching rules that decide who will be part of this group. We will go through this in more detail in the *Using instance principals to make a call to the OCI API* section of this chapter.

A dynamic group is accompanied by the required policies to access OCI resources. You can view a logical diagram of the OCI IAM in the following diagram:

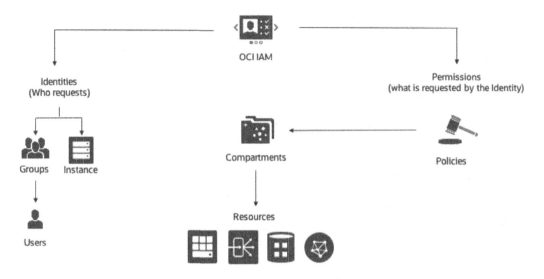

Figure 2.1 – OCI IAM login diagram

We will discuss how instance principals work in greater detail toward the end of this chapter. However, before that, let's look at how IAM works in conjunction with principals.

An IAM service authenticates a principal using three things: the username, the password, and the API signing key.

The username and password

You need to have a password to sign in to the OCI web console. The administrator of a tenancy sets a one-time password for your account. When you first log in, you will be asked to change this password.

The API signing key

You need to have an OCI API signing key when you want to send authenticated calls to the OCI API from the **Software Development Kit/Command Line Interface (SDK/CLI)**. In order to have an API signing key, you need to input an RSA key in PEM format (which has a minimum of 2,048 bits).

Let's go through the process of generating an API signing key.

Generating an API signing key

Using an API key is the standard method for OCI authentication. Every standard authentication mode (the non-standard being Swift/SigV4) uses an API key to make a signed request API call.

You can generate a key pair using `openssl`. The recommended way is to use an encrypted password while creating the key pair. Let's use the following command to generate a password-protected private key:

```
$ openssl genrsa -out private_key.pem -aes128 2048

Generating RSA private key, 2048 bit long modulus
.............................................+++
...........................+++e is 65537 (0x10001)
Enter pass phrase for private_key.pem:
Verifying - Enter pass phrase for private_key.pem:

$ cat private_key.pem
-----BEGIN RSA PRIVATE KEY-----
Proc-Type: 4,ENCRYPTED
DEK-Info: AES-128-CBC,5EE51D737AC6938FC830BF54E86ACB23

mg7euVlAV05QSdAxkjEyE6CubUjpoGSAALYOs5vIvTIamN3W7SjGtKy
WXEcv3pll
........................
cI93H0riOTlEh2cmxp97So9/O/+c3atA05ld6btsqzo9nofiR49cDoR
HSTi2nfDC
0WGOWTiNSuNhzJdE0nc9MzscTQ7fEfNCUuN+56bsjmT45wIooZrpOCq
CGUem8j/q
-----END RSA PRIVATE KEY-----
```

Change the permission of the PEM file so that only you can read the key. To do this, you can use the following command:

```
$ chmod go-rwx private_key.pem
```

Now, let's generate the public key using the following command:

```
$ openssl rsa -pubout -in private_key.pem -out public_key.pem
Enter pass phrase for private_key.pem:
writing RSA key


$ cat public_key.pem
-----BEGIN PUBLIC KEY-----
MIIBIjANBgkqhkiG9w0BAQEFAAOCAQ8AMIIBCgKCAQEAwAR9a/LRwoU
1UoyFdA+5
fIczdM4se6Yvp5dFUz5yJJu757P+3Ro8HA9qxw2UIOwQ6ADqmjQXp0t
RU27SSpJd
............
T/f99DU5pMnBR/QB1jmwN82Rym1Mx2Qx8qPqHl+isXUuiAfrHO9N/Ue
iqASU1JIc
7QIDAQAB
-----END PUBLIC KEY-----
```

The preceding command generates the key. Next, we will verify whether that key matches with the public key.

Verifying whether a private key matches a public key

There may be occasions where you might not be sure if you are using the right private key. The way in which to ensure that a private key matches a certain public key is to check the modulus and see whether it matches. The following is a set of commands that you can use to verify this:

```
$ openssl rsa -noout -modulus -in private_key.pem
Enter pass phrase for private_key.pem:
Modulus=BCB8F82B4CC2F895A34354FEB95E275605753EFB42EC22E97BFD
26522F80D09EE4C8DF932F9C7A014B4E7E2B8E61F1C26F9B64DF953A99CC
D065BE17FD719AC4EF047ECB2F176FF7EF2F1540290D324A6D998E26F14D
244C3A57FD9B453F6AFC7844578DC11C54A64095D18D65CAC3F6AA56F4F4
3D41A5E5ABEEC6CB03388B9C7141BB4F4A0A5B687FD8B84EEB7D289AFE4B
DD353508759489797DB8D304547CD8FF2E68B549198442F2133F63F13858
9337DA959890C1048BB582934379838F84482CE73FB03701B74F8D4B7679
1AA636106082E8FA5D197447F02F8A849D7FF971DE4807E979395EF52125
8C7306890E6F26317C26CFC2BAF033E699DBC969


$ openssl rsa -pubin -in public_key.pem -text -noout
```

```
Public-Key: (2048 bit)
Modulus:
    00:bc:b8:f8:2b:4c:c2:f8:95:a3:43:54:fe:b9:5e:
    27:56:05:75:3e:fb:42:ec:22:e9:7b:fd:26:52:2f:
    80:d0:9e:e4:c8:df:93:2f:9c:7a:01:4b:4e:7e:2b:
    ........
    c9:69
Exponent: 65537 (0x10001)
```

From the preceding output of both commands, you can see that the modulus of both the private and public certificate matches. However, for security reasons, we have omitted the whole output of the public key's modulus.

So, you can see how we use openssl to generate the API signing key. Now, let's generate a fingerprint and upload this to the OCI portal.

Generating a fingerprint

When you upload your public key to the identity control plane, you get a key ID in return:

- The key format is tenantId/userId/fingerprint.
- fingerprint is the fingerprint of your public key.

If you accidentally lose your key ID, then you can generate the fingerprint again using the following command:

```
$ openssl rsa -in public_key.pem -pubout -outform DER | openssl
md5 -c
d4:1d:8c:d9:8f:00:b2:04:e9:80:09:98:ec:f8:42:7e
```

Uploading the public key

To upload the public PEM key, you need to first log in to the OCI console. This is located at https://console.us-phoenix-1.oraclecloud.com/. Follow these steps:

1. Log in to the OCI console.
2. Open the **Profile** menu and click on **User Settings**.
3. Click on **API Keys**.
4. Click on **Add Public Key**.
5. Choose the **PASTE PUBLIC KEYS** option.

6. Copy the public PEM key contents.

7. Paste the copied content of the PEM file into the dialogue box and click on **Add**.

You will notice the fingerprint of the public key is displayed, as shown in the following screenshot:

Figure 2.2 – Uploading the public key

Now you are all set to use a private key and fingerprint to get yourself authenticated using the OCI CLI or other tools that require you to use an OCI API key.

In the next section, let's discuss authorization, which is a type of privilege that you need to operate on OCI resources.

Authorization

You can define what privileges you need in policies and associate them with principals. OCI authorization works on the least privilege-first approach, so you are not allowed to perform any actions.

You can specify one or more policy statements in a human-readable format. These policy statements allow you to gain access to OCI resources and outline what you can do with them.

Let's take a look at a few human-readable policy statements:

```
Allow group <group_name> to <verb> <resource-type> in tenancy
```
```
Allow group <group_name> to <verb> <resource-type> in
compartment <compartment_name> [where <conditions>]
```

You can either attach these policies to a compartment or at the tenancy level.

Organizing resources using compartments

Compartments are a hierarchical construct, that is, they are a logical boundary that groups resources, each of which can exist in only one compartment. This construct can be used for a number of purposes, including the following:

- **IAM**: This is where you can group resources in a compartment for the purpose of restricting access to those resources.

- **Metering/Billing**: You can set limits on resource usage within a compartment; alternatively, you can bill the usage within a compartment to a specific contract.

- **Visibility/Compliance/Audits**: People in a particular department should only know about the resources in their compartment. You can distinguish between resources/usage in this compartment in order to apply specific governance/compliance rules.

- **Mergers/Acquisitions/Changes**: You can move an acquired company's tenancy inside of its new parent company's tenancy; alternatively, you can remove a subsidiary's compartment from the parent tenancy.

When you sign up for OCI, Oracle will create an organization tenancy for you, by default. From an end user perspective, this is your top-level resource container. Because this is something that gets created by OCI, you should not place or create resources at this level. You have full control of all compartments (and the resources within those compartments) within the tenancy.

Just as folders are hierarchical groupings of resources that can have restrictions set upon them, but also be easily amended to meet the changing needs of the organization, so too are compartments—a hierarchical grouping of cloud resources.

Compartments allow customers to set up a logical boundary that groups resources. Each resource in OCI today must exist in only one compartment. Compartments are a hierarchical construct; they allow customers to manage their resources vertically.

Design considerations

There are certain design considerations that you have to keep in your mind while designing the compartment model. We have listed them as follows:

- Every resource resides in a single compartment, but you can share these resources across different compartments as well.

- Aside from OCI Object Storage buckets, you can't reassign a resource to a different compartment after creation.

- You can delete or rename a compartment after creation.

- A compartment can have sub-compartments. This can go down to *six levels deep*.

- If you are the administrator of the account, then you can access this compartment without a policy assigned to it. Otherwise, you need at least one policy assigned to it.

- A sub-compartment inherits access permissions from its parent compartment.

- A policy is always attached to a compartment. So, when you write an IAM policy, you have to specify which compartment you want it to act on.

- We recommend that you use a separate compartment for the network resources of differing security levels and each team/project.

When you sign up for OCI, Oracle creates a default administrators account for your tenancy. It also creates a default group of administrators as well. You cannot delete this group, and there must always be at least one member in it. If you put any other users into this group, then those users will have full access to all of the resources. By default, there will be a policy that is generated and allows administrator groups access to all resources. You cannot delete this policy, nor it can be changed. This is depicted in the following diagram:

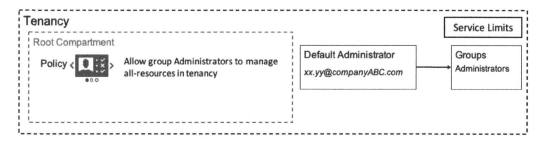

Figure 2.3 – Compartment constructs

So far, you have learned about the design considerations of compartments and have also learned how to organize resources using compartments. In the next section, we will discuss a couple of reference models that will allow you to organize your compartments based on their usage function.

Reference model of compartments

Let's take a look at an ideal reference architecture for model compartments, as depicted in the following screenshot. Here, we have created a **NetworkInfra** compartment, which has all the critical resources, and then we have divided this into another compartment layer:

- **NetworkInfra**: This is a compartment for critical network infrastructure components that are centrally managed by network administrators.

- **Dev, Test, and Prod networks**: This compartment is modeled as a separate compartment and allows you to easily write a policy about who can use the network.

- **Project (A/B/C)**: This compartment is used for the resources used by a particular team or project; it is separated for the purposes of distributed management.

The compartment design model is shown in the following diagram:

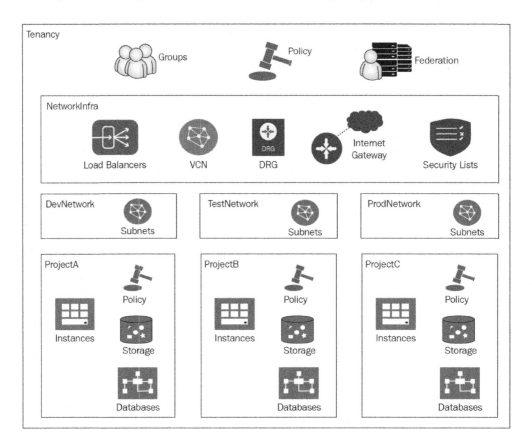

Figure 2.4 – The compartment design model

Ideally, you should use a sharable structure around the compartment for better manageability. Having said that, this will always give us the benefit of managing resources by functions than anything else, for example, having a compartment of shared IT resources and provisioning network and IT infrastructure resources onto that.

Compartment Explorer

Customers need the ability to see their entire enterprise organized by compartment so that they can easily view their allocated resources across their nested compartments. Compartment Explorer allows customers to view all the resources of a particular compartment in the context of a compartment tree. The benefit of this is that you can easily find and manipulate resources across the entire enterprise in a super convenient way. Additionally, you can view all the information of a particular resource, delete a resource, and move that resource between compartments.

The following steps demonstrate how to access the Compartment Explorer.

To check the **Compartment Explorer**, you need to first log in to the OCI console, which is located at `https://console.us-phoenix-1.oraclecloud.com/`:

1. Log in to the OCI console.
2. Open the **Navigation** menu.
3. Under **Governance and Administration**, expand **Governance** and select **Compartment Explorer**.

Here, you can see the Explorer, and from there, you can browse through your resources, as shown in the following screenshot:

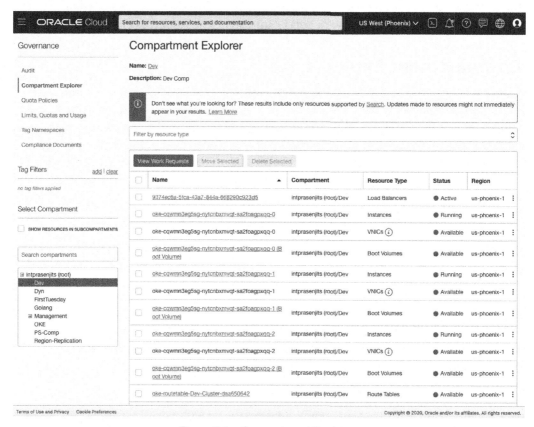

Figure 2.5 – Compartment Explorer

If you want to move a compartment to a different upper-level (that is, parent) compartment, then you need to use **Compartment Explorer**. However, keep in mind that with this movement across different compartments, you are also going to move all of the original compartment's contents to the target compartment.

However, there are restrictions when you move resources to another compartment. They are as follows:

- The name of the compartment cannot be the same when you move one compartment to another compartment. That means the parent and sub-compartment cannot have the same name.

- Additionally, you cannot use the same name in the sub-compartment when you have another sub-compartment with that name already in use. That means two sub-compartments cannot have the same name under a parent compartment.

Take a look at the following steps to learn how to move resources across compartments:

1. Log in to the OCI console.

2. Open the **Navigation** menu.

3. Under **Governance and Administration**, expand **Governance** and select **Compartment Explorer**.

4. Check which resource you want to move.

5. On the right-hand side, there is an **Action** icon, which is three dots. Click on it and select **Move Resource**, as shown in the following screenshot:

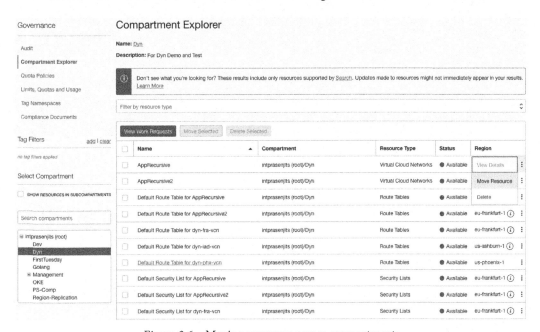

Figure 2.6 – Moving resources across compartments

6. Choose which compartment you want this resource to go to from the list. This is shown in the following screenshot:

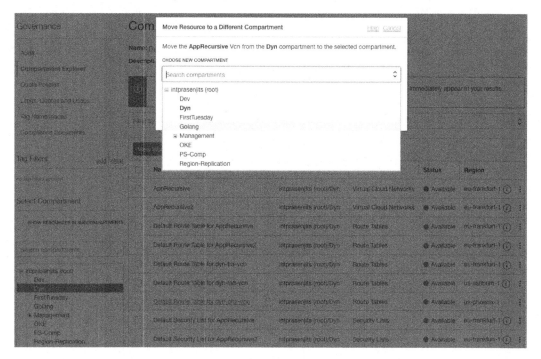

Figure 2.7 – Moving a resource to another compartment

7. Click on **Move Resource**.

In this section, you have learned how to use compartments to organize resources. In the next section, we will discuss how to secure access to the resources in these compartments using policies.

Accessing resources from compartments using a policy

A policy is an entity that specifies which groups can access specific resources, and in which ways. You tend to assign access at the compartment level, which indicates that all users in the group, to which the policy is assigned, can access all the resources within that compartment using the level of permission specified in the policy. Policies can also be applied at the tenancy level, and in such cases, the granted access is available to all compartments within the tenancy.

There are three requirements for a policy: an action or a verb, a resource type, and whether the policy is at the tenancy or compartment level. Furthermore, IAM allows granular policies, so they can be applied at either the aggregate level or the individual resource level. Polices can also include one more condition. Conditions such as *any* or *all* can be used. You can also use multiple conditions using logical *OR* and *AND* operators.

For conditions, you can use *any* or *all* with multiple conditions for a logical *OR* or *AND* operator, respectively.

Let's take a look at the structure of a policy statement:

```
Allow <subject> to <verb> <resource-type> in <location> where
<conditions>
```

Now, let's look at each part of this policy statement in detail.

Verbs

Verbs can be one of the following:

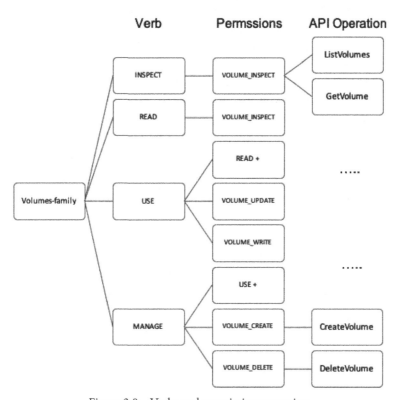

Figure 2.8 – Verbs and permissions mapping

Let's look at each of these verbs and explore what they do:

- **INSPECT**: This gives you the ability to list resources.

- **READ**: The **READ** verb also includes the **INSPECT** verb, but it also adds the ability to get user-specified metadata.

- **USE**: The **USE** verb also includes the **READ** verb, but it also adds the ability to work with existing OCI resources.

- **MANAGE**: This includes all permissions for the resource.

Permissions are the core of authorization. Permissions decide what a user can do on a given resource.

By using verbs, you can essentially simplify the process of granting access to resources. If you are sending an API request, then you need to make sure that you have access to one or more permissions.

All policy statements begin with `allow`. Therefore, by default, all access to resources within compartments is denied unless explicitly allowed by a policy statement. Here, `subject` can be a group, a comma-separated list of groups, or a special construct, such as `any-user`, which encapsulates all users within the tenancy. The `resource-type` element is the more common element of the complete list, and it currently includes approximately 12 different resource types. The `location` field of a policy statement is required, and a location can be a compartment name, a compartment ID, or tenancy, which applies to all of the compartments within the tenancy. Unlike `subject`, a comma-separated list of compartments cannot be used for the `location` field. If the same policy is to be applied to multiple compartments, multiple policy statements must be used.

The following is the list of the available resource types:

- All-resources

- Database-family

- Instance-family

- Cluster-family

- Compute-management-family

- Data-catalog-family

- DNS
- File-family
- Object-family
- Virtual-network-family
- Volume-family

Let's take a look at some of the most common policies using the verbs and resource types that we have just gone through.

In this example, we are allowing network administrators to manage a **Virtual Cloud Network (VCN)**:

```
Allow group NetworkAdmins to manage virtual-network-family in
tenancy
```

In this example, we are allowing the object writers group to write to the OCI Object Storage bucket:

```
Allow group ObjectWriters to manage objects in compartment
ABC where any {request.permission='OBJECT_CREATE', request.
permission='OBJECT_INSPECT'}
```

In this example, we are allowing OCI Block Storage and Object Storage to encrypt and decrypt volumes and buckets using customer/OCI managed keys:

```
Allow service blockstorage, objectstorage-<region_name> to use
keys in compartment ABC
```

Policy inheritance

Policy inheritance occurs between the parent compartment and the child compartment. For example, OCI has a built-in policy for administrators: `allow administrators to manage all-resources in tenancy`. Policy inheritance is responsible for the administrators' group being able to do anything in *any* of the compartments in the tenancy. This is depicted in the following diagram:

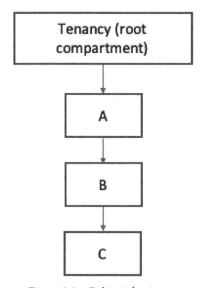

Figure 2.9 – Policy inheritance

Here, you can see that there are three levels of compartments: A, B, and C. Policies that apply to the resources in compartment A also apply to the resources in compartments B and C. If you write this policy, that is, `Allow group NewtworkAdmins to manage virtual-network-family in compartment A`, it will automatically allow the `NetworkAdmins` group to manage VCNs in compartments A, B, and C.

Policy attachment

You can assign a policy to a compartment or tenancy. If you have access to manage policies in the tenancy, and if the policy is attached to your tenancy, then you can change or delete it. Additionally, if you have access to a child compartment, and if anyone attaches a policy to the child compartment, then you can change or delete it.

In this section, we have learned about OCI IAM policies. In the next section, we will discuss the use of these policy statements in a more advanced IAM construct, called instance principals.

Using instance principals to make a call to the OCI API

Instance principals enable OCI instances to make API calls against other OCI services. Using instance principals, you can make OCI calls without the need to configure user credentials or a configuration file.

Even without instance principals, you can still achieve this by storing API credentials on each instance. However, then, you will be faced with a credential rotation problem. Additionally, auditing at the instance level is impossible since credentials are the same across hosts.

So, the ideal solution is to use instance principals that give instances their own identity. The instances that have instance principals configured become a new type of principal, and this is in addition to the existing OCI IAM user/group.

To implement an instance principal, you need to use dynamic groups, which allow policies to be defined on instances. An instance principal implements API authentication at the instance level, removing the need for any credential management.

Authorization is done via dynamic groups. You can create a principal actor by grouping OCI instances, and this is done by using dynamic groups. Here, you specify the permission to that dynamic group using an IAM-level policy. To manage the membership of this dynamic group, you need to define rules called **Matching Rules**. Resources that match the rule criteria become members of the dynamic group.

Take a look at the following diagram to understand how it actually works:

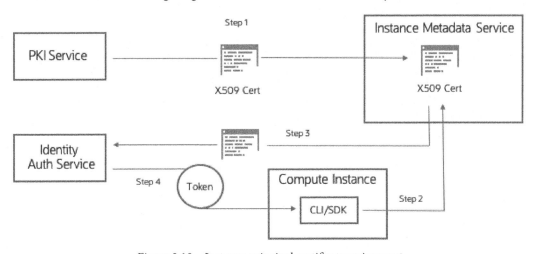

Figure 2.10 – Instance principal certificate assignment

OCI uses an internal **Public Key Infrastructure** (**PKI**) Service, which issues X.509 certificates for every compute instance. OCI's internal **Certificate Authority** (**CA**) assigns these certificates that hold information about the instance, such as the instance ID, compartment ID, and more. The OCI SDK/CLI calls the Instance Metadata Service to get this certificate, and then uses it to call the Identity Auth Service. The auth service then returns a token that this instance uses for calls to OCI APIs.

When you send OCI API calls using that token, the OCI auth service will check whether any matching policy exists. If a match is found, then it will be authorized (using the new *instances* subject).

Creating an instance principal

In this section, we will show you how to create an instance principal where an instance within OCI can access OCI Object Storage without any stored user credentials, private keys, or fingerprints. To create the instance principal, you need to first create a dynamic group. So, let's do that first.

To create a dynamic group, first, log in to the OCI console, which is located at `https://console.us-phoenix-1.oraclecloud.com/`:

1. Log in to the OCI console.
2. Open the **Navigation** menu.
3. Under **Identity**, select **Dynamic Groups**.
4. Click on **Create Dynamic Groups**.
5. Provide a suitable **Name** and **Description**.
6. In the **Matching Rules** section, type in the following:

```
ALL {instance.compartment.id = '<compartment-ocid>'}
```

Change `compartment-ocid` to your compartment OCID, as shown in the following screenshot:

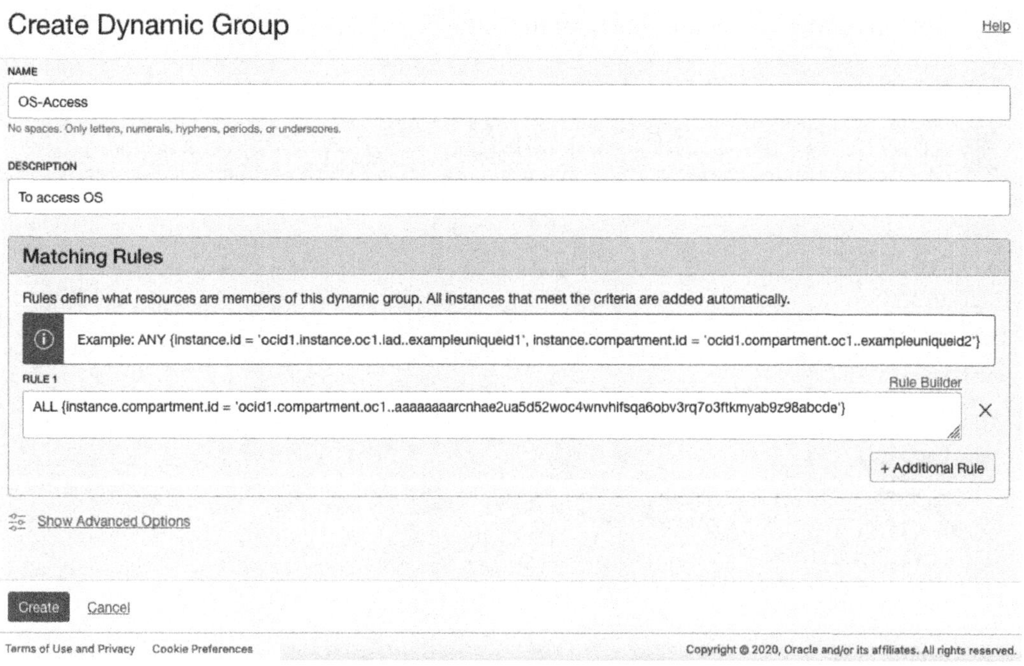

Create Dynamic Group

Help

NAME

OS-Access

No spaces. Only letters, numerals, hyphens, periods, or underscores.

DESCRIPTION

To access OS

Matching Rules

Rules define what resources are members of this dynamic group. All instances that meet the criteria are added automatically.

(i) Example: ANY {instance.id = 'ocid1.instance.oc1.iad..exampleuniqueid1', instance.compartment.id = 'ocid1.compartment.oc1..exampleuniqueid2'}

RULE 1   Rule Builder

ALL {instance.compartment.id = 'ocid1.compartment.oc1..aaaaaaaarcnhae2ua5d52woc4wnvhifsqa6obv3rq7o3ftkmyab9z98abcde'}   ✕

+ Additional Rule

Show Advanced Options

Create   Cancel

Figure 2.11 – Creating a dynamic group

7. Click on **Create**.

8. Within the **Identity** menu, click on **Policies**.

9. Click on **Create Policy**.

10. Provide a suitable **Name** and **Description**.

11. Choose the compartment that you want to attach this policy to.

12. In **Policy Statements**, write the following policies to allow the created dynamic group to manage buckets:

```
Allow dynamic-group OS-Access to manage buckets in
tenancy
```
```
Allow dynamic-group OS-Access to manage objects in
tenancy
```

The preceding details are shown in the following screenshot:

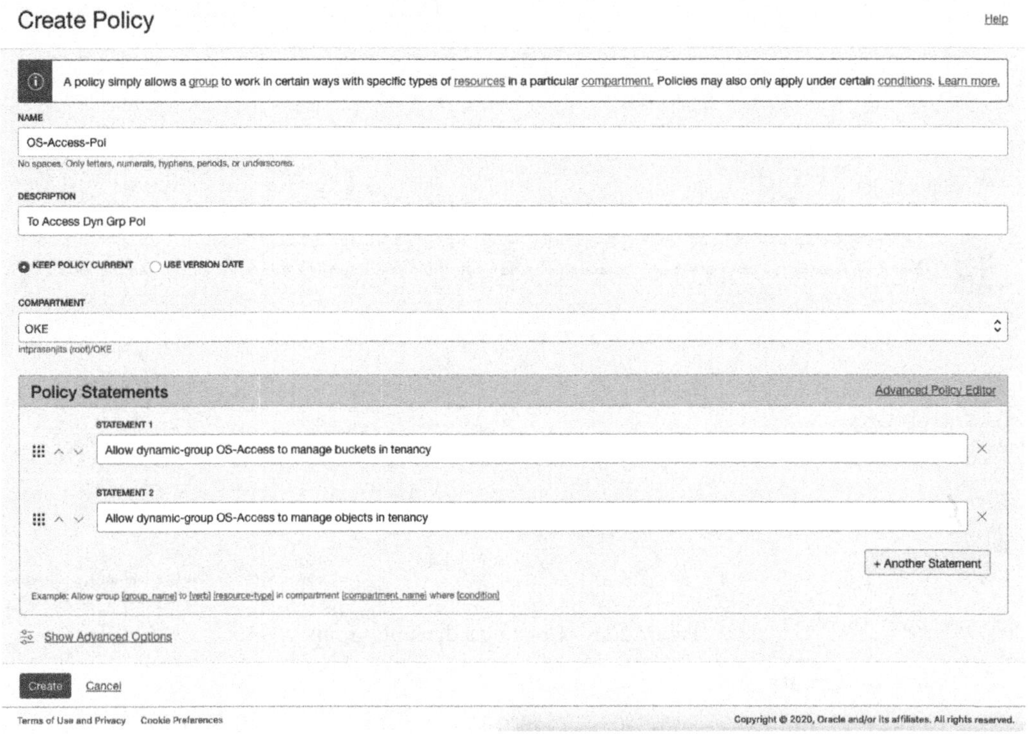

Figure 2.12 – Creating an IAM policy

13. Click on **Create**.

So, you can create a dynamic group and associate policy to give access to certain, or all, instances in a particular compartment. To test it out, you will need to create an instance and install the OCI CLI. We will go through that process in *Chapter 4, Compute Choices on Oracle Cloud Infrastructure*, and *Chapter 10, Interacting with Oracle Cloud Infrastructure Using the CLI/API/SDK*.

Once you install the OCI CLI, run the following command to authenticate against the OCI Object Storage API:

```
$ oci os ns get --auth instance_principal
{
    "data": "intprasenjits"
}
```

In this section, we have learned how to use instance principals to give access to an OCI instance to call the OCI API without carrying any credentials or configuration files. In the next section, we will discuss how you can take IAM further and bring in your own identity using federation concepts.

Federating OCI access using a third-party IdP

OCI's recommendation is to have a federation established between your existing IdP and OCI to manage the OCI console login. As an administrator, it's your responsibility to create the federated trust between your existing IdP and OCI IAM. Once this trust is established, you can create the mapping between on-premises groups and IAM groups. For enterprises that use custom policies for user authentication, a federation is super important.

OCI's best practice is to have a federation administrators' group. This should then be mapped to the federated IdP administrator group. The administrators' group from the federated IdP holds administrative privileges and can manage customer tenancy.

As a best practice, you should have access to the OCI-level tenancy administrator user. If a situation occurs where you break the federation, then you can always use this account to log in to the OCI console and fix the problem.

If you want to leverage **System for Cross-domain Identity Management** (**SCIM**), then you should federate your OCI tenancy with Oracle Identity Cloud Service. Federated users can use API keys and auth tokens, which we described earlier in this chapter, to authenticate against the OCI API and manage these settings from their **User Settings** page.

There are three ways to configure federations:

- Microsoft AD FS
- Any SAML 2.0-compliant IdP
- Oracle Identity Cloud Service

Configuring a federation

To configure a federation, you need to choose which federation you want to integrate your IAM with. In this case, we will assume that it's going to be Microsoft Active Directory. Follow these steps:

1. Log in to the OCI console.
2. Open the **Navigation** menu.
3. Under **Identity**, select **Federation**.
4. Click on **Add Identity Provider**.

5. Provide a suitable **Name** and **Description**.

6. Choose **Microsoft Active Directory Federation Service (AD FS)**.

7. Upload the FederationMetadata.xml document from your AD FS server, as shown in the following screenshot:

Figure 2.13 – Adding an IdP

8. Click on **Continue**.

9. At this stage, you will need to create a mapping of Active Directory resources with an IAM resource.

10. Under **Identity Provider Group**, provide the Active Directory group name. This is case-sensitive as well.

11. Choose the IAM group from the list under **OCI Group**.

12. Once your mapping is done, click on **Create**.

So, you have learned how to not only rely on OCI IAM constructs but bring in your own IdP as well, by integrating your IdP with OCI IAM using a federation.

Summary

In this chapter, you learned about the security fundamentals of OCI. We explained principals, compartments, policies, instance principals, and federation concepts. You have learned how to design a logical separation of resources within compartments, and then give access to certain users to perform operations on certain resources within a compartment. You have also looked at how to implement IAM to give native security access to OCI instances, so it can call the OCI API without the need to store local user credentials.

In the next chapter, we will learn how OCI implements virtual networking and some of the advanced scenarios that depict how you can connect your on-premises data center to a regional OCI data center.

3
Designing a Network on Oracle Cloud Infrastructure

Virtual Cloud Networks (**VCNs**) provide network connectivity to all of the OCI services with a fully customizable private network in the Oracle cloud. Customers can bring in their own IP segment and assign it to their VCN. They can create their own network topology using guided workflows to connect the virtual subnets with virtual routers and set up firewall rules. Optionally, the VCN can be configured to have internet access and/or VPN access. Customers can then launch bare metal or virtual machine instances in VCN subnets, and the instances will be assigned a private IP address from that same subnet. Optionally, the public IP address can also be assigned to an instance that will enable communication with the internet. Customers can also use security lists (groups of firewall rules) that can be associated with an instance. A VCN is regional and does not span multiple regions. A VCN can span across multiple **Availability Domains** (**ADs**).

In this chapter, we're going to cover the following main topics:

- High-level architecture of VCNs
- VCN components
- Connectivity choices
- Load balancing
- VCN flow logs

High level architecture of VCNs

VCNs are implemented by creating an overlay network over the substrate network that is hosting the physical hosts. The overlay network provides address space separation between the substrate network and the customer visible VCN and provides the ability to place and migrate networking resources independent of the underlying network topology.

With the overlay network, a network packet-encapsulation mechanism is used to hide the overlay IP addresses from the underlying substrate network. The packet encapsulation is implemented on a smart chip installed on the compute nodes as well as the physical nodes that act as the border between the substrate network and the external networks.

The overlay network configuration is computed centrally by the VCN Control Plane and the packet-routing rules are delivered to the compute nodes. The compute nodes use these rules to determine the encapsulation and decapsulation action to take on every packet that goes in or out. In addition, these rules are also delivered to network devices that perform encapsulation and decapsulation.

However, as the fundamentals of a software-defined network, core network devices, including switches and routers, are unaware of the overlay networking. They do not directly participate in the rule's discovery, propagation, or management and they do not implement encapsulation and decapsulation.

OCI uses the subnet to divide each VCN for further segmentation. You can either specify these subnets as AD specific or they can be *regional* (*recommended*). If you create a subnet that is AD specific, then that address space doesn't span other ADs. However, if you specify that the subnet is regional, then that address space will span across all the available ADs in that region. As you can imagine, subnets are nothing but a contiguous range of IPs. You cannot have overlapping IP addresses in the subnets.

This is what has been illustrated in the following diagram, where you can see that subnets A-C are AD specific, whereas subnet D spans the entire region:

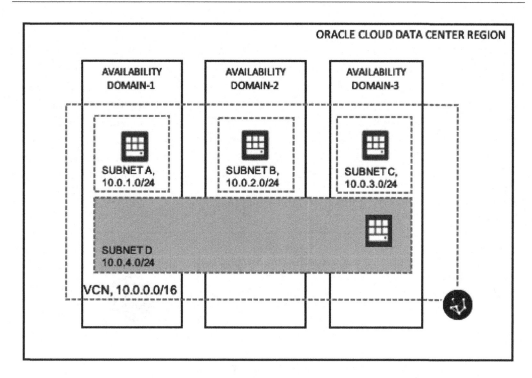

Figure 3.1 – VCN architecture

VCN components

While consuming Oracle Cloud in any form, the first thing that you need to set up is your virtual network through a VCN. This section details the various different components of the VCN.

Subnets

Instances placed onto each subnet automatically receive their network configuration from the subnet itself. However, you also have the option of manually specifying your own private IP address from the address scope of the subnet.

You can specify a subnet as either a private subnet or a public subnet:

- **Private subnet** – All the instances in this subnet get private IP addresses assigned to their attached VNICs.

- **Public subnet** – Instances placed in the public subnet not only get a public IP address assigned for external communication, but they also get a private IP address assigned to their VNICs.

VNIC

A **VNIC**, or **virtual network interface card**, is attached to an instance, and allows the instance to connect to a subnet within a VCN. This VNIC is responsible for deciding how this instance is going to be connected to the VCN and how it will send and receive network traffic. Whenever you launch an instance, the OCI Control Plane creates and attaches a VNIC to the instance. It is called a primary VNIC and you cannot remove this from the instance. Once this instance is up and running, you have the flexibility to add a secondary VNIC. You have the ability to remove it later, if you wish. You can assign this VNIC to the primary NIC's subnet, or you can choose a different subnet to attach it to.

You can see an illustration of this in the following diagram:

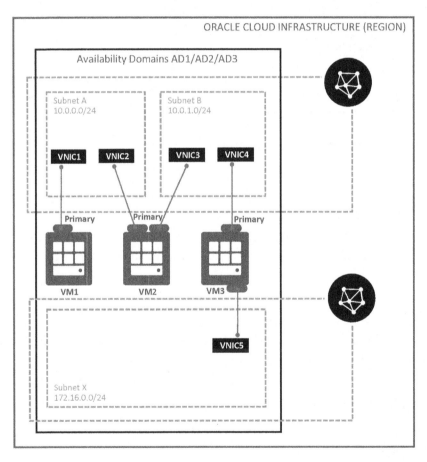

Figure 3.2 – Multiple-VNIC architecture

In the preceding diagram, you can see that you can have secondary VNICs connected to different subnets for different purposes.

Multiple VNICs on bare metal instances

Every bare metal instance has two physical NICs. But in the case of first-generation (X5 servers) bare metal hosts, only one physical NIC is active, but in second-generation (X7 servers) bare metal hosts, both of the NIC cards are set to active and each card provides 25 Gbps bandwidth. The first NIC card is set as the primary NIC card.

Each guest VM can get one or more secondary VNICs in the bring-your-own-hypervisor use case. In the case of **single-root I/O virtualization (SR-IOV)**, **virtual functions (VFs)** are used by the hypervisor to provide network access to the guest VMs, where each VF can be configured with the VLAN tag and MAC address of a secondary VNIC. You can see an illustration of this in the following diagram:

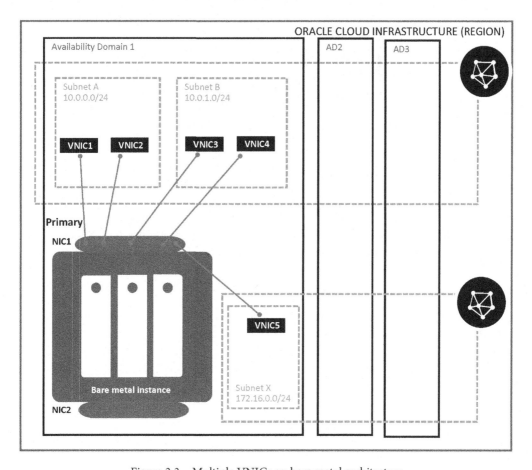

Figure 3.3 – Multiple VNICs on bare metal architecture

In the preceding diagram, you can see that a bare metal instance can have multiple VNICs and that you can use them to connect to different subnets for different purposes.

Private IP address

Each instance that you launch in OCI will have a private IP address assigned to it from the subnet IP pool. Although this is the primary IP address that gets assigned to it upon its creation, you can assign additional private IP addresses too. If you assign this instance to a public subnet and have specified that it should fetch a public IP address too, then the same NIC card will get a public IP address.

The following diagram shows an illustration of this:

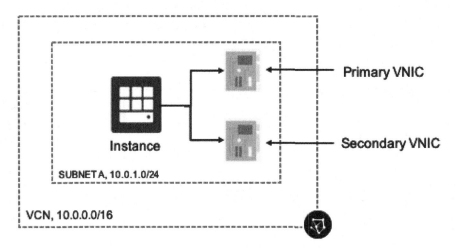

Figure 3.4 – Private IP on VNICs

In the preceding diagram, you can see that this instance has two different NIC cards and how its private IP address is assigned using the subnet's DHCP pool.

Private IP as a route target

The private IP address of an instance can be a route target as well. The main use case of this arrangement is when there needs to be a firewall appliance in the middle where every packet is checked at transit. So, your subnet's default gateway would be the private IP address of an instance other than the IP address of the internet gateway. You can see an illustration of this in the following diagram:

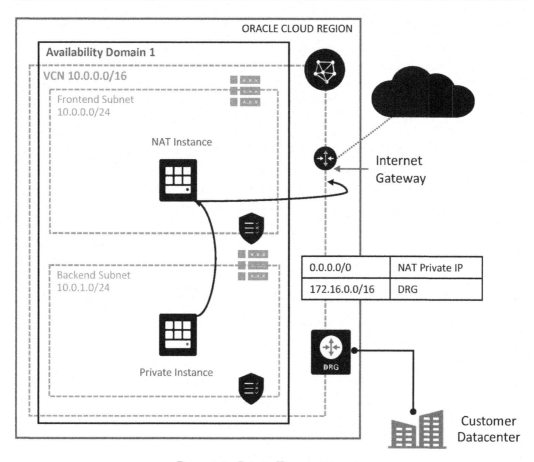

Figure 3.5 – Private IP as route target

In the preceding diagram, you can see how you can use a route rule to use a private IP as a route target and have a man in the middle to scan all of the traffic that an instance sends.

Public IP address

A public IP address is an IPv4 address that you provide to an instance so that it is reachable over the internet. You can add multiple public IP addresses to an instance's VNIC. You have the option to choose between the two available types of public IP address:

- **Ephemeral**: An ephemeral IP address is only available until the instance stays up. It's temporary in nature.

- **Reserved**: A reserved IP address is persistent in nature and doesn't depend on the instance life cycle. You also have the flexibility to detach this IP address from one instance and assign it to another instance.

Internet gateway

You need an internet gateway if you want your instances to talk to the internet and also receive traffic from internet. By design, you are bound to have only one internet gateway per VCN. To make this internet gateway effective, you need to assign a route rule to the route table of the VCN stating that this internet gateway is the next hop for the VCN. However, if you use a VCN creation wizard, then this will be done for you by the VCN itself.

You can see an illustration of this in the following diagram:

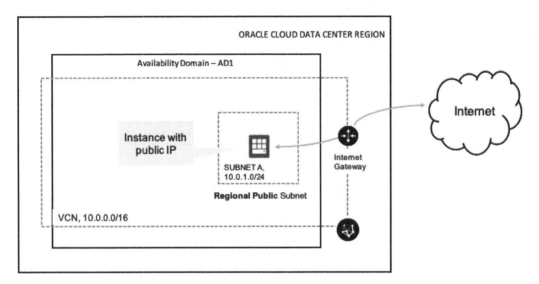

Figure 3.6 – Internet gateway

In the preceding diagram, you can see how you can use an internet gateway to send all traffic out of the VCN to the internet.

Route table

A route table, as the name suggests, is a table that has route rules, which allow instances to send traffic out of the VCN and handle traffic coming in to the VCN. You can either specify a destination CIDR or you can choose to have a private IP address as the next hop for the route rule.

At the time of the creation of the VCN, OCI will add a default route table, but you can choose to edit it any time afterwards. However, a route table is not always used, and one of the scenarios where it is not used is when the destination IP address falls under the same VCN CIDR block.

The route table must be updated to reflect your different VCN component types, such as NAT gateways, service gateways, or dynamic routing gateways.

You can see an illustration of the route table in the following diagram:

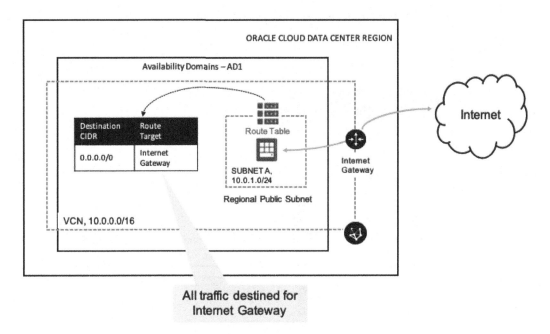

Figure 3.7 – Route table

In the preceding diagram, you can see how you should write a route rule in the route table to make the routing work. In this case, every packet for the outside world will be sent to the internet gateway and then it will go out to the internet.

Dynamic routing gateway

When you want to have connectivity for your on-premises equipment, you need to use the **dynamic routing gateway** (**DRG**). To establish the connectivity, you can either choose to connect to it via an IPSec VPN connection or a FastConnect connection. When you create a DRG and add it to the VCN, you need to create a new route rule to send the on-premises traffic via the DRG and not the internet gateway. You can only have one DRG per VCN.

You can see an illustration of this in the following diagram:

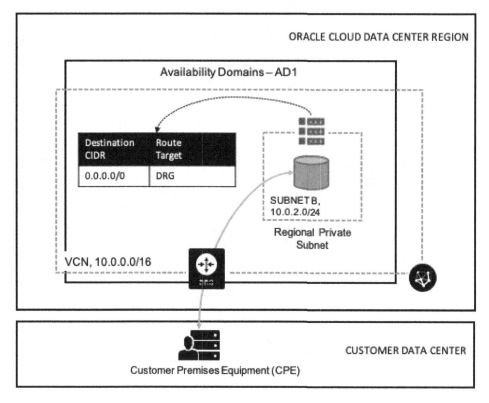

Figure 3.8 – Dynamic routing gateway

In the preceding diagram, you can see how you can use a DRG to connect your on-premises environment to the OCI. This is the same component that will be used to make either a VPN or FastConnect connection. We will discuss this later in the section on connectivity choice.

NAT gateway

Think about a use case where you don't want to expose your instance to the internet, but still want to download patches or updates. In this scenario, you just need to use an NAT gateway. It can only allow one-directional traffic—namely, outbound internet access. So, all of those private subnet instances can access the internet via an NAT gateway without having a public IP address.

You can see an illustration of this concept in the following diagram:

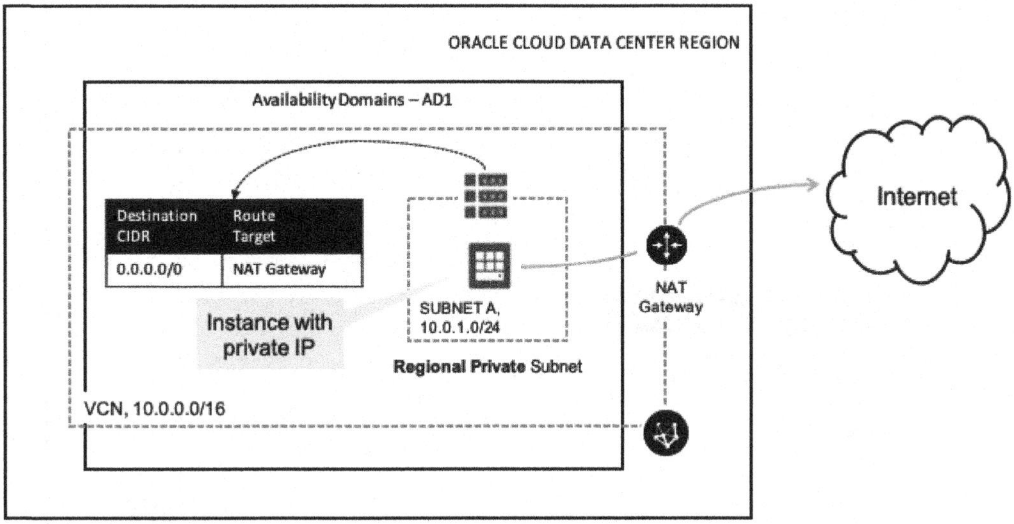

Figure 3.9 – NAT gateway

In the preceding diagram, you can see how you can use a NAT gateway to connect an instance that is connected to a private subnet to the public internet.

Service gateway

When you want to access public OCI resources, such as OCI object storage, you typically access them via the public internet. However, if you don't want your traffic to go through the public internet, you can use a **service gateway**.

This way, whenever your instance wants to access the object storage, it will never traverse the traffic through the internet, but will use the OCI network fabric to reach it instead.

You can see an illustration of the service gateway in the following diagram:

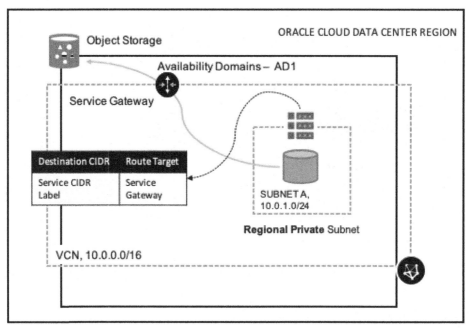

Figure 3.10 – Service gateway

In the preceding diagram, you can see how you can use a service gateway to access OCI object storage without getting routed via the public internet.

Local peering (within region)

So far, you have seen that VCNs are disjointed components in OCI. This means that one VCN cannot access other VCN resources. However, in cases where you want to run shared services within a region and host them separately on a different VCN, you need to use a **local peering gateway** (**LPG**) to connect these two VCNs together. This way, your shared resources will be available to the connected VCN's resources via a private IP address. As we are connecting two peering gateways to form the connection of two VCNs, you essentially cannot have overlapping IP addresses in the VCNs.

An illustration of the LPG is as follows:

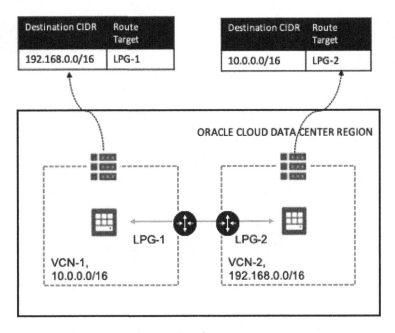

Figure 3.11 – Local peering gateway

In the preceding diagram, you can see how you can connect two VCNs in a single OCI region using a local peering gateway in the middle. You must also have proper routing rules in place to send the packets to the neighbor VCN via a particular LPG.

Remote peering (across region)

A local peering gateway is used to connect VCNs within a region inside a single tenancy. This means that it doesn't work when it comes to connecting VCNs across region, or perhaps connecting two different tenancies within a region as well. For this reason, you need to use a **remote peering gateway** (**RPG**). An RPG is implemented with a DRG. Similar to LPGs, you cannot have overlapping IP addresses for RPGs.

You can see an illustration of remote peering in the following diagram:

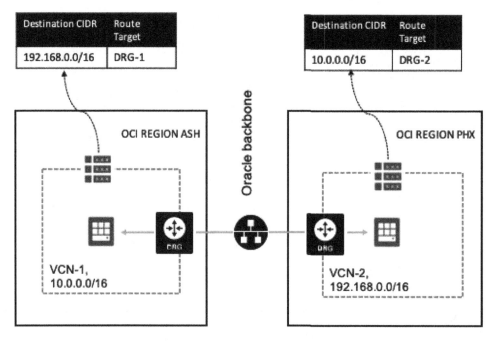

Figure 3.12 – Remote peering gateway

In the preceding diagram, you can see how you can use the Oracle backbone network to establish a remote peering connection between two VCNs located in two different regions.

Security list

The firewall is the most important function inside the virtual networking layer. OCI implements this in the form of security lists and the rules contained within them. A security list is associated with a subnet, which means that the rules will be applied to all the instances within a given subnet. You can create and assign a security list after the VCN creation if this is not done by default using the VCN creation wizard.

You can allow or restrict traffic to and from instances either within a VCN or outside of a VCN. Your specified security rules can either be stateful or stateless.

An illustration of this is as follows:

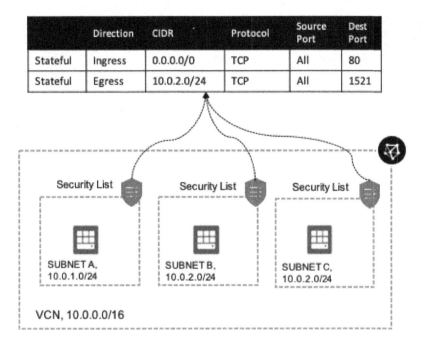

	Direction	CIDR	Protocol	Source Port	Dest Port
Stateful	Ingress	0.0.0.0/0	TCP	All	80
Stateful	Egress	10.0.2.0/24	TCP	All	1521

Figure 3.13 – Security list

In the preceding diagram, you can see how security rules are formed inside a security list that is connected to individual subnets.

Network security group

Using security lists and rules means that you have to choose resources and group them together to form a resource group on which you want to apply the security rules, as security rules are applied at subnet level. To minimize this scope, you need to use a **network security group** (**NSG**). Using an NSG, you can group resources that have similar characteristics.

You can apply NSG rules to a group of resources. Currently, this can be either compute instances, load balancers, or database instances.

As NSGs are nothing but resource groupings, you can use them as source or destination when writing firewall rules. Oracle's recommendation is to use the NSGs, which helps you to separate your application's security posture from the VCN.

You can see an illustration of this in the following diagram:

		Direction	CIDR	Protocol	Source Port	Dest Port
NSG-A	Stateful	Ingress	0.0.0.0/0	TCP	All	80
NSG-B	Stateful	Ingress	0.0.0.0/0	TCP	All	22

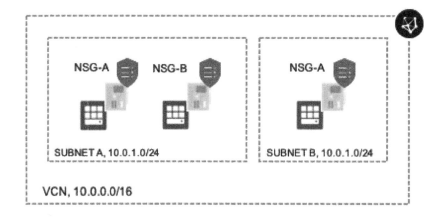

Figure 3.14 – NSG

The best solution is to use security lists and NSGs together; this way, you can create a union of the rules from both security lists and network security groups.

You can see an illustration of this combination in the following diagram:

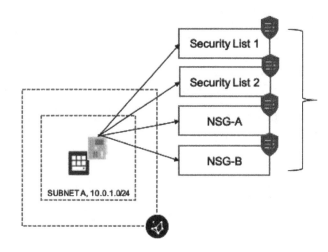

Figure 3.15 – Combination of an NSG and a security list

In the preceding diagram, you can see how we group together the NSG and security list to create a more robust security solution.

Stateful and stateless security rules

Stateful security rules track the response of the incoming traffic and whether matches allow the traffic, irrespective of the egress rules. The same approach is adopted when traffic is outbound from instances.

You can see an illustration of this in the following diagram:

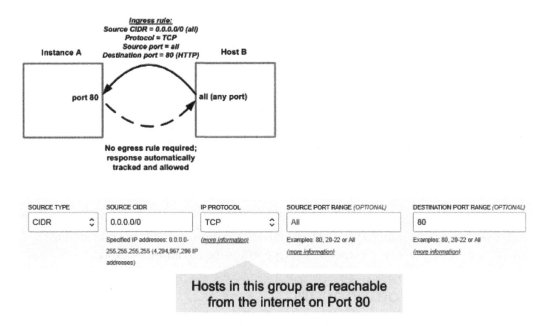

Figure 3.16 – Stateful security rules

Stateless rules work in exactly the opposite way. This means that without a matching egress rule, ingress traffic is not processed. So your incoming traffic will not be allowed by default if you don't have a matching egress rule.

Two main use cases of stateless rules are *load balancing* and *big data*. You can see an illustration of stateless rules in the following diagram:

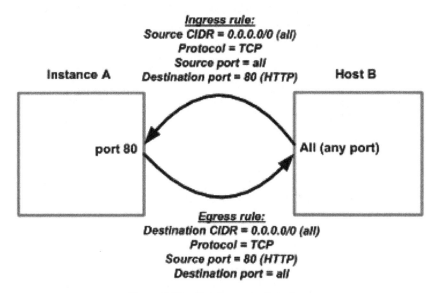

Figure 3.17 – Stateless security rules

In the preceding diagram, you can see that instance A only responds to an incoming packet at port 80, but host B responds to any port for the incoming requests.

Default VCN components

VCN has some default components:

- Default route table
- Default security list
- Default set of DHCP options

These components can't be removed, but their contents can be changed.

As the name implies, the DHCP options' job is to provide an IP addresses to the instances automatically at the time of boot up. An illustration of the default VCN components is shown in the following diagram:

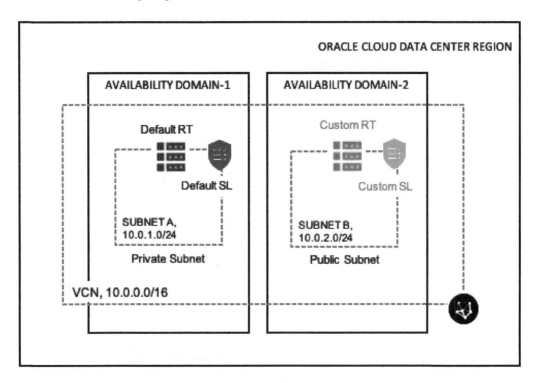

Figure 3.18 – Default VCN components

The preceding diagram shows the default components of the VCN that get created as part of the VCN creation wizard.

Reviewing the VCN components

Let's take a recap of the VCN components and their details:

- Subnets can have one route table and multiple security lists associated with it. The route table defines what can be routed out of the VCN.

- Private subnets are recommended to have individual route tables to control the flow of traffic outside of the VCN.

- All hosts within a VCN can route to all other hosts in a VCN (no local route rule required).

- Security lists manage connectivity from north to south (incoming/outgoing VCN traffic) and from east to west (internal VCN traffic between multiple subnets).

- OCI follows a white list model (you must manually specify white listed traffic flows); by default, things are locked down.

- Instances cannot communicate with other instances in the same subnet until you permit them to!

- Oracle's recommendation is to use the NSGs, which help you to separate your application's security posture from the VCN.

You can see a top-down view of the VCN in the following diagram:

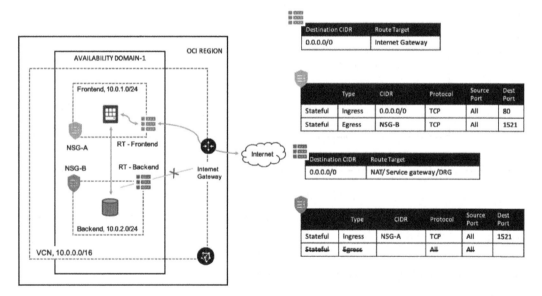

Figure 3.19 – Overall VCN

In the preceding picture, you can see a top-down view of the VCN, showing all of the aforementioned components. It is connected to the internet by an internet gateway, it has the VCN construct and the subnet, a security list, and rules, as well as routing rules. In the next section, you will see how you can connect to OCI.

Connection choices

You need to connect to OCI resources in order to access them. Without a connection in place, you cannot connect to your workloads. You can connect to your OCI resources to and from OCI using three different methods:

- Connecting through the public internet
- Connecting through a VPN
- Connecting through FastConnect

Let's discuss them in the next section.

Connecting through the public internet

Accessing an OCI instance over the public internet is pretty straightforward, and doesn't require much effort. You would need to go through the following steps to get internet access to and from the OCI instance:

1. Create a VCN and provide a CIDR range.
2. Create an internet gateway.
3. Create a route rule with traffic to the internet gateway (for all IP addresses, `0.0.0.0/0`).
4. Create security list rules to allow traffic.
5. Make sure that each instance's firewall allows the traffic as well.
6. Create a public subnet within a specific AD with the route table and security list.
7. Create an instance with a public IP address within the subnet.

You can see an illustration of this in the following diagram:

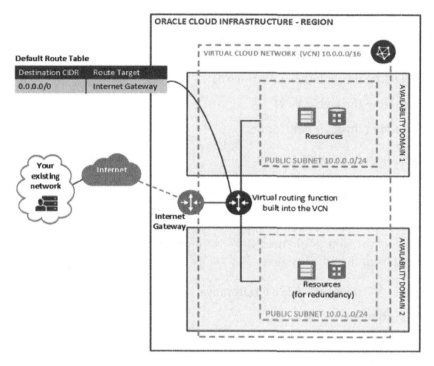

Figure 3.20 – Accessing an OCI instance over the public internet

VCN has provided a workflow to make this simple. Let's go through the following steps to create an OCI instance and access it over the public internet:

1. Sign in to the OCI console.
2. Open the navigation menu. Click **Networking** and select **Virtual Cloud Networks**.
3. Check whether you are in the correct compartment in the **Compartment** list.
4. Click **Start VCN Wizard**.
5. Select **VCN with Internet Connectivity**, and then click **Start VCN Wizard**.

    Enter the values for the following fields:

    -**VCN Name**

    -**Compartment**

    -**VCN CIDR Block**

    -**Public Subnet CIDR Block**

    -**Private Subnet CIDR Block**

Accept the default values for any other fields. You can see a sample screenshot of the workflow in the following image:

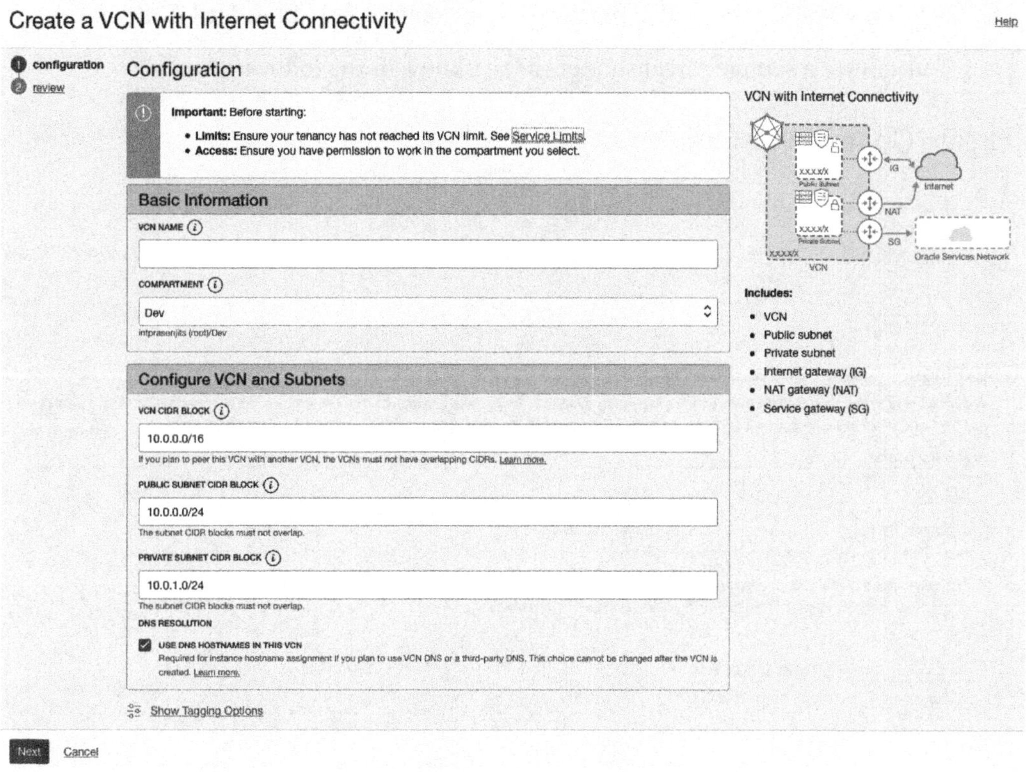

Figure 3.21 – VCN creation wizard

6. Click **Next**.

7. Click **Create** to start the workflow.

8. Once the process completes, click **View Virtual Cloud Network**.

In this section, you learned how to create a VCN and its components. Let's create an instance now and connect it to this newly created VCN.

Creating an OCI compute instance on a public subnet

To create an OCI compute instance in the private subnet, follow these steps:

1. In the console, under the navigation menu, select **Compute**, and then select **Instances**.

2. Click **Create Instance**.

3. Provide a name for the instance—for example, `Private-Instance`.

4. Select the compartment in which you want to place the instance.

5. Choose the availability domain in which you want to place the instance.

6. Select a shape for the virtual machine—for example, **VM.Standard.E3.Flex**.

    You can see a sample screenshot of the workflow in the following image:

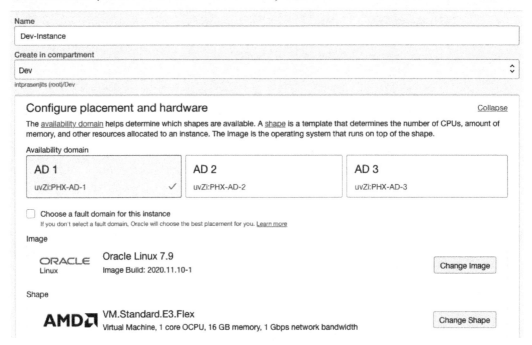

Figure 3.22 – Instance creation wizard

7. In the **Configure networking** section, select the compartment in which your VCN resides. This is typically the same compartment in which you're deploying this VM.

8. Select the **VCN**.

9. Select the compartment in which the subnet resides.

10. Select the public subnet.

11. Make sure that you have the **Assign a public IPv4 address** option selected.

12. In the **Add SSH keys** section, let OCI create an SSH key pair, and save the private key and the public key. You can see a sample screenshot of the workflow in the following image:

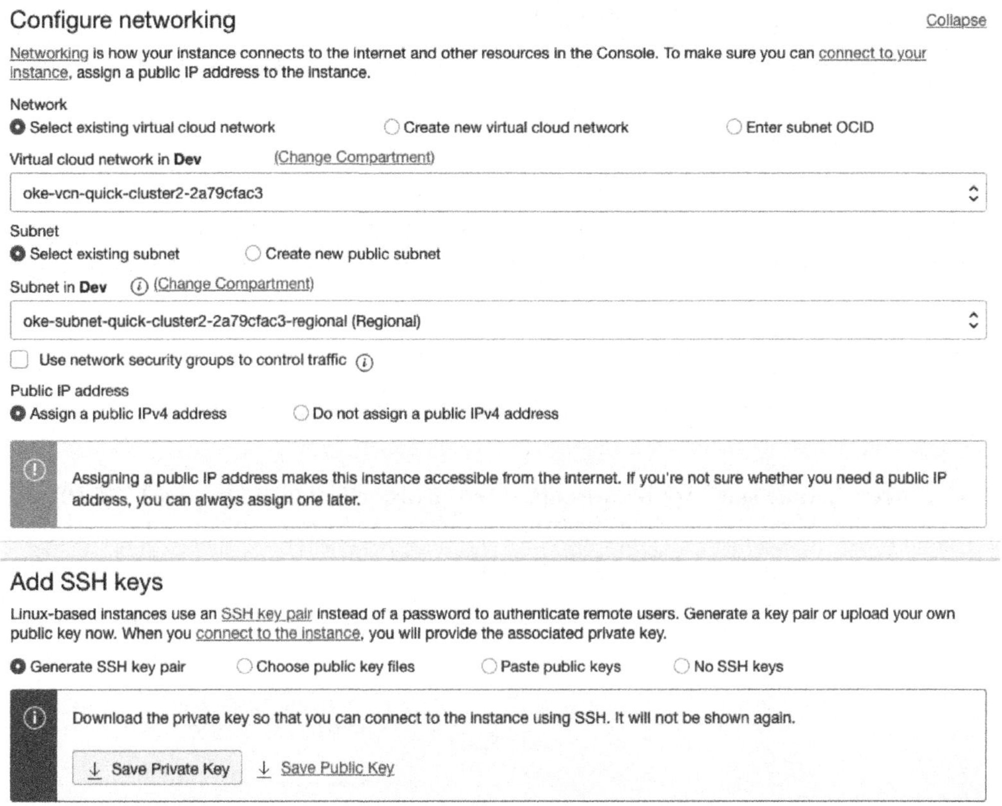

Configure networking

Collapse

Networking is how your instance connects to the internet and other resources in the Console. To make sure you can connect to your instance, assign a public IP address to the instance.

Network

⦿ Select existing virtual cloud network   ○ Create new virtual cloud network   ○ Enter subnet OCID

Virtual cloud network in **Dev**   (Change Compartment)

oke-vcn-quick-cluster2-2a79cfac3	⌄

Subnet

⦿ Select existing subnet   ○ Create new public subnet

Subnet in **Dev**   ⓘ (Change Compartment)

oke-subnet-quick-cluster2-2a79cfac3-regional (Regional)	⌄

☐ Use network security groups to control traffic ⓘ

Public IP address

⦿ Assign a public IPv4 address   ○ Do not assign a public IPv4 address

> ⓘ   Assigning a public IP address makes this instance accessible from the internet. If you're not sure whether you need a public IP address, you can always assign one later.

Add SSH keys

Linux-based instances use an SSH key pair instead of a password to authenticate remote users. Generate a key pair or upload your own public key now. When you connect to the instance, you will provide the associated private key.

⦿ Generate SSH key pair   ○ Choose public key files   ○ Paste public keys   ○ No SSH keys

> ⓘ   Download the private key so that you can connect to the instance using SSH. It will not be shown again.
>
> [↓ Save Private Key]   ↓ Save Public Key

Figure 3.23 – Instance creation wizard with networking selection

13. Click **Create**.

After the instance is created, the instance details page is displayed. Make a note of the public IP address.

In this section, you learned how to create an instance and connect it to the public-facing VCN subnet. Now let's look at how you can connect to it using SSH.

Accessing the instance over the public internet

From your local environment, use SSH to connect to the OCI instance on the public subnet (for example, JumpHost). But before you do this, you need to fix the SSH private key file permission. Let's run the following command to fix the permission and then connect to it using SSH:

```
chmod 400 <path-of-the-ssh-private-key>
ssh -i <path-of-the-ssh-private-key> opc@<public-ip-address>
```

Connecting through a VPN

The OCI VPN provides you with an IPsec connection to create a secure network tunnel between OCI and the on-premises environment. However, the network speed is not guaranteed, and depends on the internet speed.

As an architecture with no single point of failure, OCI provides you with physically redundant VPN tunnels. This means that OCI will provision two different circuits in two different availability domains (where more than one AD exists) to make a redundant VPN connection.

There are some limitations to this as well.

- An OCI VPN can only support an **Internet Key Exchange v1 (IKEv1)** using a shared secret.

- Currently, only static routes are supported (**Border Gateway Protocol (BGP)** is not supported). When you create an IPsec connection, static routes are added. These static routes can't be modified after an IPsec connection has been created.

You can see an illustration of this in the following diagram:

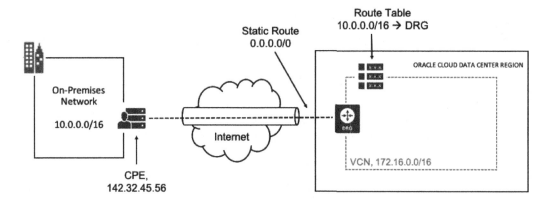

Figure 3.24 – OCI VPN setup

Customers can use a single **Customer Premises Equipment (CPE)** or a dual-head CPE for redundancy. You can see an illustration of the single-head CPE for the VPN connection in the following diagram:

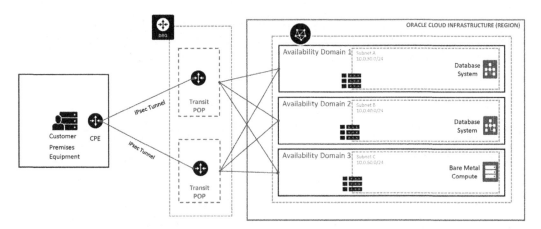

Figure 3.25 – VPN setup using single-head CPE

Additionally, you can configure two CPEs to create a **highly available (HA)** deployment in your on-premises network. The following diagram shows the recommended HA VPN deployment with three configured tunnels per CPE. This is illustrated in the following diagram:

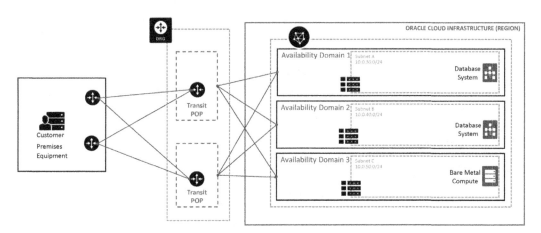

Figure 3.26 – VPN setup using multi-head CPE

The customer can use private subnets as well by using a *bastion host* connected to a public and a private subnet (multiple NICs). You can use a private subnet with a VPN connection to on-premises subnets as well. You can see an illustration of this in the following diagram:

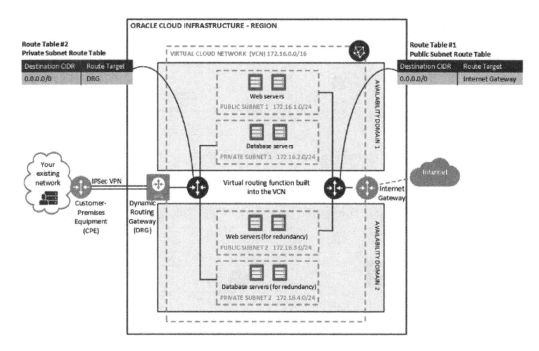

Figure 3.27 – VPN with a public and private subnet

In the preceding diagram, you can see how a customer can establish a VPN connection and then use a private and public subnet to differentiate the workload connectivity option.

Connecting through FastConnect

As you have noticed, the IPsec VPN connection doesn't provide guaranteed bandwidth, and depends on the public internet speed. If you want a dedicated and high-bandwidth connection, you need to choose a FastConnect connection. Customers can connect to OCI directly or via pre-integrated network partners. OCI supports port speeds of 1 Gbps and 10 Gbps increments. It doesn't have any charges for inbound/outbound data transfer and uses the BGP protocol for traffic routing. You can see an illustration of the FastConnect connection in the following image:

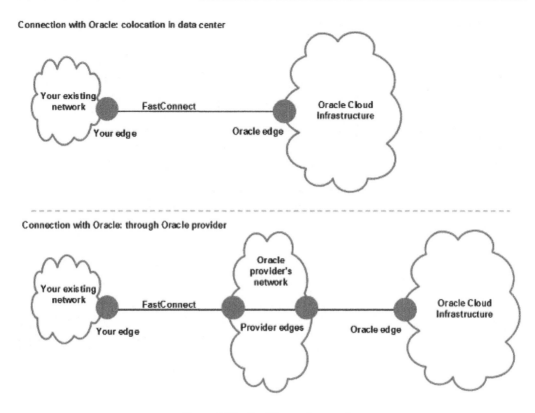

Figure 3.28 – FastConnect scenarios

The preceding image shows the connection options using either a co-located datacenter or a provider connection in the middle.

Let's now discuss the virtual circuit, as this is something that you will create to make the connection.

Virtual circuit

The virtual circuit is the key component of establishing the single and logical connection between the customer's on-premises network (typically using an edge router) and the DRG deployed on OCI. To establish this virtual circuit, you need information from the customer, Oracle, and a service provider. You can create more than one virtual circuit to segregate different organization functions. This segregation also provides redundancy. FastConnect uses the BGP routing protocol to establish this connection.

FastConnect using scenarios

Customers can choose between two kinds of peering for FastConnect connection.

Private peering:

- Extension of the on-premises network to the OCI VCN
- Communication across the connection with private IP addresses

Public peering:

- To access public OCI services, such as object storage, OCI console, or APIs over dedicated FastConnect connection
- Doesn't use DRG

You can see an illustration of the private and public peering for FastConnect connection in the following image:

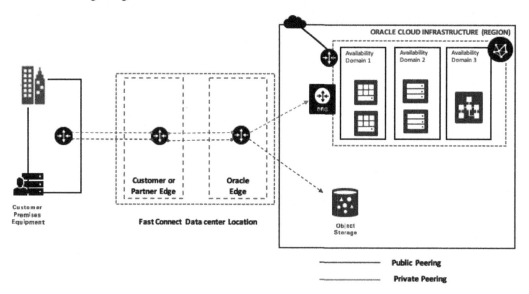

Figure 3.29 – FastConnect private and public peering

In this image, you can see that you can use public peering to access more public-facing OCI services, such as OCI object storage, and use private peering to access the other resources, such as instances, via a DRG.

In this section, you have learned about the different ways to connect to the OCI. In the next section, we will discuss how you load balance those incoming connections to your backend servers.

Load balancer

A load balancer's responsibility is to balance the network traffic between the clients and the backend. However, they do a number of other things as well:

- Service discovery
- Health checks
- Algorithms

Let's look at the benefits of using a load balancer:

- **Fault tolerance and HA** – You can use different algorithms to load balance the backend servers to provide fault-tolerant and highly available web services.
- **Scale** – You can add more backend resources when the load increases.
- **Naming abstraction** – You can use a load balancer and provide FQDN out of the load balancer listener IP address without knowing the instance's private IP address.

These are the generic benefits and use cases of any load balancer. Let's look at what the OCI load balancer does.

OCI provides this load balancer as a managed service offering for you to provide resilient web service experience to your client. It supports both private and public load balancers and also supports TCP, HTTP/1.0, HTTP/1.1, HTTP/2, and WebSocket protocols. For security, you can choose between SSL termination, end-to-end SSL, and SSL tunneling. Apart from standard layer-3/4 features, OCI also supports layer-7 capabilities, such as session persistence and content-based routing.

Unlike other cloud providers' models of using two different load balancers for network load balancing and application load balancing, OCI provides a single load balancer to achieve both of these objectives. For guaranteed and prewarm bandwidth requirements, OCI also provides different shapes of load balancer, such as 10 Mbps, 100 Mbps, 400 Mbps, and 8 Gbps. You have full flexibility to switch to a different shape at any time without any disruption.

In the next section, let's discuss the different formats of the available load balancers. We will also discuss the layer 3/4 load balancer and how it is different to the layer 7 load balancer, which uses cookie-based session persistence, virtual host-based routing, and so on. We will also discuss how to secure the connection using SSL termination.

Public load balancer

As you can tell from its name, the public load balancer is for public use, which means that you can use the public load balancer to receive traffic using a public IP address before sending it to the backend servers. As it's a regional service, you can either provision a regional subnet or provide multiple subnets from different ADs.

Using the principle of fault tolerance, OCI creates two different load balancer instances and deploys them in multiple availability domains. This way, it can switch to the other load balancer instance in case a disaster strikes, such as when one AD becomes unavailable.

An illustration of the public load balancer is shown in the following figure:

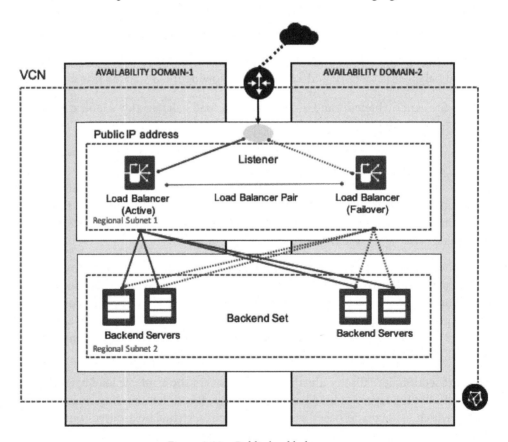

Figure 3.30 – Public load balancer

In the preceding image, you can see that there are two load balancer heads that have been placed on a single public regional subnet, which is in turn load balancing incoming traffic to four different backend servers that are connected to another public regional subnet.

Private load balancer

A private load balancer balances the load between the instances that are hosted in the private subnet. This means that you can only access this load balancer from the same VCN on which it is hosted. Using the principle of fault tolerance, OCI creates two different load balancer instances, and deploys them in multiple ADs. This way, it can switch to the other load balancer instance in case a disaster strikes, such as when one AD becomes unavailable.

An illustration of the private load balancer is shown in the following figure:

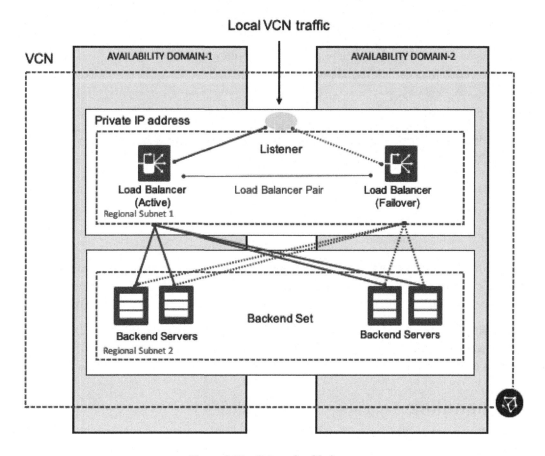

Figure 3.31 – Private load balancer

From the preceding image, you can see that there are two load balancer heads that have been placed on a single private regional subnet, which is in turn load balancing incoming traffic to four different backend servers that are connected to another private regional subnet.

Load balancing policies

There are three load balancing policies that OCI supports:

- **Round robin**: This is the default algorithm, and sends the incoming traffic randomly to the backend server set. Once it sends the first round of packets, it repeats the same order again.

- **IP hash**: The incoming IP address will be used to create a hash to send the traffic to the same backend server.

- **Least connection**: This algorithm chooses the backend server that has the fewest active connections to send the incoming traffic to.

While layer-3/4 load balancing happens over the policy algorithm and weight, HTTP load balancing considers cookie-based persistence.

Health check

The health check performs the availability check of the backend server. You can activate the health check for the following:

- Backends

- Backend set

- Overall load balancer

A load balancer IP can have up to 16 listeners (port numbers). Each listener has a backend set that can have 1 to N backend servers. The health API provides a four-state health status (ok, warning, critical, and unknown). The health status is updated every three minutes.

The health API displays the health of a load balancer instance in relation to its backends. Customers can utilize the health API to build their own notification and monitoring systems or integrate it with their existing systems.

SSL handling

Certificates are the main requirement for using SSL on the OCI load balancer. Certificates will contain the public key, private key, and CA portion of it, but you can upload and attach the certificate bundle with the listener after it is created. However, for the best user experience, you should upload it to the portal before you create the listener or backend set.

You need to make sure that the OCI load balancer does not have the capability to create any SSL certificates at all. This means that you must have it created beforehand. You can either use a CA to generate the certificates or you can use self-sign certificates.

Let's look at the three different types of SSL handling of an OCI load balancer:

- **SSL termination** – In this mode, your connection is not encrypted between the load balancer and the backend set, as the termination of the SSL connection happens at the load balancer layer.

- **SSL tunneling** – In this mode, you will have an SSL connection only between the load balancer and the backend servers.

- **End-to-end SSL** – As you can tell from the name, this is the most efficient way of load balancing as it not only encrypts the traffic from your client to the load balancer, but also from the load balancer to the backend servers.

Session persistence

Session persistence sends the incoming packets from a single originating source to a single backend server. For URLs where you rely on caching, such as in logging sessions or shopping carts, having a single backend server responding to the same originating client can help boost performance. For this, session persistence is the key feature.

OCI load balancer supports cookie-based session persistence. This works at layer 7 (HTTP). However, session persistence doesn't work if the client doesn't accept cookies.

You can configure cookie-based session persistence either on the OCI load balancer level or at the backend set level. You need to specify two parameters while configuring this. These are as follows:

- **Cookie name**: Either this can match the exact name of the cookie or it can match all to establish session persistence.

- **Fallback**: The fallback setting decides what the load balancer should do in the case that the original backend server that the session persistence was originally established with is not available.

Request routing – virtual hostnames and path routing

The request routing feature allows users to route traffic based on certain request parameters:

- Hostname (HTTP requests): **virtual hostnames**
- The HTTP(s) request's path: **path routing**

Let's look at both of these in detail.

Virtual hostnames

A virtual hostname is another way to provide an identifier to any of the *OCI LB listeners*. So, you can set different hostnames for different applications that get served by your backend set. A virtual hostname only operates at layer 7 (HTTP and HTTPS) and does not support layer 4 (TCP). Enterprises use a single load balancer to host multiple apps, with each app identified by hostname. There are three advantages to this approach:

- **Single associated IP address** – This makes the process of network-ACL configuration simpler.
- **Single bandwidth/shape** – Multiplexing many apps in a single shape/size provides customers with the flexibility of better managing the aggregate bandwidth demands, and also improves overall utilization.
- **Shared backend set definition** – This enables the administrative simplification of managing the set of backends under a single resource.

Without virtual hostnames, customers have to instantiate different load balancers for each application. This would lead to administrative pain points related to IP address management and network/ACL configuration.

The OCI load balancer service supports three matching variants for virtual hosts' hostnames in the following order:

1. Exact matching (for example, `login.example.com`)
2. Longest wildcard starting with asterisk (`*.example.com`)
3. Longest wildcard ending with asterisk (`login.example.*`)

Path routing

Typically, applications have different routing path sets for various different modules (for example, `/login`, `/app`, or `/static`), and requests for each of these endpoints need to be routed to different backend sets. Without path-based routing, different endpoints would need to be represented by different port numbers.

If the customer wants to differentiate traffic between two backend sets, their options would be either using different listeners for each backend set, which requires a different port for each listener, or different load balancers for each set of traffic.

Neither of these workarounds are suitable as they require clients to hit different endpoints, either a different port or a different load balancer altogether.

You need to use *path routing* for these scenarios. The load balancer matches this path routing string with an incoming URL path to decide which backend set it has to send the request to. A *path route rule* has four different pattern-matching types:

- **EXACT MATCH** – This rule applies when an exact match is found for the path string:

  ```
  ^<path_string>$
  ```

- **FORCE_LONGEST_PREFIX_MATCH** – This rule applies when a longest match of the beginning string is found at the URI path:

  ```
  <path_string>.*
  ```

- **PREFIX_MATCH** – This rule applies when a given string matches the beginning portion of the incoming URI path:

  ```
  ^<path_string>.*
  ```

- **SUFFIX_MATCH** – This rule applies when a given string matches the ending portion of the incoming URI path:

  ```
  .*<path_string>$
  ```

All of these route rules are only applied at layer 7, which is HTTP and HTTPS. You have no control over layer 4, which consists of the TCP packets using these rules. The maximum number of path rules that you can have is 20, while you can have 1 path route set per listener.

You have seen how the OCI load balancer handles the incoming traffic and provides various options to handle and secure the connections. In the next section, we will discuss how these traffic flow help you to diagnose connectivity issues and how important flow logs are.

VCN flow logs

VCN flow logs keep detailed records of every flow that passes through your VCN and present this data for analysis in the OCI Logging service. The data includes information about the source and destination of the traffic, along with the quantity of traffic and the *permit* or *deny* action taken, based on your network security rules. You can use this information for network monitoring, troubleshooting, and compliance. Through integration with the logging service, you can view, search, and retrieve log files.

Customers can use the *service connector* to create the object storage bucket and archive the data, as well as use the Oracle Streaming service to deliver the data to a third-party log analysis tool of their choice.

At a high level, the following steps show how flow logs will collect data:

1. Flow logs will send data every minute to OCI Logging for VNICs.

2. OCI Logging will index flow the log data every 10 mins and serve it to the customers.

3. Data sent to the logging service will be indexed and then shown via the logging UI.

4. Users can search to show all IP addresses, and these addresses can be exported once via CSV or JSON.

5. Data is retained for 30 days by default, and customers can choose to extend this period to up to 6 months.

6. If customers need to retain data for archival purposes, they must use a service connector to use object storage or streaming:

   Object storage – The service connector will read data from indexed logs and then export the flow log data every 10 mins or every 10 GBs, whichever comes first. It uses OCI Object Storage to store this flow log.

   Streaming – Integration with the streaming service will use the same 1-minute interval. Flow logs will send data every minute to the OCI Logging service, and then the customer can set up a connector using the *service connector* to connect it to the streaming service.

Customers can gain insight into their network traffic utilization by consulting flow logs for the subnets in their VCNs.

A flow log file is a list of flow records. Each record indicates the number of TCP or UDP packets that were seen during a collection window for a particular tuple of source and destination IP addresses and ports. It also includes time information, along with the protocol code, byte count, and whether the packets were accepted or rejected due to security rules.

To enable flow logs on a subnet, the customer goes to the central OCI Logging UI and selects the subnet as the resource they wish to monitor. Successfully enabling flow logging on a subnet will result in log files being stored in their chosen bucket and being viewed via the UI.

Each instance in a VCN has one or more VNIC The networking service uses security lists to determine what traffic is allowed through a given VNIC. When you attach a VNIC to a subnet, it will be subjected to all the security lists associated with that subnet.

Configuring VCN flow logs

VCN flow configuration is done through the OCI Logging service. Let's configure the VCN flow logs:

1. Log in to the OCI console.

2. Open the menu. Select **Logging** and then select **Log Groups**.

3. Click on **Create Log Group**.

4. Provide a **Name** and **Description** and click on **Create**.

    It will take you to the details of the Log Group. From here, select **Logs** from the **Resources** section. Here, we need to **Enable Service Log**.

5. Click on **Enable Service Log**.

6. Select **Virtual Cloud Network (subnets)** as the **Service**.

7. Select the subnet that you want to monitor from the **Resource** dropdown.

8. Under the **Configure Log** section, select **Flow Logs (All records)** under the **Log Category**.

9. Provide a **Log Name** and click on **Enable Log**. You can see an example of this in the following screenshot:

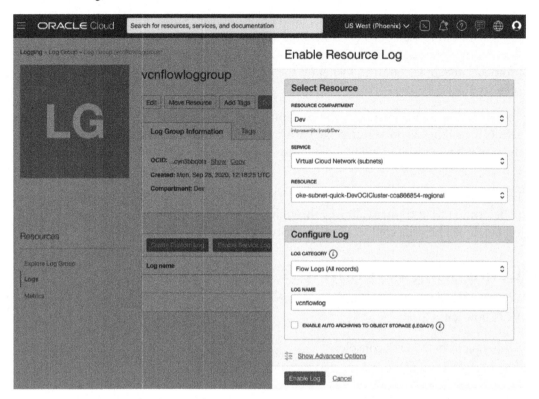

Figure 3.32 – Enable VCN flow logs

10. After five minutes or so, you will see that the VCN flow logs have started pouring in to the **Explore Log** section. You can see an example of this in the following image:

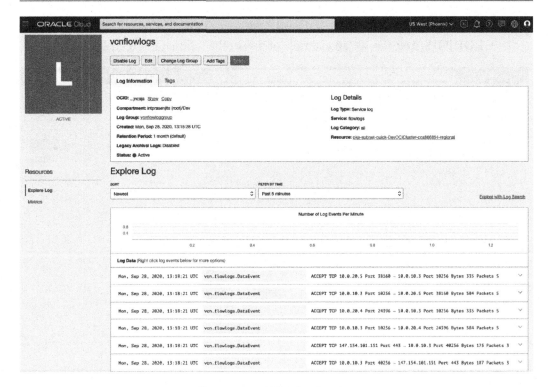

Figure 3.33 – VCN flow log data

11. From here, you can click on the **Explore with Log Search** button to go to the **Search** section under **Logging**.

12. Here, you can filter the logs by IP or by action taken on the packer flow.

13. You can click on the **Visualize** tab and create a visualization using **INTERVAL** and **GROUP BY**. You can see an example of this in the following screenshot:

Figure 3.34 – VCN flow log data visualization

So, you can see that by using VCN flow log data, you can find anomalies easily and visualize what is happening in your VCN.

Summary

In this chapter, you learned the foundation of OCI–namely, VCN. We explained the overall VCN architecture, along with the VCN components and different connection options. You also learned about the concepts of the OCI load balancer and how you can use the VCN flow log for troubleshooting and finding anomalies.

In the next chapter, you will see the various compute choices that you have in OCI and how you can leverage them in your use cases.

4
Compute Choices on Oracle Cloud Infrastructure

One of the core services from **Oracle Cloud Infrastructure (OCI)** is the OCI Compute service, which helps you provision and manage compute instances. As it is an on-demand service, you can fulfil your application requirements at any time by launching an instance of your choice. Once you have the instance up and running, you can control it fully. You can access these instances securely and even manage their life cycles, which means you have control over starting, stopping, and deleting these instances.

You can also choose various types of persistence storage that you can attach to these instances, such as block volumes, file storage, object storage, archive storage, and more. Although there are certain high performing NVMe disk-attached instances to help you meet your performance goal, they are lost when you terminate those instances. For those instances, you should add block volumes to back up your data.

In this chapter, we're going to cover the following main topics:

- Introducing the different OCI compute instance types

- Understanding instance operating system images

- Creating similar instances using instance configuration and instance pools

- Connecting to instances using instance console connection

Introducing the different OCI compute instance types

OCI is the only public cloud that supports bare metal and VMs using the same set of APIs, hardware, firmware, software stack, and networking infrastructure. You can see the two models in the following diagram:

Figure 4.1 – Compute instance types

Bare metal instances are instances where customers get the full server. This is also referred to as a single-tenant model. The advantage here is that there is no performance overhead, no shared agents, and no noisy neighbors. For performance and isolation requirements, this is the best instance type. You can see an example of this in the following diagram:

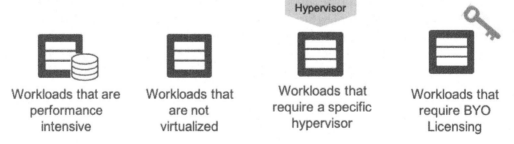

Figure 4.2 – Various workloads for bare metal

On the other spectrum is **virtual machines** (**VMs**), where the underlying host is virtualized to provide smaller VMs. This is also referred to as a multi-tenant model. The advantage here is flexibility in regard to what instance shapes are used. A VM instance is a piece of virtual hardware that shares the physical compute with other VM instances. OS virtualization helps you run multiple virtual machines on top of a physical piece of hardware and share the physical space among them. Logically speaking, these VM instances are isolated.

If you do not have strict or very high performing applications, then this is the best type of instance to use. You can dynamically choose how much CPU and memory to use in these instances and based on your computing power, the network bandwidth available in these instances also varies. Since these instances run on the same type of physical infrastructure, they leverage the same backend infrastructure that created the foundation of Oracle's second-generation cloud.

Dedicated VM hosts (**DVH**) is yet another type of OCI compute instance. On DVH, you can run your VMs so that they will be treated as single-tenant VMs. These instances will not be sharing the underlying physical compute with other customers. If you have compliance and regulatory requirements for isolation, then DVH instances are the most suitable. DVH help you be flexible in terms of licensing because you can meet either node-based licensing or host-based licensing using this offering. The following is a logical diagram of a DVH:

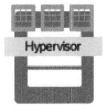

Figure 4.3 – Dedicated VM host

In the next section, we will look at instance shapes.

Understanding instance shapes

Based on your application's performance requirements, you have the power to decide on the form of these compute instances. Here, you'll select the amount of CPU cores you wish to use, the amount of memory that you just want for your instances, and so on. Network bandwidth increases linearly with the amount of CPU cores you have per instance. OCI has a good number of compute instance shapes that can help you satisfy your application's performance requirements. Let's observe them.

Standard shapes

Standard shapes are for general-purpose workloads. You can meet the requirements of a large range of applications and use cases using these shapes. You can either choose a fixed CPU and memory type for standard shapes or choose a flexible instance type that's powered by an AMD Rome processor.

Standard shapes VMs start from 1 CPU and can go up to 64 CPUs, with the memory starting from 1 GB and going up to 1,024 GB. You can choose either flexible shapes, which are flexible in terms of the amount of processor and memory you can have, or you can go for a fixed amount of CPU and memory. You can also choose instances that are powered by Intel Skylake-based processors. Legacy standard type instances are based on X5 and X7 types of hardware. You can see the AMD Rome-based standard shapes and how you can use the slider to choose the number of resources in the following screenshot.

AMD EPYC processor-powered instances have different use cases. The AMD EPYC bare metal server (64 cores, 512 GB RAM, 2 x 25 Gbps bandwidth, 75 vNICs) is available to customers for $0.03 core/hour (this price is at the time of writing this book). These instances are there to help you cut down on your bill. Also, from a support perspective, it supports **E-Business Suite**, **JD Edwards**, and **PeopleSoft**. You can also run **Cloudera**, **Hortonworks**, **MapR**, and **Transwarp**.

The following screenshot shows various AMD Rome processor-based compute instances on OCI:

Browse All Shapes

A shape is a template that determines the number of CPUs, amount of memory, and other resources allocated to a newly created instance. See Compute Shapes for more information.

Instance type

Virtual Machine	Bare Metal Machine
A virtual machine is an independent computing environment that runs on top of physical bare metal hardware. ✓	A bare metal compute instance gives you dedicated physical server access for highest performance and strong isolation.

Shape series

AMD Rome	Intel Skylake	Specialty and Legacy
AMD Customizable OCPU count. For general purpose workloads. ✓	(intel) Fixed OCPU count. Latest generation Intel Standard shapes.	Earlier generation AMD and Intel Standard shapes. Always Free, Dense I/O, GPU, and HPC shapes.

You can customize the number of OCPUs and the amount of memory allocated to a flexible shape. The other resources scale proportionally. Learn more about flexible shapes.

NUMBER OF OCPUS

1	16	32	48	64	64

AMOUNT OF MEMORY (GB) (i)

1	256	512	768	1024	1024

Network Bandwidth (Gbps): 40.0 (i)   Max. Total VNICs: 24.0 (i)

Figure 4.4 – Standard shapes

There are standard types of shapes that are specifically designed for **Always Free Tier** services. This is a micro VM that has just 1 CPU and 1 GB of memory.

Let's create a standard OCI compute instance:

1. Sign into the OCI console.
2. Open the navigation menu, select **Compute**, and then select **Instances**.
3. Click **Create Instance**.
4. Provide a **Name** and select a **Compartment** where you want to deploy it.
5. In the **Availability Domain** section of the **Configure placement and hardware** section, choose where you want to place the AD. Additionally, you can click on the **Choose a Fault Domain for this Instance** checkbox and select a **Fault Domain** from the drop-down menu.
6. Select an **Image** for the operating system that you want to deploy. We will talk about the different types of images in the next section. By default, it will be the latest **Oracle Linux** image.

7. In the **Shape** section, by default, the **VM.Standard.E3.Flex** shape type will be selected, which has 1 core OCPU, 16 GB memory, and 1 Gbps network bandwidth shape. Click on **Change Shape** if you want to change it to a different one. You can either select another type of standard shape or use the slider to change the allocated OCPU and memory for this default instance type. You can see an example of this in the following screenshot:

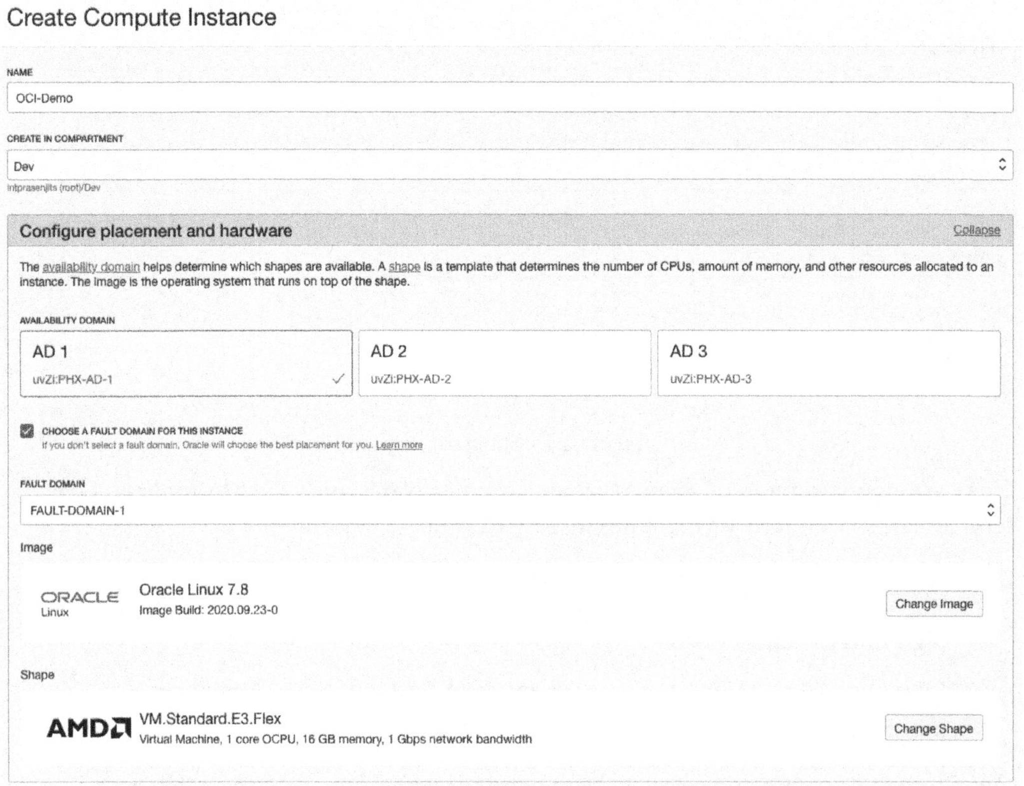

Figure 4.5 – Create compute instance wizard

8. In the **Configure Networking** section, choose the Virtual Cloud Network and the subnet that you want to connect this instance to.

9. Select the **Assign a Public IP Address** radio button to have access to this instance over the public internet.

10. Select **Generate SSH Key Pair** if you're unsure of how to generate an SSH key pair to access this instance.

11. Click on **Save Private Key** and **Save Public Key** so that you can use these keys to connect to this instance. You can use these keys to provision other instances in the future. You can see an example of this in the following screenshot:

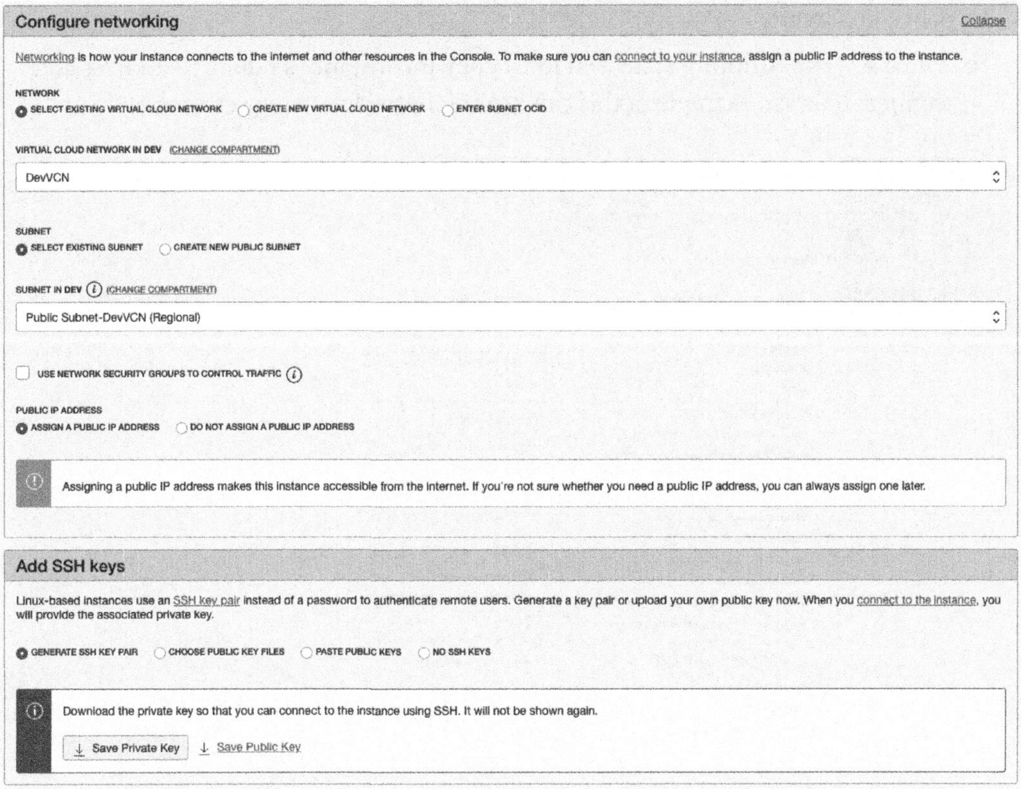

Figure 4.6 – Create compute instance wizard – Configure networking section

12. Optionally, you can **Specify a custom Boot Volume size**. While creating this instance, you can choose the default boot volume size of this instance or a custom boot volume size up to 32 TB.

    If you are provisioning a Linux image-based instance, then you must set your custom boot volume size so that it's more than its default volume size, which is 50 GB. If you want to create an instance based on Windows operating system images, then the same rule applies; that is, you must set the custom boot volume size so that it's more than the default boot volume size, which is 256 GB.

    The reason behind setting up this default boot volume size is so that you have enough space for Windows patches and a page file.

13. Optionally, you can specify **Use in-transit encryption**. In-transit encryption allows to encrypt the volume when it's being created.

14. Optionally, you can specify **Encrypt this volume with a key that you manage**.

15. Click on **Create**.

16. Once it is in a **Running** state, you must copy the instance's public IP address and connect to it. An example of this can be seen in the following screenshot:

Figure 4.7 – Instance details

With that, you have learned how to create an instance using standard shapes. In the next section, we will talk about DenseIO shapes.

DenseIO shapes

When you design instances for giant applications such as large databases, big data applications, or if you are planning to run applications that have strict requirements in terms of high-performance local storage, then you need to go for DenseIO shapes. DenseIO shapes come with NVMe-based SSDs that are locally attached. You can get up to 52 physical CPU cores and 768 GB of memory. It also has 51.2 TB of locally attached SSDs and 2 x 25 Gbps networking bandwidth.

DenseIO shapes come in both bare metal and VM instance types. Let's create an OCI compute instance of the DenseIO type. There are extra steps that need to be performed, including creating a volume out of the available NVMe disk and formatting it with a filesystem before you can use that space:

1. To create an instance of the DenseIO type, follow the same procedure that we described in the *Standard shapes* section, but choose DenseIO as the image type. For this example, we will create an instance of **VM.DenseIO2.8**. You can see an example of this in the following screenshot:

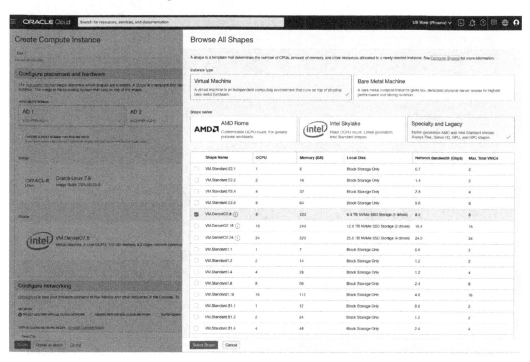

Figure 4.8 – DenseIO type of virtual instance

2. Copy the public IP address of this instance and log into it using `ssh`:

```
ssh -i <path-of the-private-key> <username>@<public-ip-
address>
```

3. Once you've logged into the DenseIO instance, you need to create a filesystem and mount the NVMe disks. Let's do that now:

```
sudo fdisk -l
```

```
sudo lsblk
```

```
sudo mkdir /mnt/nvme
```

```
sudo mkfs -t ext4 /dev/nvme0n1
```

```
sudo mount /dev/nvme0n1 /mnt/nvme
```

You can see an example of the output in the following screenshot:

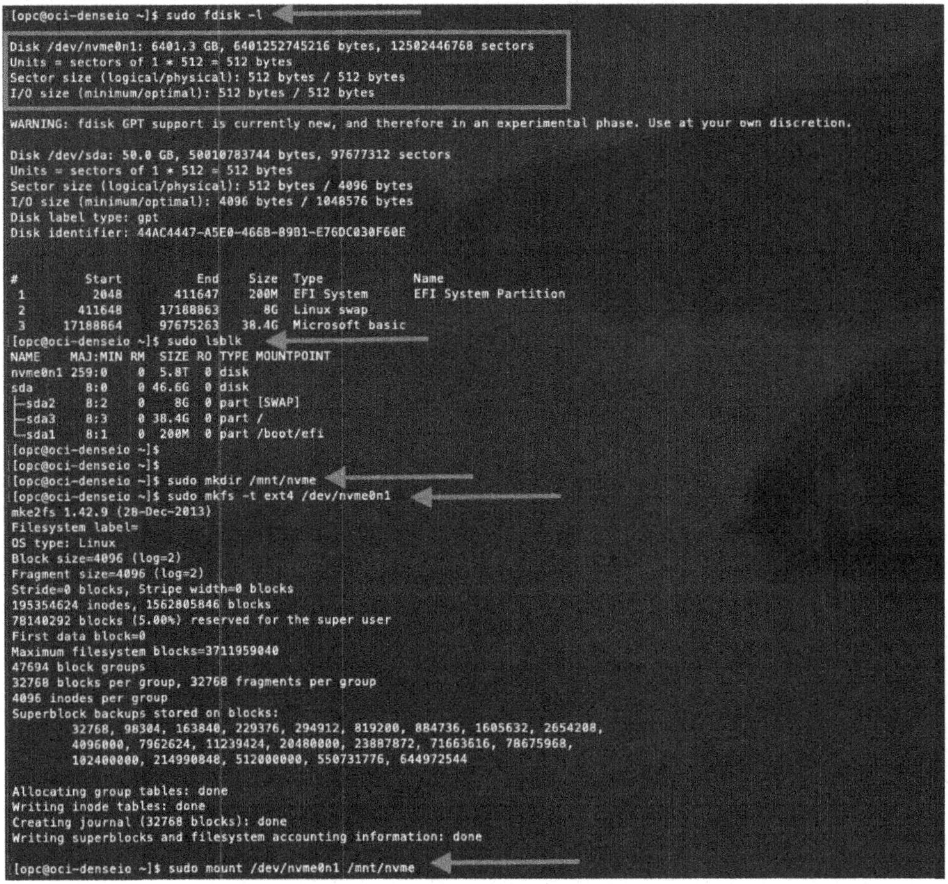

Figure 4.9 – DenseIO NVMe disk mounting

4. At this point, your disk has been formatted and mounted. However, it is not protected from hardware failures. For NVMe disk hardware failures, you should choose to create a software RAID solution on them.

In the next section, we will look at GPU shapes.

GPU shapes

GPU shapes are required when you plan to run hardware-accelerated workloads. GPU shapes come with processors from both Intel and AMD and NVIDIA graphics processors.

At the time of writing, there are three different types of GPU shapes available, as follows:

* 2nd-generation GPU shapes that have NVIDIA Tesla P100 GPUs
* 3rd-generation GPU shapes that have NVIDIA V100 GPUs
* 4th-generation GPU shapes that have NVIDIA A100 GPU chipsets

You can either choose a standard operating system and then install the NVIDIA GPU drivers on top of it or you can choose **NVIDIA GPU Cloud** (**NGC**). NGC provides you with GPU-optimized cloud instances that you can use for deep learning and scientific computing.

NVIDIA worked along with OCI engineering in an effort to provide cloud-ready Tesla, Volta, and Pascal GPU shapes. As a result, when you run these instances and then run NGC containers, you get optimum performance for deep learning applications.

Creating a GPU-based instance is same – you just need to choose the OS image and the GPU instance type and then create the instance. An example of this is shown in the following screenshot:

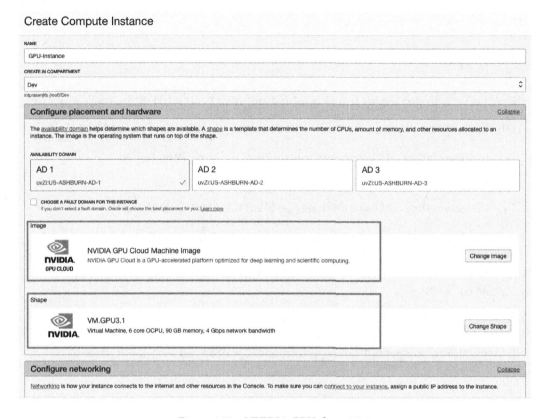

Figure 4.10 – NVIDIA GPU shape VM

In this section, you learned about GPU shapes. Now, let's discuss HPC shapes.

High performance computing (HPC) shapes

If you have an application that requires high frequency processor cores and cluster networking since this application will be performing parallel computing, then HPC shapes are the most suitable. You can only choose bare-metal instances for HPC shapes. You can see an example of how to select HPC shapes while creating a bare-metal instance in the following screenshot:

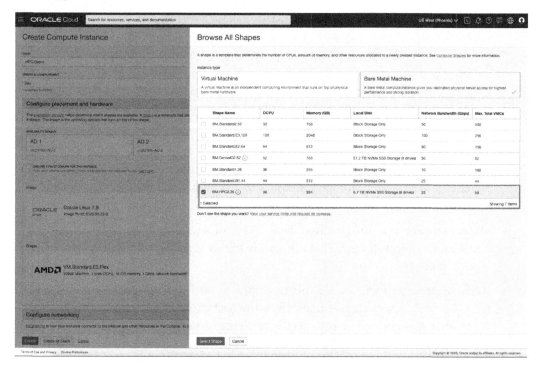

Figure 4.11 – HPC shape bare-metal instance

Most customers will go for some kind of external storage attachment for the compute shapes. In the next section, we will discuss those options.

Storage for compute instances

In the previous section, we discussed different types of instances and their different shapes. However, one thing that you must consider is the data persistence of these instances. None of these instances can give you data persistence. So, you need to rely on an externally attached storage type to persist the data. There are four different types of external storage that you can have, and they are as follows:

- **Block volume**: OCI block volumes are backed by iSCSI storage targets that are hosted on top of the same underlying network infrastructure. You can dynamically provision and manage block volumes. Furthermore, you can attach these block volumes to one instance or, for clustering purposes, to more compute instances. OCI also provides paravirtualized attachment for block volumes, which simplifies the configuration steps of block storage by removing the extra commands. However, if you want to provision block volumes for performance, then this is not ideal as it adds to the overhead of virtualization.

- **File storage**: OCI file storage is based on the NFS protocol. It is not only cost-effective and a durable storage solution, but it is highly scalable, secure, and an enterprise-grade network filesystem.

- **Object storage**: For unstructured data storage of any content type, you should choose OCI object storage. This is not only highly scalable but a high-performance storage platform.

- **Archive storage**: If you are looking to archive your data in an unstructured format, then the OCI archive storage platform is the best choice. The archive storage's scope is regional. It is not tied to any specific compute instance.

Although we will cover these specific storage types in the next chapter, let's learn how to create a block volume and then attach it to a compute instance and access the filesystem:

1. Sign into the OCI console.
2. Open the navigation menu, select **Block Storage**, and then select **Block Volumes**.
3. Click **Create Block Volume**.
4. Provide a **Name** and select a **Compartment** where you want to deploy it.
5. Select an **Availability Domain** where you want to deploy it.
6. Under the **Volume Size and Performance** section, select the **Default** option and make sure that the IOPS and throughput is proportionate to the volume's size.
7. Optionally, select **Backup Policy** in **Compartment**.

8. Click on **Create Block Volume**. You can see some example output of this in the following screenshot:

Figure 4.12 – Create Block Volume wizard

9. Once it has been provisioned, you can click on **Attached Instances** from the left-hand side tree.

10. Click on **Attach to Instance**.

11. Here, you can select an **Attachment Type**, which should be either **iSCSI** or **Paravirtualized**.

12. You can select an **Access Type** from here. By default, it is set to **Read/Write**.

13. Click on the **Select Instance** option and then select the instance that will be connected to this block volume from the dropdown.

14. Optionally, you can choose **Require CHAP credentials**.

15. Select a **Device Name** from the drop-down list.

16. Click on **Attach**. You can see some example output in the following screenshot:

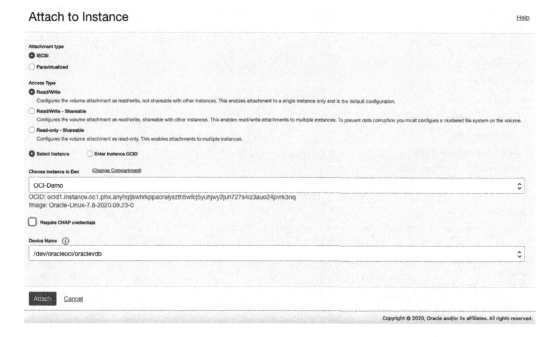

Figure 4.13 – Attach to Instance wizard

17. To attach this block volume to the operating system, you need to copy the commands that OCI provides. To do that, click on the three little dots on the **Attached Instances** page and select **iSCSI Commands & Information**. You can see some example output in the following screenshot:

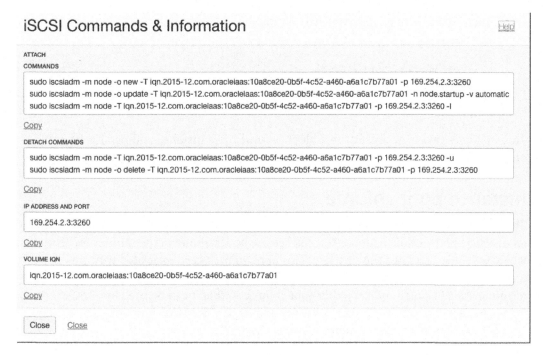

Figure 4.14 – iSCSI commands

18. Log into your instance via SSH if it is a Linux box and then run the commands shown in the previous step. You can see some example output in the following screenshot:

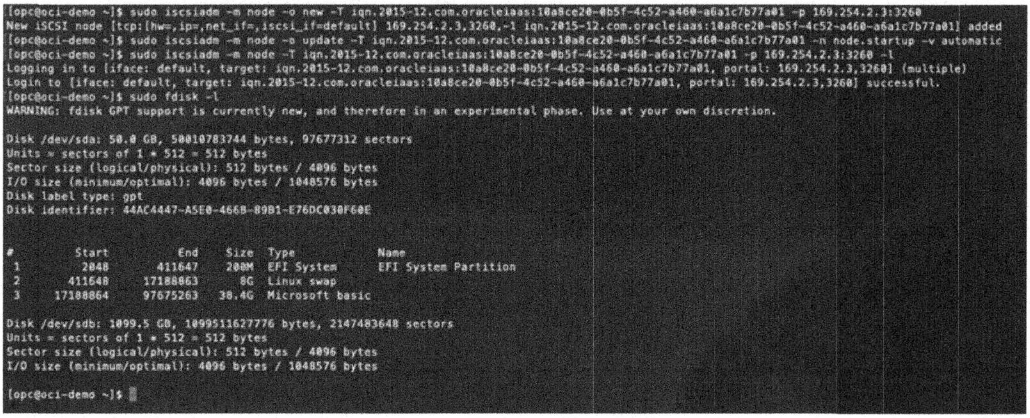

Figure 4.15 – iSCSI attach commands

19. Then, run the following standard commands to format this disk with the `ext4`
    filesystem type and mount it on a directory:

```
sudo mkdir /mnt/block
sudo mkfs -t ext4 /dev/sdb
sudo mount /dev/sdb /mnt/block
```

This way, you can create and attach a block volume to an instance and persist the data
on it.

Instance boot volume

The instance boot volume comes from the same block storage backend where you launch
an instance in any of the regions. You can see the boot volume in the same compartment
where you have launched the instance. This boot volume gets associated with this
instance. You can use it within this instance as this instance's boot volume or you can
terminate this instance and keep this boot volume so that it can be used by another
instance. That way, you can preserve the OS and its configuration and other data as well.
You can use that in another instance if you wish to.

There are primarily two use cases for boot volumes, as follows:

- **Instance scaling**: In the previous section, we mentioned that you can keep the boot
  volume while terminating an instance to preserve it. The main use case here is to
  use this boot volume to create another instance of a different configuration. You can
  choose to either upgrade the resources that have been assigned to it or cut down on
  the resources. So, instance scaling is a perfect use case where the boot volume is a
  key feature. The good news is that you can even switch between VM and bare-metal
  instances using this boot volume.

- **Troubleshooting**: If you want to troubleshoot cases where instances are not booting
  up because of some issues in the boot volume itself, you can detach the boot volume
  and attach it to another instance as a data volume to troubleshoot this. Once you
  have finished troubleshooting, you can attach it back to the same old instance and
  boot up.

Let's look at using boot volumes in an instance:

1. Sign into the OCI console.

2. Open the navigation menu, select **Compute**, and then select **Boot Volumes**. Here
   you can see all the existing boot volumes and their details. You can see an example
   in the following screenshot:

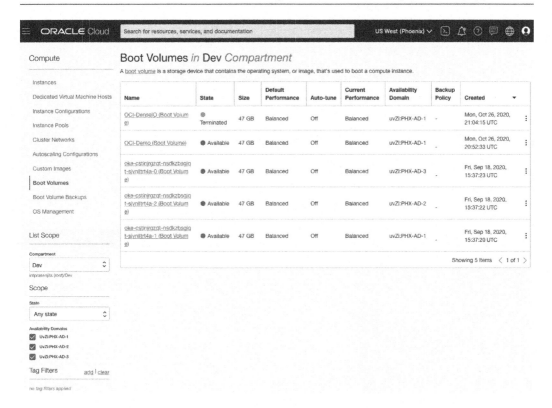

Figure 4.16 – List of boot volumes

Let's terminate an instance but preserve the boot volume to spin up another instance of a different config.

3. Open the navigation menu, select **Compute**, and then select **Instances**.

4. From the list of instances, select the instance that you want to terminate, click on the three little dots, and select **Terminate**.

5. Do not select the **PERMANANTLY DELETE THE ATTACHED BOOT VOLUME** checkbox. Instead, click on **Terminate Instance**. You can see an example of this in the following screenshot:

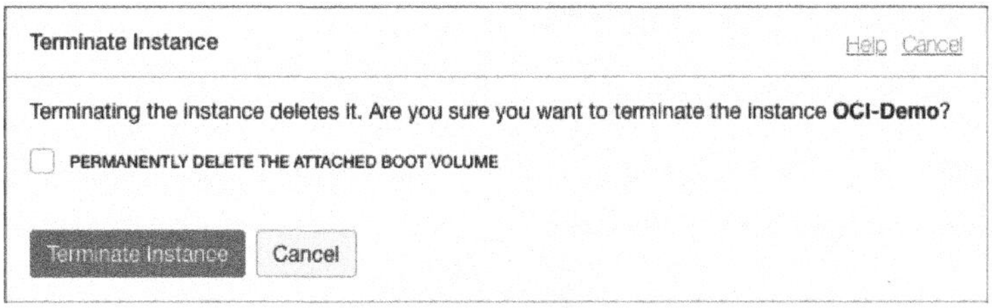

Figure 4.17 – Terminate Instance window

6. Once it has been terminated, you can go back to the boot volumes section (*step 2*) to see that the boot volume does exist.

7. Click on **Create Instance**.

8. Follow the same procedure for everything else, as described in the *Creating an instance* section.

9. In the **Image** section, click on **Change Image**.

10. Click on the **Boot Volumes** tab.

11. Select the boot volume from the list and click on **Select Boot Volume**. You can see an example of this in the following screenshot:

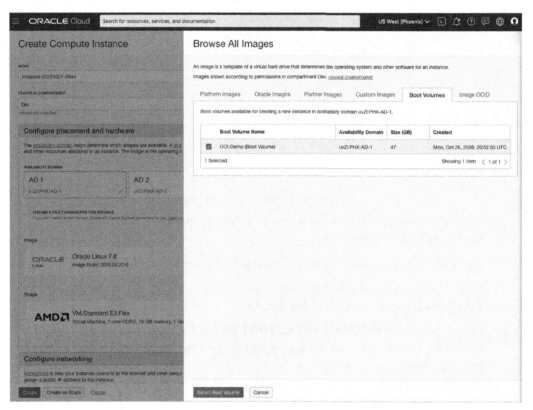

Figure 4.18 – Instance creation using an existing boot volume

12. Choose the shape that is appropriate for your workload and follow the configure of the options before clicking on **Create**.

With that, you have learned how to use the boot volume for various purposes. In the next section, we will talk about instance images.

Understanding instance operating system images

An instance image holds the operating system and other tools and software that go with it. Images can be Oracle-provided, Custom, or BYOI. You can choose an image from either Oracle Linux, Microsoft Windows, Ubuntu, or CentOS. As far as security concerns go within those images, Oracle adds rules within those images that restrict anyone else but the root on Linux instances (and administrators on Windows instances) from making outgoing connections to the iSCSI network endpoint (`169.254.0.2:3260`), which serves the instance's boot and block volumes.

For a maximum security posture, OCI's recommendation is not to tamper with any of the default operating system firewall rules as these may expose the risk of non-admins accessing the boot disk and other filesystems. This is also valid when you're creating a custom image from this.

Let's look at some of the characteristics of these images.

The following are characteristics of Oracle-provided Linux images:

- A new user, named `opc`, will be added to the instances that are created from Oracle Linux or CentOS images.
- A new user, named `ubuntu`, will be added to the instances that are created from Ubuntu images.
- By default, these users will get `sudo` privileges and can use SSH v2 to log into these instances.
- By default, an instance firewall will allow SSH access; that is, access to the instance over port `22`.
- Provide a startup script using `cloud-init`.

The following are characteristics of Oracle-provided Windows images:

- A new user, named `opc`, will be added to the Windows instances and for authentication, you will get a **one-time password (OTP)**.
- These instances will have a Windows Update utility installed so that you can get the latest Windows updates from Microsoft.

Now, let's look at custom images.

Custom images

You can also use custom images. Think about a base OS image that you want to use to spin up hundreds of instances that has been tuned to your requirements, installed software, and other configurations. This is one of the main use cases for custom images. This is where you take an instance's boot disk to create and launch many other instances with similar OS configurations.

When you start creating a custom image from an existing instance, that instance goes through life cycle operations; that is, it shuts down on its own and remains unavailable until the ongoing operation is complete. This instance will start up when the process has completed.

However, you cannot create a custom image from the attached block volume. If you want to attach the secondary volumes, you will need to clone or back them up and then attach them to the newly created instance. A custom image cannot exceed 400 GB. For security reasons, you are not allowed to export Windows custom images out of the tenancy. You can see a logical representation of a custom image in the following diagram:

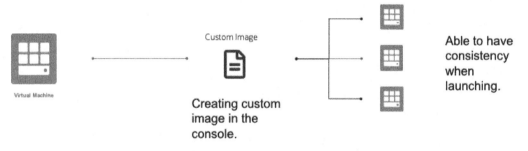

Figure 4.19 – Custom image

Let's create a custom image from an existing instance and use that to spin up another instance:

1. Sign into the OCI console.

2. Open the navigation menu, select **Compute**, and then select **Instances**.

3. Click on the VM that is going to be your base VM image.

4. On the **Instance Details** page, click on the **More Actions** menu and select **Create Custom Image**. You can see an example of this in the following screenshot:

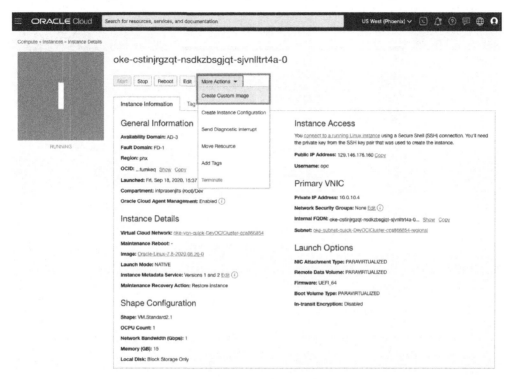

Figure 4.20 – Custom image creation

5. Select the compartment where you want to create this image and provide a **Name**.

6. Click on **Create Custom Image**. This is going to take some time. As described earlier, this VM is going to stop and start in the meantime as well.

7. Once complete, click on **Custom Images** from the **Compute** navigation menu. Here, you can see the custom image listed. You can see an example of this in the following screenshot:

Figure 4.21 – Custom Images list

8. Let's use this image and create an instance. Go to the **Instances** section of the **Compute** navigation menu.

9. Click on **Create Instance**.

10. Follow the same procedure that was described in the *Understanding instance shapes* section.

11. In the **Image** section, click on **Change Image**.

12. Go to the **Custom Images** tab and select the custom image from the list. You can see an example of this in the following screenshot. Click on **Select Image**:

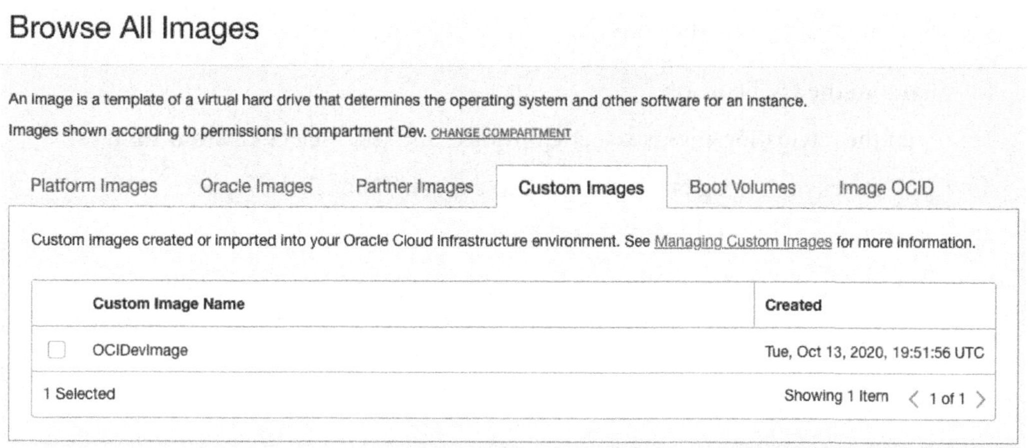

Browse All Images

An image is a template of a virtual hard drive that determines the operating system and other software for an instance.

Images shown according to permissions in compartment Dev. CHANGE COMPARTMENT

| Platform Images | Oracle Images | Partner Images | **Custom Images** | Boot Volumes | Image OCID |

Custom images created or imported into your Oracle Cloud Infrastructure environment. See Managing Custom Images for more information.

Custom Image Name	Created
☐ OCIDevImage	Tue, Oct 13, 2020, 19:51:56 UTC

1 Selected   Showing 1 Item   ‹ 1 of 1 ›

Figure 4.22 – Instance creation using a custom image

13. Click on **Create**.

In this section, you learned how to efficiently create a custom image from an existing VM and use that to instantiate other instances, all while keeping the same configuration.

Image export and import

The image export and import capability lets you share custom operating system images across different tenancies and OCI regions. Image import/export uses the OCI Object Storage service.

You can import Linux and Windows operating system. It supports the following mode:

- **Emulation mode**: In emulation mode, VM I/O devices, such as disk, network, and CPU and memory are implemented in software. Emulated VMs can support almost any x86 operating system. However, these VMs are slow.

- **Paravirtualized**: These VMs include a driver specifically designed to enable virtualization.

- **Native mode**: Similar to a **hardware virtualized machine (HVM)**, it offers the maximum performance for modern operating systems.

Let's export an image using the console:

1. Sign into the OCI console.

2. Open the navigation menu, select **Compute**, and then select **Custom Images**.

3. Click the custom image that you want to export. Then, click **Export**.

4. Select **Export to an Object Storage bucket**.

5. Choose the object storage bucket from the drop-down list. Optionally, you can specify a name for this exported image. You can see an example of this in the following screenshot:

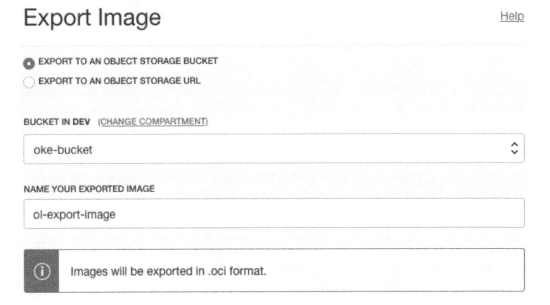

Figure 4.23 – Export Image wizard

6. Click **Export Image**.

With that, you've learned how to quickly export an image and use that in either a different region within the same tenancy or in other tenancies.

Bring Your Own Image (BYOI)

If you have an operating system that is not available on OCI, you can use the BYOI feature to get that onto OCI, as long as OCI supports the underlying hardware.

BYOI can help with the following scenarios:

- Lift-and-shift applications

- Support for old and new OSes

- Experimentation using different versions of an OS

- Maximum flexibility of the underlying infrastructure

> **Note**
> When you bring in your own custom images, you need to comply with the licensing of those OS images on your own.

The following is a logical diagram of the image export and import process. Here, a customer exports their on-premises image onto a qcow2 image and uploads it to OCI object storage. Then, they can create a custom image out of it and use it to create an instance:

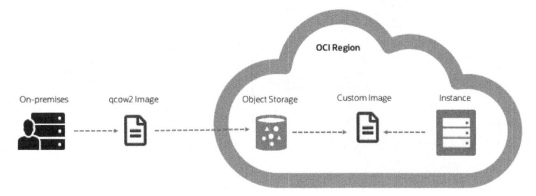

Figure 4.24 – Image export/import process

So, you've learned about exporting a custom image and importing it to OCI. In the next section, we will discuss the process of bringing your own hypervisor.

Bring Your Own Hypervisor (BYOH)

In a BYOH scenario, each guest VM can get one or more secondary **virtual NIC cards (VNICs)**. If SR-IOV **virtual functions (VFs)** are used by the hypervisor to provide network access to the guest VMs, each VF can be configured with the VLAN tag and MAC address of a secondary VNIC. The guest VM can have a private IP and a public IP associated with it. However, make sure that you know the limits of the VNICs for each shape type.

So, to illustrate this, we can have multiple virtual network interfaces in different subnets and those VNICs can each be associated with a different guest VM. This can be seen in the following diagram:

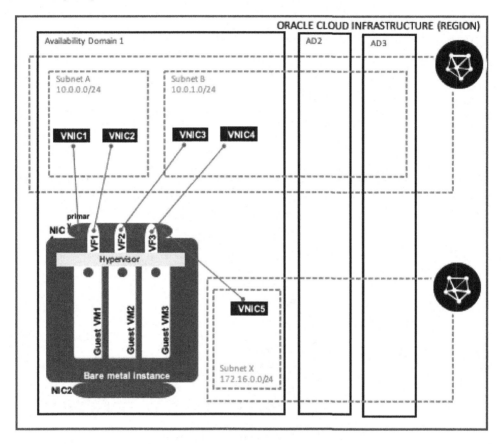

Figure 4.25 – Bring Your Own Hypervisor

In the preceding diagram, you can see how the VNICs are connected to different subnets and how that is translated for the guest VMs inside it.

OCI supports three types of hypervisor that you can bring over to OCI:

- **Oracle Virtual Machine (OVM)**
- KVM
- Microsoft Hyper-V

BYOH will give you the flexibility to customize your VM shape while selecting the amount of CPU and memory required for your workload.

Since this is a unique feature of OCI, you can leverage services such as block volume and network interfaces that can be directly attached to the virtual machines you created on top of your hypervisor. This allows them to communicate with other resources and instances provisioned in OCI. There are two benefits of this:

- You can extend the same configuration and the workload that's running on on-premises on OCI.

- Using this feature, you can install legacy OS images using pre-packaged VMs.

To speed up the hypervisor configuration, OCI offers a pre-built image for the KVM hypervisor. This image is part of the Oracle Partner catalog and provides a set of tools you can use to interact with your provisioned virtual machines.

At the time of writing, OCI supports BM Standard and BM. DenseIO shapes are used as part of the deployment.

Creating similar instances using instance configuration and instance pools

If you want to create a template configuration that will be used to create multiple OCI instances, then instance configuration is your friend. It is a template for configuration that we can use to create similar OCI instances. You can specify configuration for which OS image to choose, different shapes and their resource allocation, different block volume sizes, and so on.

These templates can be created using an existing OCI instance or using the OCI CLI. When you launch an instance using this instance configuration, OCI creates the resources that are defined within that template config.

You can see a logical representation of this in the following diagram:

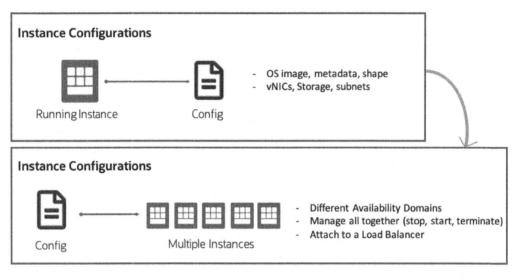

Figure 4.26 – Instance configuration

OCI uses this instance configuration to create and manage identical instances in a logical group. This is known as an instance pool. The main use case for an instance pool is horizontally scaling OCI instances. An instance pool scales these identical instances up and down based on either a schedule or performance metrics.

Let's look at the use cases for both of these options:

- **Instance configurations**:

  - Create a configuration file out of an existing instance.

  - Create a baseline configuration for instances.

  - Use this configuration file to provision OCI instances using the OCI CLI as well.

  - Instance creation automation using a base template for the configuration and resources.

- **Instance pools**:

  - You can manage and scale a group of OCI instances using a configuration template.

  - You can distribute these instances across different availability domains within a region to maintain high availability.

  - You can scale out and in of these instances based on a schedule or performance metric.

With that, you've learned how instance configuration and instance pools both work together to create similar instances at scale. However, there are other factors in play here, such as scaling this configuration using metric-based scaling.

Compute instance metrics

Compute metrics are critical components of your architecture design. With metrics, you can see how your instances are performing based on CPU, memory, disk, and network usage. You can also take some actions based on the metrics that are displayed for each compute instance.

Each instance will provide information about all the components associated with it, such as network and storage components.

To monitor the overall compute instances, including their health, capacity and performance, you need to use **metrics**, **alarms**, and **notifications**.

Here is a logical representation of how to map the instances and their available metrics:

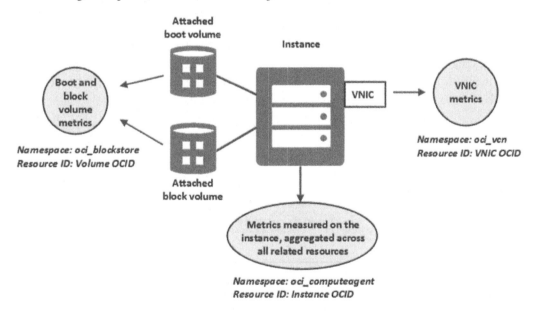

Figure 4.27 – Instance metrics

In this section, you learned how to combine instance configurations and instance pools, and then have a metric to trigger the instance creation automatically using them. In the next section, we will show you how to do this.

Autoscaling configurations

In the previous section, we explained how to use instance configurations and instance pools. In this section, we will talk about how you can combine those two to scale an instance pool in and out using autoscaling configuration.

Autoscaling lets you choose schedule or performance metrics such as CPU and memory utilization (this is handled by the OCI monitoring service) to automatically adjust the amount of compute instances in the pool.

There is an order that OCI sets up when the instances scale back in. This is how the extra instances are going to be deleted. First, OCI balances the number of instances across the availability domain and then narrows down to the fault domain. Even within a fault domain, when you need to scale back those instances, it chooses the oldest instance to delete first.

You have the option to choose which performance metric to choose when it comes to the autoscaling configuration. Then, you can decide on a threshold percentage, after which the autoscaler will start adding instances automatically. Once the threshold comes down below the threshold percentage, it will start deleting them.

The OCI monitoring service aggregates these metrics into 1-minute periods and then averages them across the instance pool. Autoscaling doesn't immediately kick in; it waits for the threshold to breach three consecutive times, which is the average of 1 minute's worth of data over 3 minutes. Then, the autoscaling event is triggered:

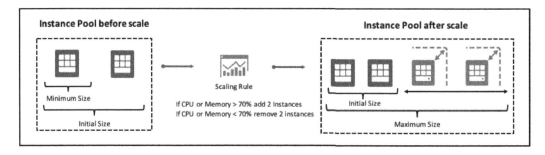

Figure 4.28 – Instance pool

Let's create an instance config and an instance pool and then perform the instance autoscaling configuration:

1. Sign into the OCI console.

2. Open the navigation menu, select **Compute**, and then select **Instances**.

3. Select the instance that you want to create a config from. Click on the **More Actions** menu on the **Instance Details** page and click on **Create Instance Configuration**.

4. Select the compartment where you want to create this config in from the dropdown and provide a **Name**.

5. Click on **Create Instance Configuration**.

6. You will be redirected to the **Instance Configuration Details** page. From here, click on **Create Instance Pool**.

7. Select the compartment a provide a **Name** for it. Select **Instance Configuration** from the dropdown and specify **NUMBER OF INSTANCES** to be provisioned. Click on **Next**. You can see an example of this in the following screenshot:

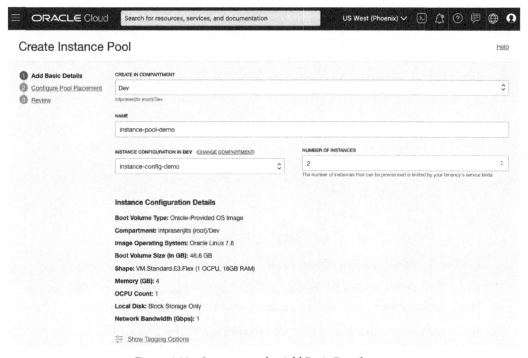

Figure 4.29 – Instance pool – Add Basic Details page

8. On the **Configure Pool Placement** page, select your **AD**, **FDs**, and which **VCN** and **subnet** you want to connect the primary NIC to. Since we have selected two instances, you can see that we are distributing it to two different ADs and two different FDs within them. Click on **Next**. You can see an example of this in the following screenshot:

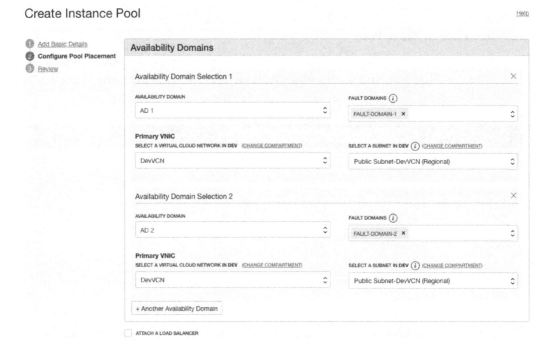

Figure 4.30 – Instance pool – Configure Pool Placement page

9. Review the details and click on **Create**.

10. You will be redirected to the **Instance Pool Details** page. From here, click on the **More Actions** menu and select **Create Autoscaling Configuration**.

11. Select the Compartment and provide a **Name** for it. Then, select the existing **Instance Pool** from the dropdown. Click on **Next**. You can see an example of this in the following screenshot:

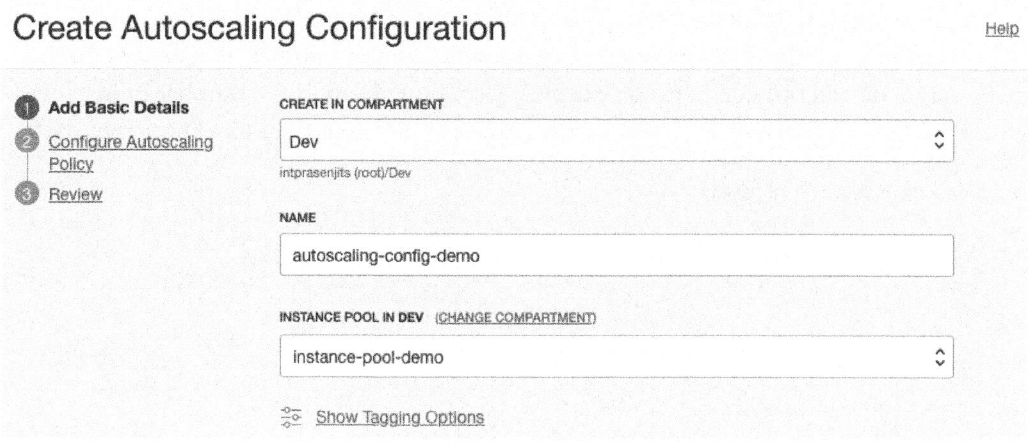

Create Autoscaling Configuration

① **Add Basic Details**

② Configure Autoscaling
     Policy

③ Review

CREATE IN COMPARTMENT

Dev

intprasenjits (root)/Dev

NAME

autoscaling-config-demo

INSTANCE POOL IN DEV (CHANGE COMPARTMENT)

instance-pool-demo

Show Tagging Options

Figure 4.31 – Autoscaling – Add Basic Details page

12. In the **Configure Autoscaling Policy** section, select **Metric-based Autoscaling**.

13. Provide a **Name** and select **COOLDOWN IN SECONDS** (by default, it is **300** seconds).

14. Choose **CPU utilization** for **PERFORMANCE METRIC**.

15. In the **Scale-out rule** section, provide a threshold percentage (for example, 70%) that will be used to trigger the autoscaling function.

16. Provide the number of instances to add. For an example, when autoscaling starts, it will add **1** instance.

17. The same goes to the **Scale-in rule** section. Provide a threshold percentage such as 50%. So, in this case, when the compute instances are only 50% utilized, the instances that were scaled out will be scaled in.

18. Provide the number of instances to remove. For example, when scale-in starts, it will remove **1** instance.

19. In the **Scaling limits** section, provide the minimum number of instances to maintain. In this case, set it to **2**. Provide a maximum number of instances. In this case, we will provide **4** instance limits. Also, provide an initial number of instances. In this case, set it to **2**. You can see an example of this in the following screenshot:

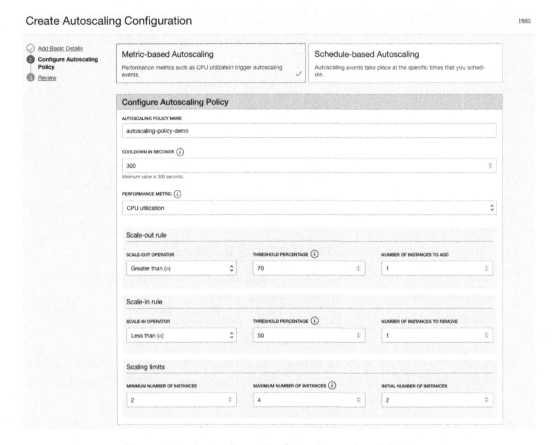

Figure 4.32 – Autoscaling – Configure Autoscaling Policy page

20. Click on **Next**.

21. Review the details and click on **Create**.

With that, you've learned how to create an autoscaling configuration and let OCI handle the horizontal scaling of OCI compute instances.

Connecting to instances using an instance console connection

When you're working with deploying compute instances, you can get in situations where the compute has failed to boot because of a misconfiguration in the OS, or there's a problem with a specific driver that could not load during boot. When this happens, your instance will be stuck and you won't have network access.

So, with instance console connections, you can access your instance in the same way you would using a serial console. You will be able to access an instance even if you don't have network connectivity and then gain access to the instance screen. From there, you can, for example, access the root filesystem to fix a misconfigured file or even replace your SSH key.

OCI offers two ways to connect to console connections: using SSH or using VNC.

Using this console connection, you can do the following:

- You can either add an SSH key or reset the SSH keys for the default `opc` user.

- You can edit system configuration files.

- When you import a customized image and that does not boot up, you can SSH to the console of it to troubleshoot.

- If there is an issue with an existing instance no longer responding, you can log into the console.

Let's create a console connection and then log into the instance console. Follow these steps:

1. Open the navigation menu, select **Compute**, and select **Instances**.

2. From the list of instances, click on the instance name that you want to create the console connection for.

3. On the **Instance Details** page, under the **Resources** section, click **Console Connection**, and then click **Create Console Connection**.

4. Specify the public key portion of the SSH key and then click **Create Console Connection**. You can see an example of this in the following screenshot:

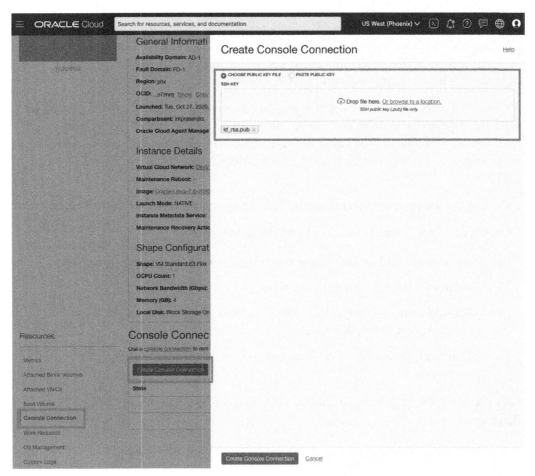

Figure 4.33 – Create Console Connection page

> **Note**
> This SSH key can be different than the one you used to launch your instance.

5. Once the console connection job has completed, its status will change to **ACTIVE**.

Now that you have created the connection, let's connect to the instance. We will show you how to do this in the next section.

Connecting to the serial console from macOS or Linux OS

You need to use an SSH client to connect to the serial console of the instance. By default, macOS and Linux distribution has an `ssh` client installed:

1. In the console, in the **Resources** section of the **Instances Details** page, click **Console Connections**.

2. Click on the **Actions** icon, and then click **Copy Serial Console Connection for Linux/Mac**.

3. Open a Terminal window and paste in the command that you have copied in *step 2*. Press *Enter*. You can see an example of this in the following screenshot:

Figure 4.34 – Console connection from Mac

4. If you get a `Permission denied (public key). Key_exchange_ identification: Connection closed by remote host` error, you should include the identity file flag, `-i`, in the connection string to specify the SSH key to use. You must do this for both the SSH connection and the SSH `ProxyCommand`. This is shown in the following code:

```
ssh -i /<path>/<ssh_key> -o ProxyCommand='ssh -i
/<path>/<ssh_key> -W %h:%p -p 443...
```

For security reasons, you should delete the console connection once you have finished troubleshooting. If you do not do that, then OCI will terminate the serial console session after 24 hours.

Summary

In this chapter, you learned about the compute choices that you have in OCI. We explained the different types of compute instances that you can use, as well as the different type of shapes they can have. We also described how to use different OS images while creating these instances, such as Oracle-Provided images, custom images, and so on. You also learned how to export/import images for image portability across regions and tenancy. We then discussed instance config, pools, and autoscaling. Finally, you got to grips with console connections and how to use them to troubleshoot instance issues.

In the next chapter, we will cover the various storage choices that you have in OCI and how to leverage them in your use cases.

5
Understanding Oracle Cloud Infrastructure Storage Options

Data in your overall cloud computing system is the most critical part of your application. **Oracle Cloud Infrastructure** (**OCI**) storage options give you multiple options and flexibility to store your digital data in a logical representation of the storage pools. OCI's physical storage options span across multiple backend storage devices and their categories are also very different from their use cases. Whether you want super-performing local data storage within your compute box or you want highly scalable and performant storage, OCI has it all covered. In fact, OCI also offers very low-cost storage for backing up your application data. OCI has vast storage options to choose from for your various needs, providing Block Volume, Local NVMe, **File Storage Service** (**FSS**), Object Storage, and Archive Storage storage options.

OCI's Block Volume service lets you attach a volume to an instance, move that across to a different instance, and also change the performance characteristics of it—for example, changing it to extreme performance. You can choose local NVMe for higher **input/ output operations per second (IOPS)** performance where data locality is a requirement. OCI's FSS provides durable, scalable, secure, and enterprise-grade network filesystems, whereas you can choose Object Storage for fast, immediate, and frequent access to data as objects, and Archive Storage for rare access to data that is stored there, such as backup data. However, by nature, Archive Storage is set up to prevent data being stored for a long period of time.

By the end of this chapter, you should be able to choose between the Block Volume, Object Storage, File Storage, and Archive Storage options.

In this chapter, we're going to cover the following main topics:

- OCI Block Volume
- OCI File Storage
- OCI Object Storage

OCI Block Volume

To understand the service, let's begin by understanding what a block volume is. A **block volume** is a type of block device that is used as data storage. The OCI Block Volume service uses **Internet Small Computer Systems Interface (iSCSI)** to deliver features and performance. OCI Block Volume has been carefully designed for the security and durability of data and lets you create block volumes and attach them to your compute instance. The OCI Block Volume service delivers a simple, scalable block volume service that fulfills all your workload performance needs. You can treat this volume as your regular hard drive once you attach it to an instance. The Block Volume service utilizes industry-leading highest performance **Non-Volatile Memory Express (NVMe)** drives and is offered over the network using the standard iSCSI protocol.

The Block Volume service serves both the boot volume (for the **operating system (OS)** disk) and the block volume (applications data). As the name suggests, it lets you store your application data independently and beyond the lifespan of compute instances. This means that even if you shut down or terminate your instance, your block storage data remains.

OCI Block Volume storage uses a fixed-size block for consistent performance. As iSCSI works on the network layer, the OCI Block Volume storage service also uses the same network backend (OCI **virtual cloud network**, or **VCN**) that an instance uses for connectivity. Not only that—OCI also offers the **paravirtualized** attachment of block volumes.

However, there are some restrictions. Not all instances can use paravirtualized block volumes. To use these, your instances must be provisioned using Oracle-provided images. Because OCI Block Volume storage operates at a raw-storage level, it performs consistently. OCI Block Volume storage performance is linear with the size of the storage, which means that, as the size of the storage grows, so does the level of IOPS that you can get out of it. It's so flexible that you can create a volume, attach it to an instance, and also move those block volumes whenever you need to. This total flexibility enables you to meet your applications' storage requirements.

These are typical use case scenarios for **Block Volume**:

- When you want persistent and durable storage for your application data
- If you want to expand an instance's local storage
- When you want to scale your instances

In the following diagram, you can get a high-level view of how an instance gets connected to a block storage and gets the boot volume and block volume for data from the same storage backend:

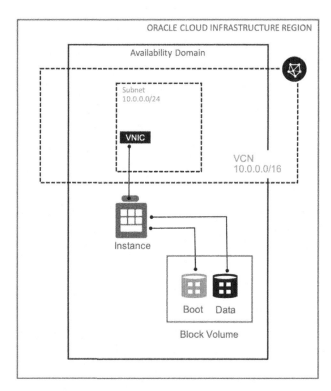

Figure 5.1 – Block storage overview

The Block Volume service is configurable from 50 **gigabytes** (**GB**) to 32 **terabytes** (**TB**), which is a huge range when you see it from an application's data requirement perspective. However, not only that: it also provides 32-volume attachment per instance. That means you can have 1 **petabyte** (**PB**) (32 GB x 32 volume) of block volume attached to an instance.

From a performance perspective, it is linear to the size of the storage. However, that is also dependent on an instance's shape because the shape decides the network speed of the instance. You can achieve 60 IOPS per GB of block volume for a **Balanced Performance** profile, at a maximum of 25,000 IOPS for **Balanced Performance** and 35,000 IOPS for **Higher Performance**. From a throughput perspective, you can achieve 480 **kilobytes per second** (**KBps**) per GB of block volume at a maximum of 320 **megabytes per second** (**MBps**) for a **Balanced Performance** profile. For a **Higher Performance** profile, this is 600 KBps per GB of block volume at a maximum of 480 MBps.

It is durable as well because OCI keeps multiple replicas across multiple storage server backends in an **availability domain** (**AD**). You also have an option to encrypt the volume at transit or at rest.

As you can imagine, the storage servers are hosted in a particular AD and connected to the AD local VCN, thus you can only access a volume from an instance hosted in the same AD and not from another AD.

Creating a block volume

So far, you have seen an overview of block storage and its use cases and performance criteria. In this subsection, we will go through creating a block volume and then attach it to an instance.

Let's create a block volume and connect to an instance, as follows:

1. Sign in to the OCI console.

2. Open the **Navigation** menu. Under **Core Infrastructure**, go to **Block Storage** and click **Block Volumes**.

3. Click **Create Block Volume**.

4. Provide the volume information, as follows:

    a. **Name**—Provide a name for the volume.

    b. **Compartment**—Choose a compartment where it is going to be created.

    c. **AD**—Select the AD where it should be provisioned.

    d. **Volume Size and Performance**—Either chose the **Default** size (which is 1,024 GB, and you can see the calculated performance numbers) or choose **Custom** and provide the size that you want. The benefit of choosing **Custom** is that you can choose **Higher Performance** with the same size of storage to satisfy your application requirement. You can see a sample output in the following screenshot:

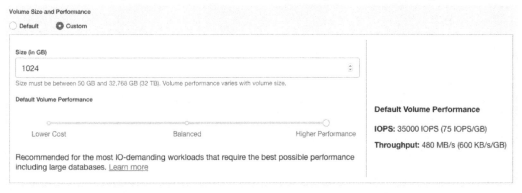

Figure 5.2 – Custom storage options for Higher Performance

    e. **Backup Policy**—You can choose a backup policy from the list. We will discuss volume backups in detail in our upcoming section.

    f. **Encryption**—You can either choose to encrypt this volume using Oracle-managed keys or customer-managed keys.

5. Click on **Create Block Volume**. You can see the overall workflow in the following screenshot:

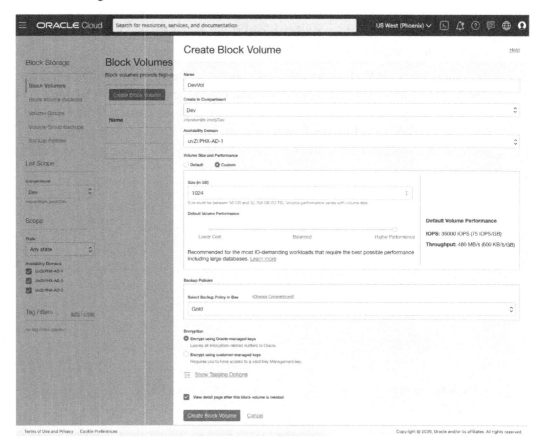

Figure 5.3 – Block volume creation workflow

So, you have now created a volume. Let's see how you can resize it if you have to.

Resizing a block volume

OCI also provides an online and offline volume resize feature through which you can enhance the performance of the block volume, or you can let OCI choose the performance based on your workload requirement and save money on it.

Let's perform an online resize of a block volume, as follows:

1. Sign in to the OCI console.

2. Open the **Navigation** menu. Under **Core Infrastructure**, go to **Block Storage** and click **Block Volumes**.

3. Click the **Actions** menu of the block volume that you want to resize and click on **Edit**.

4. On the **Edit** screen, you can increase the size of the volume and also choose the **Default Volume Performance** type.

5. Set **Auto-tune Performance** to **On**. This will help you to lower the cost when you detach the volume from an instance. It will retain this setting when you reattach it.

6. Click on **Save Changes**. You can see a sample output in the following screenshot:

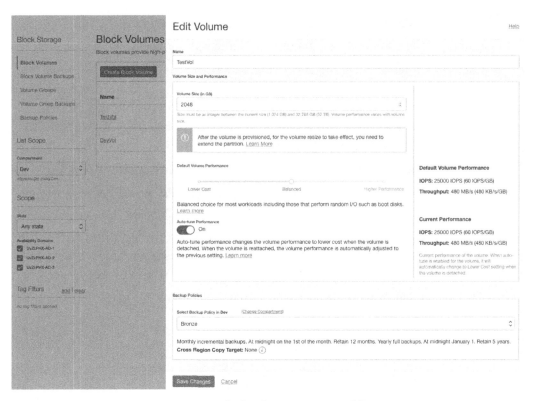

Figure 5.4 – Block volume creation workflow

You can see how you can use this resizing feature to keep a balance between performance and money for the block volume. Let's now see how you can attach this volume to an instance.

Attaching a block volume to an instance

There are two ways to attach a block volume to an instance. Either you can go to the **Instance Details** page and connect an existing block volume or you can go to the **Attached Instances** screen under the **Block Volume Details** page and do it. Let's go through the second option, as follows:

1. From the **Block Volume Details** page, go to the **Attached Instances** page. Click on **Attach to Instance**.

2. Depending on the type of the image to create the instance, select either **iSCSI** or **Paravirtualized**. We will choose **iSCSI** as that will walk you through the process of running iSCSI commands to mount the volume within the OS.

3. Choose an access type. In this case, we will show you the **Read/Write** method. If you want to create a cluster filesystem where you can simultaneously read and write data from multiple instances, then choose **Read/Write Shareable**. For a witness kind of a disk, you can choose a volume of **Read-only Shareable**. We will discuss this later in the chapter.

4. Choose the **Select Instance** option and select an instance from the dropdown.

5. You can optionally check the **Require CHAP credentials** option. We are not going to do this for this exercise.

6. Choose a device from the **Device Name** dropdown. If you select a provided device path, it becomes persistent between instant reboots. This is very important when you create a partition and filesystem and mount it inside the guest OS.

7. Click on **Attach**. You can see a sample output in the following screenshot:

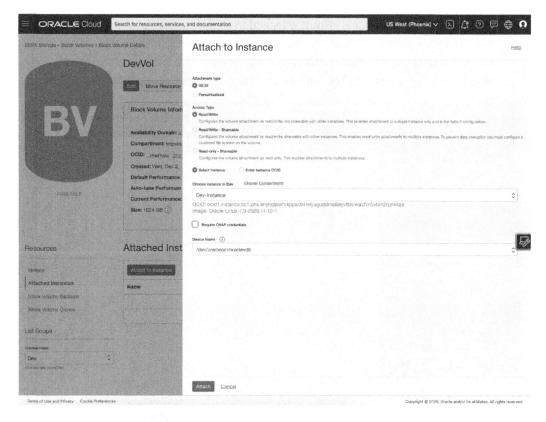

Figure 5.5 – Block volume attachment to instance

8. Once it is attached, you need to log in to the instance separately, using **Secure Shell** (**SSH**).

9. Copy the iSCSI connect command to connect the guest OS to the block volume. To do that, click the actions icon (three dots) next to the volume you're interested in, and then click **iSCSI Commands and Information**.

10. Copy the commands from the **Commands** section and paste it into a terminal window where you are logged in to the Linux instance.

11. This way, you will have the volume attached to the instance. But that's not all—you need to create a partition and filesystem and mount it within the guest OS as well. To do that, follow the standard method of creating a partition, create a filesystem, and mount it on the guest OS. You can see an example output in the following screenshot:

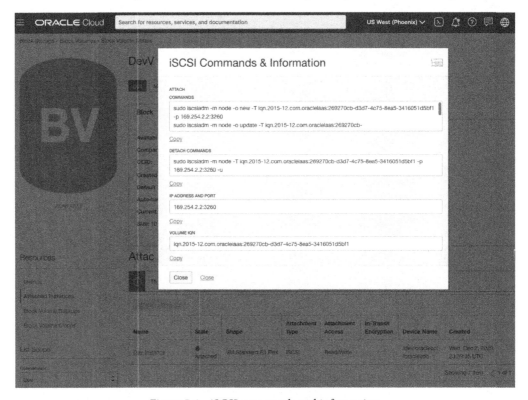

Figure 5.6 – iSCSI commands and information

So, you can see how easy it is to create a block volume, attach it to an instance, and then mount it within the filesystem. In the next section, let's talk about block volume backup operations.

Backing up and restoring a block volume

Block volumes allow you to take snapshots and point-in-time backups at any time. An interesting thing about volume backups is that they are differential and automatically managed, so a number of volume snapshot backups will chain to form the most recent backup, saving you space, time, and cost. The backup service manages these incremental backups for users. Backups go into the backup section of the storage service, which is based on Object Storage and gets encrypted as well. You can also copy the backup of a volume from one region to another.

When the time comes to restore, these backup/snapshots are automatically maintained so that any restorations will match the volume state at the time of the last snapshot. Users don't have to keep track of those incremental backups. Block volumes can be restored to the same or a different AD and reattached to the original instance or a new one.

You can see a logical representation of the backup operations of a block volume in the following diagram:

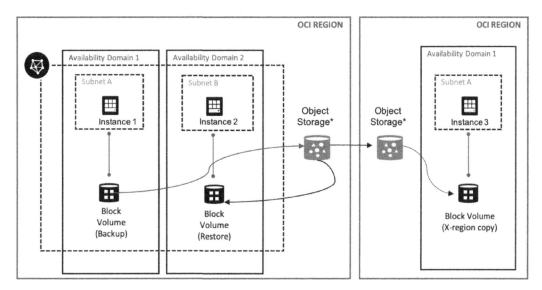

Figure 5.7 – Block volume backup operations

The preceding diagram shows how **Instance 1** is connected to **Block Volume (Backup)** and getting backed up to the Object Storage bucket, and it's getting used to restore it to **Instance 2**. Also, note how the **Object Storage** bucket is getting replicated to a different region so that you can have a **disaster recovery (DR)** copy of this data in a different geographical region.

You can either initiate a backup manually or you can assign a policy that defines a set backup schedule.

There are two backup types (manual configuration) available in the Block Volume service, outlined as follows:

- **Incremental**: Only the changes since the last backup will be backed up.
- **Full**: As the name suggests, this backup includes all changes.

You can choose to create a custom type of backup policy and let the policy drive the replication, schedule, and so on. OCI provides one more level of backup and restoration, and that is using a pre-defined policy.

There are three backup policies, outlined as follows:

- **Bronze**: Monthly incremental backups, whereby your data is retained for 12 months. For a full yearly backup, it is retained for 5 years.

- **Silver**: Weekly incremental backups, whereby your data is retained for 4 weeks. It includes capabilities from the Bronze category.

- **Gold**: Daily incremental backups, whereby your data is retained for 7 days. It includes capabilities from the Silver and Bronze categories.

Apart from schedule- and policy-based backups, you can always choose to get a manual backup done. Here is how it should be done:

1. Sign in to the OCI console.

2. Open the **Navigation** menu. Under **Core Infrastructure**, go to **Block Storage** and click **Block Volumes**.

3. Click on the **Actions** menu of the volume that you want to take a backup of and click on **Create Manual Backup**. You can see a sample output in the following screenshot:

Figure 5.8 – Block volume manual clone

4. Provide a name for the backup and choose a type from the **Backup Type** dropdown. This can either be **Full Backup** or **Incremental Backup**.

5. Click on **Create Block Volume Backup**. You can see a sample output in the following screenshot:

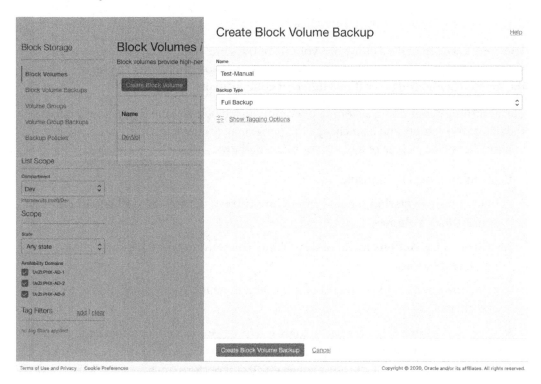

Figure 5.9 – Block volume manual clone workflow

So, you can see you have a choice when protecting your block volume data—either you can let OCI take a backup automatically using the policy and schedule or you can manually take a backup as well. In the next section, we will talk about another way of having a backup copy of your block volume.

Cloning a block volume

The Block Volume service also allows you to clone a block volume, whereby a cloning operation makes a copy of an existing block volume. It's a point-in-time direct disk-to-disk deep-copy process. When you initiate a clone operation, it just creates a cloned volume and initiates a data copy operation in the background. Once the copy is done, no data will be copied again from the source.

You are allowed to make a clone of a volume in the same region and same AD as the source volume. However, if you have adequate permission, then you can create a clone of the source volume and place it in a different compartment.

The best thing about doing a cloning operation on a block volume is that you can increase the size of the volume and also change the performance characteristics of the cloned volume. Let's take a clone of a block volume, as follows:

1. Sign in to the OCI console.

2. Open the **Navigation** menu. Under **Core Infrastructure**, go to **Block Storage** and click **Block Volumes**.

3. Click on the **Actions** menu of the volume you want to take a backup of and click on **Create Clone**.

4. Provide a name and choose a compartment in which you want this clone to be created.

5. For the **Volume Size and Performance** setting, you can either choose the **Default** option, which will keep the same characteristics as the source volume, or you can click on **Custom** and choose a volume size and performance.

6. For this example, click on **Custom** and change any of the characteristics of the volume (size or performance).

7. Select an **Encryption** type and click on **Create Clone**. You can see a sample output in the following screenshot:

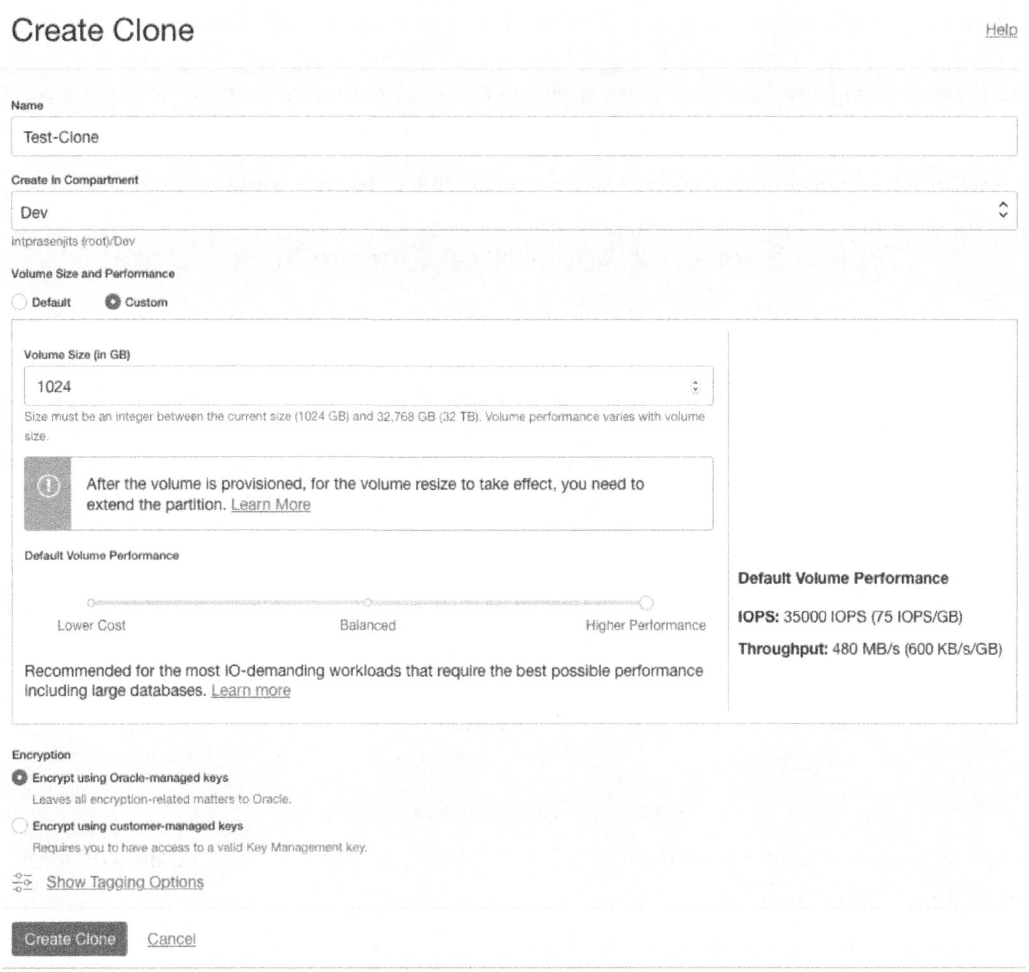

Create Clone

Name

Test-Clone

Create In Compartment

Dev

intprasenjits (root)/Dev

Volume Size and Performance

( ) Default   (●) Custom

Volume Size (in GB)

1024

Size must be an integer between the current size (1024 GB) and 32,768 GB (32 TB). Volume performance varies with volume size.

> (!) After the volume is provisioned, for the volume resize to take effect, you need to extend the partition. Learn More

Default Volume Performance

Lower Cost   Balanced   Higher Performance

Recommended for the most IO-demanding workloads that require the best possible performance including large databases. Learn more

Default Volume Performance

IOPS: 35000 IOPS (75 IOPS/GB)

Throughput: 480 MB/s (600 KB/s/GB)

Encryption

(●) Encrypt using Oracle-managed keys
    Leaves all encryption-related matters to Oracle.

( ) Encrypt using customer-managed keys
    Requires you to have access to a valid Key Management key.

Show Tagging Options

[Create Clone]   Cancel

Figure 5.10 – Creating a clone of a block volume

So, you can see that by cloning, you can create a bigger volume, change the performance characteristics, and at the same time keep a backup of the volume as well. In the next section, we will discuss how you can group these volumes together to perform the operations we have discussed so far.

Volume groups

The OCI Block Volume service lets you group together block and boot volumes from multiple compartments across multiple compute instances in a volume group. Volume groups are essential when you create volume group backups and clones.

We can manually trigger a full or incremental backup of all the volumes in a volume group, leveraging a coordinated snapshot across all the volumes. Volume groups help to manage the life cycle of enterprise applications because these enterprise applications require multiple volumes across multiple compute instances to function effectively.

You can see a logical representation of volume groups in the following diagram:

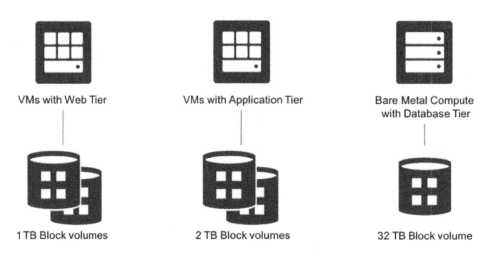

Figure 5.11 – Volume groups overview

The preceding diagram shows the grouping of volumes that are getting tied up with a set of **virtual machines** (**VMs**).

Let's quickly create a volume group from the OCI console, as follows:

1. Sign in to the OCI console.

2. Open the **Navigation** menu. Under **Core Infrastructure**, go to **Block Storage** and click **Block Volumes**.

3. Click on the **Volume Groups** section and click on **Create Volume Group**.

4. Provide a name and choose a compartment in which you want this volume group to be created.

5. Choose an AD from where you want to pick up the volumes.

6. In the **Volumes** section, make selections from the **Compartment** and **Volume** dropdowns. You can click on + **Volume** to add multiple of them.

7. Click on **Create Volume Group**. You can see a sample output in the following screenshot:

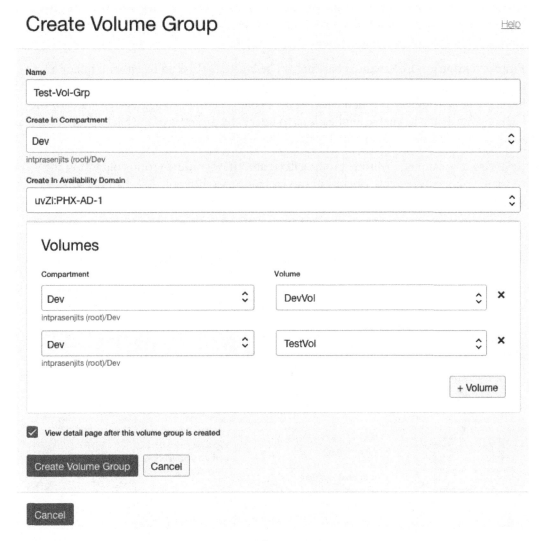

Figure 5.12 – Volume group creation

In this section, you have seen how to group volumes together to perform a backup of the volumes together.

Volume groups for coordinate backups

A volume group is used when you want to create a one-time backup of all the volumes, and as a result it generates a volume group backup. You can then use this volume group backup to create a new volume group, and to do so you need to restore all the data for volumes that are in the volume group.

From a volume group, a manual backup can be created. This can be either a full or an incremental backup (a full backup is required to have happened before an incremental backup can be triggered). When backing up a volume group, an aggregated state for the backup is available to enable applications to query the progress of the backup, in particular to figure out when the coordinated backups have been completed.

Restoring a backup of a volume group will create a new volume group containing the restored volumes. A restore operation can be made to a different AD than the source volume group, but this must be in the same region.

You can see an overview of this in the following diagram:

Volume Groups for Coordinated Backups

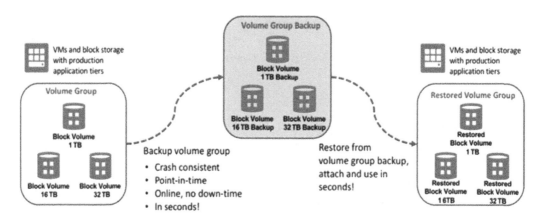

Figure 5.13 – Volume group coordinated backup

In the preceding diagram, you can see how a volume group is getting backed up and then restored to a different volume group.

We have discussed backup options, so let's now discuss cloning options.

Volume groups for coordinate clones

A coordinate clone is a deep disk-to-disk copy of an entire volume group. This creates a new completely isolated volume group and a new set of volumes that are also completely isolated from their corresponding source volumes.

There is no delay in a cloning operation, which means it is immediate, and right after initiating a cloning operation, you can access the cloned volume group and cloned volumes within that. While you access the volume groups and clone volumes, your data gets copied in the background. The time it takes to finish the actual data copy depends on the amount of data that you are copying across—for example, copying 1 TB of data can take up to 15 minutes.

You can see an overview of this in the following diagram:

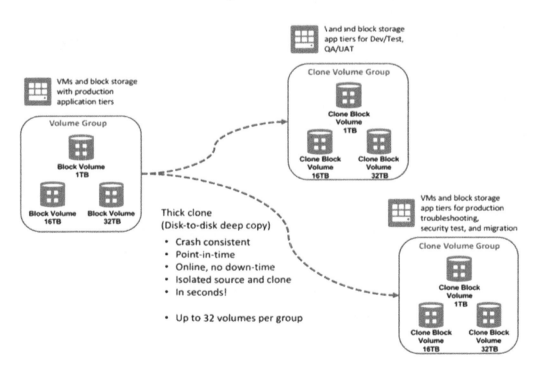

Figure 5.14 – Volume group cloning operation

The preceding diagram shows the coordinated clone operations of a volume group.

In the next section, you will see how you can attach one block volume to multiple instances.

Block Volume operations – shared multi-attach

The OCI Block Volume service has the capability to let you attach one single block volume to multiple instances. You can attach a volume in either R/O or R/W mode. The main use case of a shared volume is a cluster filesystem.

> **Important note**
>
> One thing that you have to keep in mind is that the Block Volume service does not provide the capability for concurrent writes on this block device, so you need to install a cluster filesystem on top of the block volume.

You can see a logical representation of a shared multi-attach volume in the following diagram:

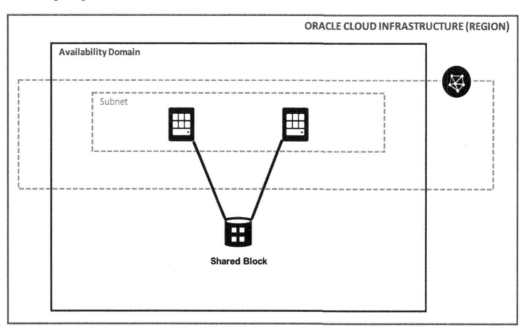

Figure 5.15 – Shared block volume attachment

In the preceding diagram, you can see that two different instances are connected to the same shared block volume in a single AD.

So, not only can you have performance and capacity, but you can also have other options, such as a cluster-aware application running on the OCI block volume too.

OCI File Storage Service

The OCI FSS is an enterprise-grade network filesystem, and at the same time, it is durable, scalable, and secure as well. As it's a network file storage service, it utilizes the same VCN backbone to serve, so you can use any instance type, be it bare-metal or VM, or even containers as well. If you implement VCN peering or a FastConnect or **Internet Protocol Security** (**IPsec**) VPN, then you can even access the filesystem from outside of the host VCN.

It's so massively scalable that you can even connect thousands of compute instances to the filesystem. It uses the **Network File System version 3.0** (**NFS v3.0**) protocol, and for the locking mechanism, it uses **Network Lock Manager** (**NLM**). For the best reliability, OCI uses five-way replication of the filesystem and stores it in different fault domains. For data protection, it uses snapshots; you can have 10,000 snapshots per filesystem. For security, it employs 128-bit data-at-rest encryption for all filesystems and metadata.

These are the main use cases of File Storage:

- Oracle applications lift and shift
- General-purpose filesystem
- Big data and analytics
- **High-performance computing** (**HPC**) scale-out applications
- Test/dev databases
- Microservices and containers

Creating a filesystem

A filesystem in the OCI FSS is a primary resource for storing files. To access your filesystems, you need a new or an existing mount target. You can have 100 filesystems per mount target. You can see an overview of a filesystem in the following diagram:

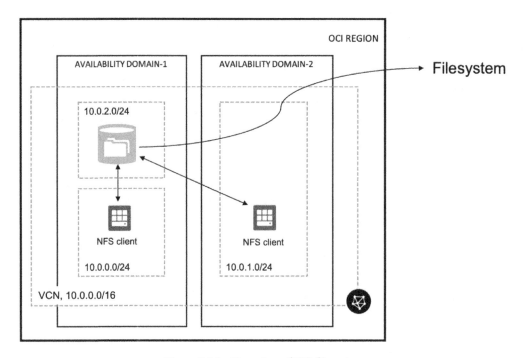

Figure 5.16 – Overview of FSS filesystem

To have access to this filesystem, you need mount points. Mount targets are NFS endpoints that are connected to your choice of VCN. These mount targets have an IP address and **Domain Name System (DNS)** name that you can use in your mount command.

Each mount target requires three private IP addresses in the subnet; you can't use a /30 subnet or smaller subnets for the mount targets. Out of those three, two of the IP addresses are used during mount target creation, and the third IP is used for **high availability (HA)**.

However, you need to be careful placing NFS clients and mount targets in the same subnet as that can cause IP conflicts, as users are not shown which private IPs are used for the mount targets. To avoid this, place the FSS mount target in its own subnet, where it can consume IPs as it needs.

Before we proceed further and discuss filesystem security, let's first create a filesystem and a mount target, as follows:

1. Sign in to the OCI console.

2. Open the **Navigation** menu. Under **Core Infrastructure**, go to **File Storage** and click **File Systems**.

3. Click on **Create File System**.

4. By default, OCI will provide all the required information—for example, name of the filesystem, encryption type, and export path—and will also create a mount target along with this.

5. However, you can click on the **Edit Details** link to edit each section. You can see a sample output in the following screenshot:

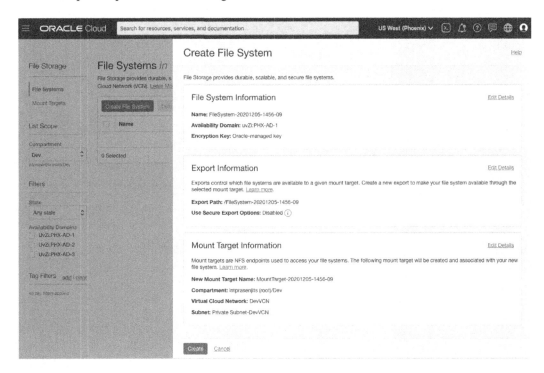

Figure 5.17 – Creating a filesystem

6. Click on **Create**.

The preceding steps will let you create a filesystem but it is not mounted to any instance, and the VCN security list is also not prepared for it to be mounted. Let's do that now, as follows:

1. Sign in to the OCI console.

2. Open the **Navigation** menu. Under **Core Infrastructure**, go to **File Storage** and click **File Systems**.

3. Click on **File System** to go to the **Filesystem details** page.

4. From the **Resources** section, click on **Exports**.

5. Click on the export that was created while creating the filesystem.

6. Click on **Mount Commands** and you will see the **Mount Commands** details screen. You can see an example screenshot here:

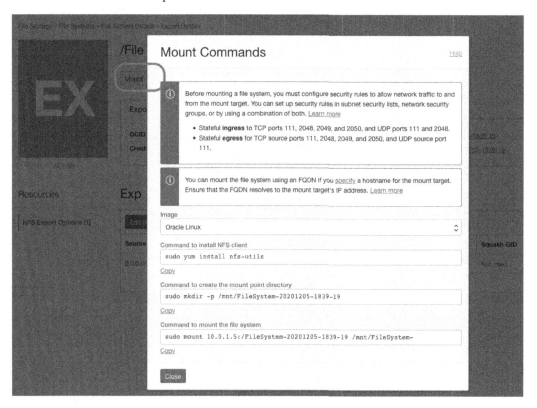

Figure 5.18 – FSS mount command screen

7. From here, you can see that you have to create a couple of security rules in your subnet to allow this mount target to be connected to the instances.

8. Open up the security list according to the given ports and traffic direction.

9. Choose the OS image and copy and run the commands inside the guest OS to mount the filesystem.

Filesystem security

A security list can be used as a virtual firewall to prevent NFS clients from mounting an FSS mount target (even in the same subnet). FSS needs these ports to be opened:

- Stateful ingress **Transmission Control Protocol** (**TCP**) ports 111, 2048-2050

- Stateful ingress **User Datagram Protocol** (**UDP**) ports 111 and 2048

- Stateful egress TCP ports 111, 2048-2050

- Stateful egress UDP port 111

However, using a security list to block unwanted traffic to a filesystem is not ideal because you can either allow access or block whole access to the mount target. Therefore, this will be applicable on all filesystems associated with it.

In a multi-tenant environment, you should use an NFS export option to limit how a client is able to connect to a filesystem.

By default, an NFS export option will allow full access for all NFS clients. You can see an example of that configuration in the following screenshot:

Exports

Source	Ports	Access	Squash	Squash UID	Squash GID
0.0.0.0/0	Any	Read/Write	None	Not used	Not used

Showing 1 Item

Figure 5.19 – NFS export option

Let's look at an example where the following applies:

- **Client X**, assigned to 10.0.0.0/24, requires **Read/Write** access to **filesystem A**, but not **filesystem B**.

- **Client Y**, assigned to 10.0.1.0/24, requires **Read** access to **filesystem B**, but no access to **filesystem A**.

- Both filesystems **A** and **B** are associated with a single mount target.

You can see an example of the preceding scenario in the following diagram:

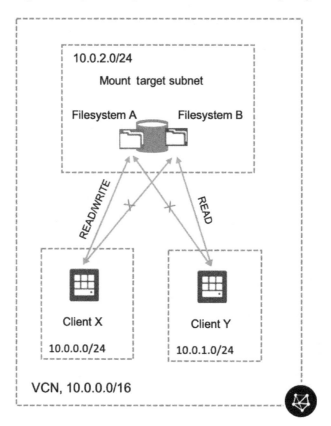

Figure 5.20 – Export option rule

You need to run the following commands to make it happen. To do that, you can use OCI Cloud Shell:

```
oci fs export update --export-id <FS_A_export_ID> --export-
options '[{"source":"10.0.0.0/24 ","require-privileged-
source-port":"true","access":"READ_WRITE","identity-
squash":"NONE","anonymous-uid":"65534","anonymous-
gid":"65534"}]'
```

You have just allowed an `export` option from a particular subnet; let's do that for the other one as well, as follows:

```
oci fs export update --export-id <FS_B_export_ID> --export-
options '[{"source":"10.0.1.0/24 ","require-privileged-
source-port":"true","access":"READ_ONLY","identity-
squash":"NONE","anonymous-uid":"65534","anonymous-
gid":"65534"}]'
```

The preceding commands will update **NFS Export Options** to allow specific clients to use only specific mount targets.

With this, we have concluded our discussion on the OCI FSS. In the next section, we will go through OCI Object Storage.

OCI Object Storage

In our earlier section, we discussed high-performance, durable, secure, and scalable storage solutions, but OCI has lot more to offer. OCI offers "hot" storage that is frequently accessed and "cold" storage that is less frequently accessed.

These are two different storage tiers that are performant as well, outlined as follows:

- **Object Storage**: This tier of storage is what you need when you require fast, immediate, and frequent access to data.

- **Archive Storage**: This tier of storage is what you need when you don't require frequent access to data, but the retention period for this type of data is long.

The OCI Object Storage service is an internet-scale, high-performance storage platform. If you think about storing unlimited bytes of unstructured data, such as images, media files, logs, and backups, then this is an ideal solution.

Data in object storage is managed using an **application programming interface (API)** and standard **HyperText Transfer Protocol (HTTP)** verbs. This service is regional. OCI Object Storage not only provides object storage but also provides an archive storage solution at a low cost for less frequently accessed data. You can either put the objects (your data) onto the object storage and have it as public-facing or you can put the data onto private access. If it is put onto **Private access** mode, you can use an **OCI service gateway** to access this data from the OCI resources. You can create a replication policy and have the objects copied over to a different region. You can also give pre-authenticated access to either a whole bucket or a specific object. For larger files, you can use a multipart upload as well.

There are three resources in the OCI Object Storage service, outlined as follows:

- **Object**: Objects are nothing but data, regardless of content type. Each object is composed of data and metadata.

- **Bucket**: A bucket is what you store your objects in. You have to store all of your objects (that is, your data) in a bucket.

- **Namespace**: This is a top-level container and refers to all buckets and objects. Each tenancy has a unique namespace that spans across all compartments and regions. You cannot customize, change, or request a namespace name change.

Let's create an object storage bucket and upload a file (as an object) to the bucket, as follows:

1. Sign in to the OCI console.

2. Open the **Navigation** menu. Under **Core Infrastructure**, go to **Object Storage** and click **Object Storage**.

3. Click on **Create Bucket**.

4. Provide a name for the bucket, and then choose a storage tier from either
    Standard or **Archive**. You can check **Emit Object Events**, which is needed when
    you run automation based on object upload. You can also choose **Enable Object
    Versioning**—choose an **Encryption** method and click on **Create Bucket**. You can
    see a sample output in the following screenshot:

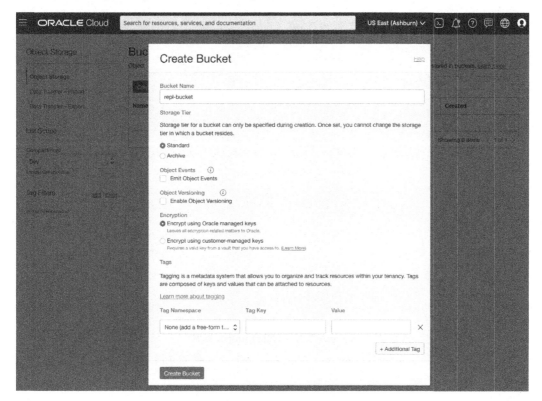

Figure 5.21 – Creating an Object Storage bucket

You have just created a bucket. Now, it is time to upload some objects to it, as follows:

1. From the **Object Storage Bucket Details** page, select **Objects** under the
    Resources section.

2. Click on **Upload**.

3. Select a file or drag a file onto the **Choose Files from your Computer** section.

4.   Click on **Upload**. You can see a sample screenshot of this operation here:

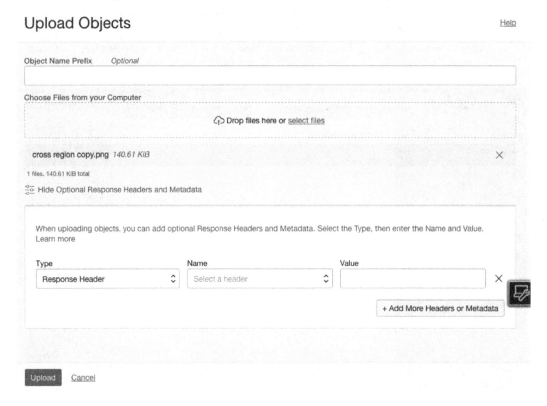

Figure 5.22 – Uploading objects

So, you have just created a bucket and uploaded some objects, but you did not provide access to it. So, let's see what we can do about that.

Pre-authenticated requests

The OCI Object Storage service provides **pre-authenticated requests** (**PARs**). PARs help you to access either an object or a bucket without having your own credentials to access it. You can either create a PAR for a whole bucket or you can choose individual objects to grant access as well.

Let's provide access to the just-created object, as follows:

1.   From the **Object Storage Bucket Details** page, select **Objects** under the **Resources** section.

2.   Click on the **Actions** menu of the object you want to create a PAR for.

3. Click on **Create Pre-Authenticated Request**.

4. Provide a name for the PAR. By default, it will show this as an **Object** PAR, but you can choose **Bucket** as well.

5. Choose an access type: either read, write or read, or both read and write.

6. Choose an expiration time. By default, it will give you 7 days' access to this object. You can see a sample output in the following screenshot:

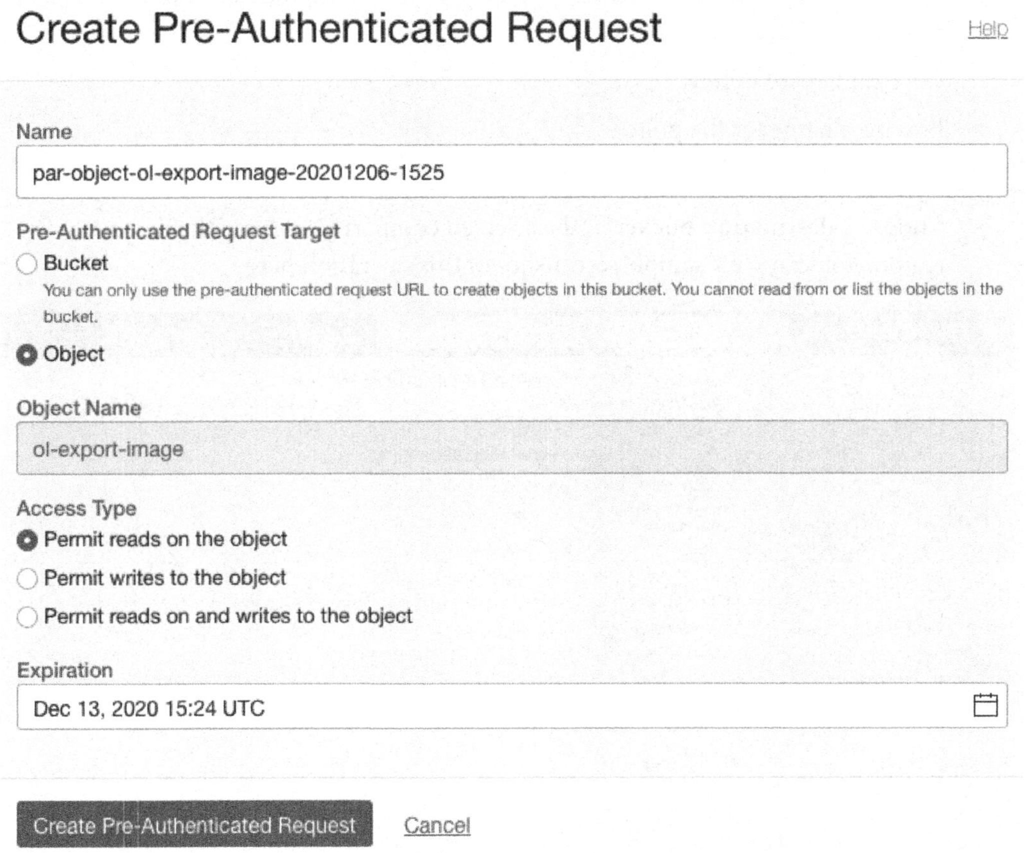

Create Pre-Authenticated Request

Help

Name

par-object-ol-export-image-20201206-1525

Pre-Authenticated Request Target

◯ Bucket

You can only use the pre-authenticated request URL to create objects in this bucket. You cannot read from or list the objects in the bucket.

🔘 Object

Object Name

ol-export-image

Access Type

🔘 Permit reads on the object

◯ Permit writes to the object

◯ Permit reads on and writes to the object

Expiration

Dec 13, 2020 15:24 UTC

Create Pre-Authenticated Request   Cancel

Figure 5.23 – Creating a PAR

7. Click on **Create Pre-Authenticated Request**.

This way, you can have public access to any object for a specified period of time.

Cross-region copy

OCI Object Storage provides you with the ability to copy objects across regions using a replication policy. You have an option to choose between either copying objects to another bucket but in the same region or to another bucket but in a different region. However, you cannot copy objects from Archive Storage.

Let's perform a cross-region copy of the objects, as follows:

1. From the **Object Storage Bucket Details** page, select **Replication Policy** under the **Resources** section.

2. Click on **Create Policy**.

3. Provide a name for the policy.

4. Choose a **destination region**.

5. Choose a **destination bucket** in the selected compartment from the destination region. You can see a sample screenshot of this operation here:

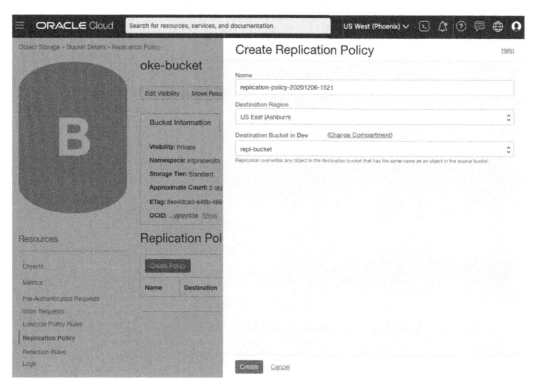

Figure 5.24 – Cross-region copy of the objects

6. Click on **Create**.

Multipart upload

A multipart upload is basically a parallel operation through which your objects will be uploaded to a bucket in parts so that the time to upload large objects can be reduced. There are four steps to a multipart upload, outlined as follows:

1. **Create object parts**—A multipart upload is performed when you upload objects larger than 100 **megabytes** (**MB**). At a maximum, an individual part of the data can be of 50 GB in size, or it can be as small as 10 MB. In this phase, the multipart upload will assign part numbers from 1 to 10,000 to the object.

2. **Initiate an upload**—Once the multipart upload engine creates a chunk, then a **REpresentational State Transfer** (**REST**) API called `CreateMultipartUpload` will be called to initiate a multipart upload.

3. **Upload object parts**—After the initialization, this engine initiates an `UploadPart` request for each object part upload. The best part of this is that if there are any hiccups such as network errors, then you can restart the failed upload of that individual part instead of the entire upload.

4. **Commit the upload**—Lastly, when every part is uploaded, this engine will complete the multipart upload by committing it, adding a bullet on the checksum, and so on.

Summary

In this chapter, we have learned the various different options for storing your application data in OCI. OCI not only provides best-in-class storage options but also offers various flavors of storage to have every aspect of your application's storage requirements satisfied. So, you can either choose high-performance block storage or super-elastic file storage to keep your application data very local to your instances. You can also choose the Object Storage tier for your unstructured data or the Archive Storage tier to keep your backup costs under control.

In the next chapter, you will see which database choices you have.

Section 2: Understanding the Additional Layers of Oracle Cloud Infrastructure

In the second part of this book, you will understand the more advanced concepts of **Oracle Cloud Infrastructure (OCI)**, learning about the database choices in OCI, the basics of cloud-native application patterns, and how can you build and run serverless applications. We will also look at managing OCI infrastructure as code, interacting with them using the CLI, API, and SDK, and lastly, how to build a hybrid cloud model using the OCVS solution.

The following chapters are in this section:

- *Chapter 6, Understanding Database Choices on Oracle Cloud Infrastructure*
- *Chapter 7, Building a Cloud-Native Application on Oracle Cloud Infrastructure*
- *Chapter 8, Running a Serverless Application on Oracle Cloud Infrastructure*
- *Chapter 9, Managing Infrastructure as Code on Oracle Cloud Infrastructure*
- *Chapter 10, Interacting with Oracle Cloud Infrastructure Using the CLI/API/SDK*
- *Chapter 11, Building a Hybrid Cloud on Oracle Cloud Infrastructure using Oracle Cloud VMware Solution*

6
Understanding Database Choices on Oracle Cloud Infrastructure

Oracle Cloud Infrastructure (**OCI**) provides a range of database services, and these are categorized as autonomous and co-managed database services. Despite the type of database service, these databases are designed to be robust so that enterprises can use them on a cloud scale. The Oracle Database service is backed by a robust infrastructure and is capable of handling mission-critical production workloads. This includes three availability domains and multiple regions. Currently, active redundancy can be implemented with features such as Data Guard configured to operate across all availability domains.

The networking that backs these database systems, along with every other system in OCI, is fully non-blocking and fully contextualized (multi-tenant with full isolation between networks). Speeds go from a minimum of 10 gigabits up to dual 25 gigabits per host, along with dedicated **InfiniBand** (**IB**) for cluster and storage networking for **Real Application Cluster** (**RAC**) and Exadata shapes.

Isolation is accomplished through off-box networking, which allows bare-metal hosts along with database systems such as Exadata to participate in virtual networks without needing virtual-switch software installed on the host.

At a very high level, there are three types of database systems offered by OCI. First, the bare-metal database systems come in a single-node shape. The second type of system is in the form of **virtual machine** (**VM**)-based shapes that support single- and two-node cluster operations. The third type of Oracle Database system in OCI is Exadata, which comes in quarter-, half-, and full-rack shapes.

In this chapter, we're going to cover the following main topics:

- Discussing OCI database choices
- Managing Oracle's Autonomous Database service

Discussing OCI database choices

Earlier, you learned that OCI databases predominately come in three different options. These database systems are protected by two- or three-way mirroring. In two-way mirroring, all the data gets mirrored, which means there are two copies of the same data. In three-way mirroring, you get additional protection from a bad disk sector in one disk and the failure of another disk. The database systems can be brought up as standalone or in a RAC cluster that is entirely configured and managed by the database service. In addition to RAC, Exadata systems are also available.

Because the systems are fully managed, they are **Maximum Availability Architecture** (**MAA**)-compliant.

Dynamic **central processing unit** (**CPU**) and storage scaling features are available, as well as the ability to upsize Exadata deployments across shapes. CPU core usage can be changed hourly to right-size the database system.

For security, there are several features and capabilities. These are a part of the identity services element, such as users, groups, compartments, and policies that can share or isolate the database system with fine-grained role-based controls. There is also networking security, implicit isolation, and off-box network virtualization—as well as security lists and on-host firewalls—in place.

Along with the policies and network security, there is a complete auditing service that tracks all actions of the users, whether through the **application programming interface** (**API**) or the console.

At the database level, encryption is on by default. Data at rest is transparently encrypted. Backups done to the object store are encrypted, and communications with the database service are encrypted by default.

Licensing flexibility is also available with **Bring Your Own License** (**BYOL**), so you can either use the database service with included licenses or bring existing Oracle licenses to the host for use on the cloud. All the database systems in OCI can be managed by tools such as Enterprise Manager, SQL Developer, and so on, just as with a regular on-premises database.

Let's look at the choices one by one. First, let's discuss VM database systems.

VM database systems

Database VMs offer a wide range of flexibility for the database service. Not all workloads need dedicated bare-metal servers. Customers ask for a cost-effective, easy-to-get-started, and durable database option that is well suited to a variety of workloads, ranging from **proof of concept** (**POC**) **development/testing** (**dev/test**) environments to production applications. VM-based database shapes can accommodate these workloads.

The database service on VMs is fully featured. While these instances run on VMs, the software can be configured with Standard, Enterprise, High, and Extreme editions. The database service on VMs is built on the same high-performance, enterprise-secure-grade, highly durable, and highly available cloud infrastructure used by all OCI services.

You will find the following two types of database systems running on VMs:

- A one-node VM database that is deployed using one VM

- A two-node VM database that is deployed using two VMs and then clustered using Oracle RAC

You will get a single database in a VM database offering. However, you can choose to allocate more computing power using different shapes of VM for these databases.

You can choose the storage size of the VM database system, but once deployed, you cannot change the number of CPUs allocated to this. You also have the ability to choose an older database when you select a VM database.

For the better **high-availability** (**HA**) architecture, OCI puts two VMs in two different availability domains when you select a two-node RAC cluster VM database. You can also configure Data Guard between these two VMs.

Let's look at the storage architecture of VM database systems. The OCI VM database system uses **Automatic Storage Management (ASM)**, which in turn uses Block Volumes to mirror the data. ASM directly interfaces with the disks and inherently uses the triple-mirroring capability of the OCI block storage. The actual data and recovery data uses independent block storage volumes, where it's ASM's job to monitor these storage volumes for hard and soft failures. Disks are mounted on **ASM Cluster File System (ACFS)** or another filesystem providing maximum **input/output (I/O)**. Some resources such as wallets are mounted in a common store along with database homes (binaries), but the **DATA** and **RECOVERY** areas are found within ASM. You need to have this storage architecture for VM RAC database systems. You can see a logical representation of this storage architecture in the following screenshot:

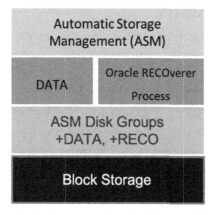

Figure 6.1 – VM database storage architecture

Storage is continuously monitored for any failures with the disks. These disks refer to **Non-Volatile Memory Express (NVMe)** and **solid-state drives (SSDs)**. In the case of VM shapes, block volumes are used, which is NVMe-based, and multiple block volumes are brought in and managed the same way as these disks.

Any disks that fail will be managed. Space is reserved for rebalancing, so the amount of free space is calculated based on that reservation. Whenever the shapes list a maximum amount of usable space in **DATA** and **RECO**, these reservations for rebalancing are already considered.

The root user has complete control over the storage subsystem, so customization and tuning are possible, but the service sets these up by default in an optimal way.

Up to now, you have learned how VM database systems work on OCI for customers who don't have a requirement to run it on bare-metal servers. In the next section, we will talk about bare-metal database systems.

Bare-metal database systems

A bare-metal database system comprises a 1-node database system. OCI uses Oracle Linux 6.8 as the base operating system for this bare-metal box and uses locally attached NVMe disks for storage. OCI recommends this for test and dev environments because of its lower cost. You can restore the database using a backup onto a different server, in case a failure happens.

As with other services, this is also manageable via the OCI **REpresentational State Transfer** (**REST**) API console, but note that you can also use Enterprise Manager, Enterprise Manager Express, SQL Developer, and the database **command-line interface** (**CLI**) to manage this database offering.

Let's look at the physical architecture of a bare-metal database system. You can see a logical representation of this in the following screenshot:

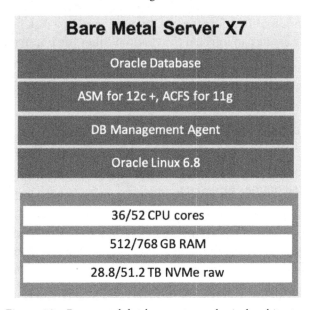

Figure 6.2 – Bare-metal database system: physical architecture

Now, let's look at the storage architecture of a bare-metal database system. You can see a logical representation of this in the following screenshot:

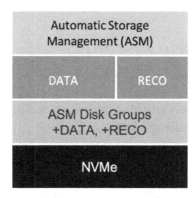

Figure 6.3 – Bare-metal database system: physical architecture

You can see that the ASM manages a large part of storage management. ASM manages the mirroring of NVMe disks, where disks are partitioned in such a way that one mirror is for DATA and one is for RECO. ASM also monitors the disks for hard and soft failures. It proactively puts the disks that get failed, have been predicted to fail, or are performing poorly into offline mode and performs corrective actions. On a disk failure, the database system automatically creates an internal ticket and notifies the internal team to contact the customer.

Let's look at Exadata database systems now.

Exadata database systems

In addition to VMs, bare-metal hosts, and bare-metal RACs and VMs, Exadata is also available on OCI. The Exadata systems are provided in three shapes, and all of them have all Exadata's advanced options turned on.

These are physical Exadata engineered systems that come with IB networking and scalable compute and storage nodes that can run on OCI without modification. Exadata database systems have complete isolation of tenants. Whenever partial shapes of Exadata are used, tenants are completely isolated.

Exadata on OCI gives all the features, performance, and capabilities of on-premises Exadata but with the flexibility of the cloud. All the installation, from systems to firmware, to operating system install and maintenance to patching, is managed by Oracle and presented as a public cloud service.

You can choose from three different Exadata database offerings—a quarter-rack, half-rack, and full-rack Exadata database, where you will get physical compute nodes and storage servers as part of the configuration you choose. It is very nice to be able to try out Exadata for your database needs on the cloud without having to deal with procuring a physical Exadata database.

Each compute node is configured to have root access to a virtual context running on the compute hosts. In case you need to install and run other software and tools, OCI has provided you root access to these nodes. This root access is only limited to the operating-system level, and you can't alter configuration for physical hardware, switches, **power distribution units (PDUs)**, **Integrated Lights Out Manager (ILOM)**, and storage servers. Not only do you have root access to the operating system, but you will also get admin access to the database, which you can connect to using either its private or public **Internet Protocol (IP)** address.

Database administration is the customer's job, whereby they are responsible for creating tablespaces, users, and so on. It is also the customer's job to control the recovery of the database in case of a failure, plus they also are in charge of the automated maintenance of the database.

Exadata DB systems on OCI benefit from having the **Identity and Access Management (IAM)** service, which helps create policies on which users and groups can perform actions on Exadata and database systems. You can have compartments and **virtual control networks (VCNs)** for these database services and either isolate or share them.

All the virtual cloud network capabilities and advantages are added to the Exadata and database systems. You do not have to use a public IP address for any of the instances if you do not want to. You can use a **virtual private network (VPN)** and FastConnect to connect to your on-premises environments. Because of the capabilities of OCI, we can have the application tier seamlessly running on VMs while the database is running on bare metal.

So, you can see that for different use cases, you have different database choices in OCI. In the next section, we will discuss Oracle's Autonomous Database service.

Managing Oracle's Autonomous Database service

Unlike other databases that you have learned about so far, where each database is individual, Autonomous Database is a set of OCI databases whereby each database has been built to serve a particular type of workload. For data warehouse workloads, which are an analytical type of workload, OCI provides **Autonomous Data Warehouse (ADW)**.

However, if you are looking for a database to support more transactional data, then OCI has the **Autonomous Transaction Processing (ATP)** database service.

The third member of the family is **Autonomous JSON Database**. This is built for applications that have **JavaScript Object Notation (JSON)**-centric schema requirements. This service also offers document APIs and native JSON storage.

The OCI Autonomous Database offering is fully managed like the other Oracle services. As it is autonomous in nature, you have no responsibility to configure and manage any hardware and don't even need to install any software. The CPU and storage capacity are scalable.

With Autonomous Database, you don't need to do the following tasks:

- Back up the database
- Patch the database
- Upgrade the database
- Tune the database

Let's create an autonomous transaction processing database on OCI, as follows:

1. Sign in to the OCI console.
2. Open the navigation menu, select **Oracle Database**, and then **Autonomous Database**.
3. Click on **Create Autonomous Database**. You can see a sample screenshot here:

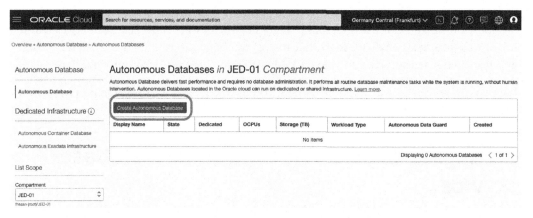

Figure 6.4 – Creating an autonomous database

4. Choose which compartment you want this database to be in.
5. Provide a display name and a database name.

6. From the **Choose a workload type** section, select **Transaction Processing**.

7. From the **Choose a deployment type** section, select **Shared Infrastructure**.

8. From **Choose database version**, choose the latest available database. At the time of this writing, the available option was **19c**.

9. Provide the **OCPU count** and **Storage (TB)** requirements. By default, both are set as **1**.

10. Check the **Auto scaling** checkbox if you want OCI to handle the scale-up operation when the load increases. You can see a sample output in the following screenshot:

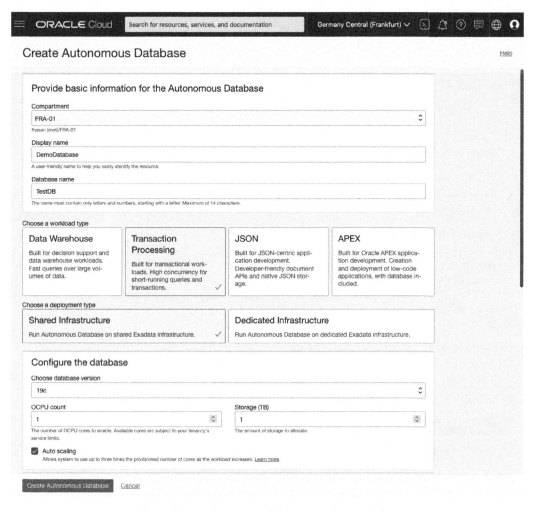

Figure 6.5 – Autonomous database creation workflow

11. Provide a password for the admin user.

12. Choose the **Secure access from everywhere** option under the **Access Type** heading. This is to simplify our testing option.

13. Select **License Included** as that is the easiest way to provision this database.

14. Click on **Create Autonomous Database**. You can see a sample output in the following screenshot:

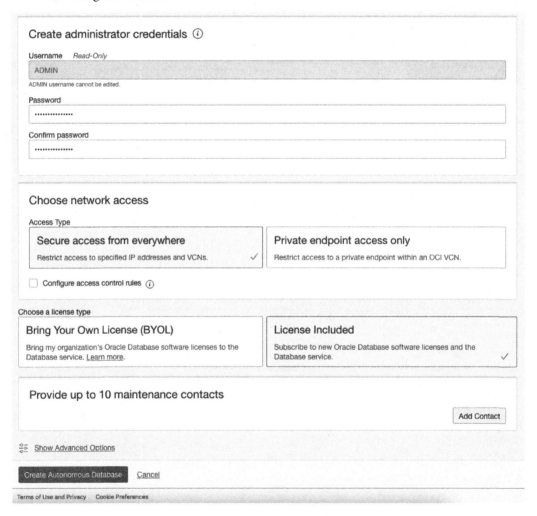

Figure 6.6 – Autonomous database creation workflow (continued)

15. Once it is finished, you will see the database available for consumption.

16. From the **Autonomous Database Details** screen, you can go to **SQL Developer Studio** to run a query from the web browser.

17. Click on the **Tools** tab and click on **Open Database Actions** from the **Database Actions** section. You can see a sample output in the following screenshot:

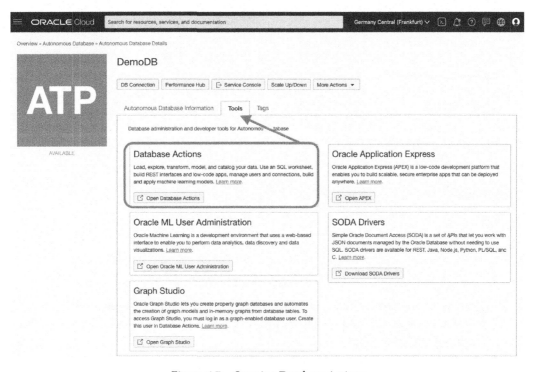

Figure 6.7 – Opening Database Actions

18. Provide a username and click on **Next**. Provide a password and click on **Sign in**.

19. Select **SQL** from the **Development** section. You can see an example output in the following screenshot:

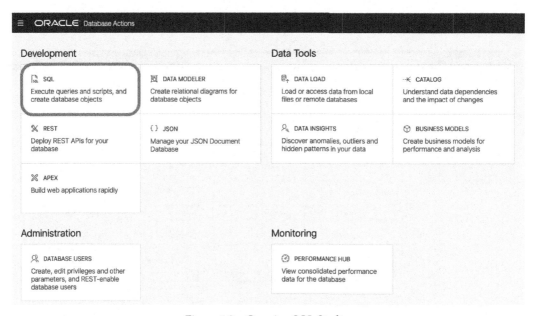

Figure 6.8 – Opening SQL Studio

20. Here, you can run any query or run any **Structured Query Language** (**SQL**) script to create database-related resources such as a table. You can see a sample output in the following screenshot:

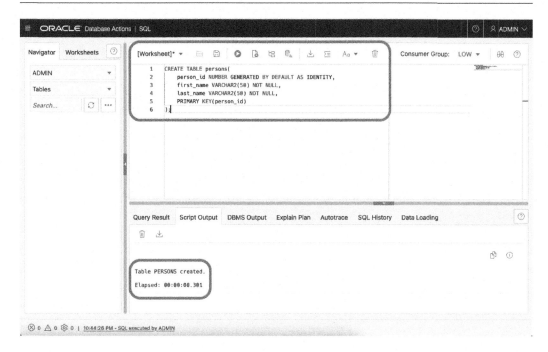

Figure 6.9 – Running SQL query

So, you can see how you can easily provision an autonomous database on OCI and use provided tools to manage the database as well.

Summary

In this chapter, you have learned about the various choices you have for adopting a particular database based on your workload type and how OCI can take care of database operations using the Autonomous Database service.

In the next chapter, you will see how you can build a cloud-native application on OCI.

7
Building a Cloud-Native Application on Oracle Cloud Infrastructure

Software development methodologies have changed a lot in the last two decades. Containers and microservices-based software development have taken the front seat. It has not only set foot in the startup world, but also expanded into large enterprises. Enterprises that were previously hesitant to look at this new model of building applications are now beginning to learn this and are changing their method of software delivery. Large IT enterprises are developing their own solutions for a hybrid model; that is, their solution not only caters to the on-premises software model, but is scaling to cloud-based models as well – they are being delivered as containers and being orchestrated using container orchestration services such as Kubernetes.

OCI provides **Oracle Container Engine for Kubernetes**, or **OKE** for short, which is a fully managed service that's highly scalable, highly available, and secure for deploying your microservices-based applications at scale. But this is not enough. OCI provides other methods so that we can have an environment where we can choose to be fully cloud native. In this chapter, we would show the use cases for cloud native applications and their evolution. We will also focus on why we need to adopt containers and container orchestration.

In this chapter, we're going to cover the following main topics:

- Evolution of cloud-native applications
- Storing application images on the OCI registry
- Deploying microservices on Oracle Container Engine for Kubernetes
- Exposing microservices using the OCI API gateway

Evolution of cloud native applications

Large enterprises are realizing the power of quickly innovating using their existing investments. To keep up this speed of innovation, they are moving on and performing cloud-native application development, where they can deliver their investments using built-in open source and open standards frameworks. But what are cloud-native applications? Cloud-native applications are built to provide consistent development, automation frameworks, and a seamless experience in a private, public, or hybrid cloud model. These applications achieve these benefits by providing self-serve, on-demand resource provisioning, and automated life cycle operations.

With this agility in mind, every cloud provider has their own methods of providing managed services, all while offering to help these large enterprise companies get started on this journey. Here, having a managed Kubernetes offering is the key to success.

Oracle knows that data is the lifeblood of cloud businesses. It ties them to their customers, their supply chain, their finances, and more. Oracle has built their cloud to support all the functionality and performance that their customers have had in their own data center, but with the benefits of increased agility and being able to eliminate mundane tasks such as managing hardware and facilities, upgrades, patches, and capacity forecasting. Oracle has deep expertise in this and provides cloud-specific automation to make migration possible, without any risks or high costs being involved. They offer tools to connect their cloud to their customer's data center, which makes migrating the workload easier. Everything OCI runs in their cloud is consistent with what customers run in their own data centers, including the Oracle database itself, the surrounding ecosystem of tools, such as **Real Application Cluster** (**RAC**), Data Guard, and Golden Gate, and all the third-party data and management tools their customers use.

Oracle has ensured that customers won't take a step backward in terms of performance when they move to the cloud. They have given customers the ability to run Exadata engineered systems as cloud services, thus offering the highest level of performance and scalability for Oracle workloads, something that is widely used in on-premises environments and not available on any other cloud. OCI has also built a cloud network with a massive interconnect bandwidth and no resource over-subscriptions to ensure that noisy neighbor problems aren't an issue, and also that the high performance they deliver doesn't vary based on external factors.

Once you get to the OCI, then the innovation behind this kicks into higher gear. Customers have a full range of options to deprecate and eliminate their data centers if they choose to, or to keep them running for some workloads, with deep compatibility and connectivity options from the Oracle Cloud. OCI allows customers to expand their curation of data with deep analytics and integration options. This helps them get onto Oracle's new autonomous database cloud services, which eliminate tedious management tasks and represent the future of enterprise data management. Customers can also expand the network of applications that are surrounding their data with cloud native functionality, which allows them to build new innovative approaches to managing and making use of data, including our Kubernetes-based container service, their flexible Oracle function capabilities, as well as a broad ecosystem of third-party options that unlock new value from data.

Let us show you the evolution of the application deployment in organizations during past 3 decades:

- During the 80's and the mid 90's, we saw that customers ran monolithic applications running on top of physical servers. They were developed using waterfall methodologies.

- During the end of the 90's until the millennium, customers started heavily using Unix/Linux operating systems, and we saw the emergence of virtualization (VMware and KVM). During this time, applications started using agile methodologies.

- Since 2010, we have seen a revolution and modernization of applications. Cloud computing has replaced a major chunk of data centers. This has led to applications being built around microservices that have been containerized, while developers and operations work toward an agile DevOps environment.

This is the modern application stack, which enables DevOps and microservices and runs on containers in the cloud. Thus, a new generation of applications are being created in the cloud and will only be running in the cloud. These are known as **cloud-native** applications.

Oracle has introduced a portfolio of products to address each of these building blocks. In this chapter, we will focus on containers. With the introduction of Oracle's managed container services, OCI is well positioned to support these modern approaches to software development and operations.

The following diagram shows the current software development and deployment model trend:

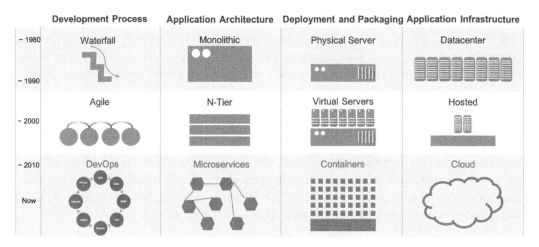

Figure 7.1 – History of software development model

There is a wide range of use cases that containers (we will be using Docker containers as a use case in this chapter) can be applied to, but as soon as their scale increases, orchestration becomes necessary. With Kubernetes, a Docker infrastructure can be made to scale and support much more advanced use cases.

Oracle's strategy for container-based services focuses on the leading technologies for containers and orchestration, which is Docker and Kubernetes. With these technologies, you can create applications at any scale, from simple DevOps setups to global mission-critical enterprise applications. Because the technologies are so widely used, they support a truly hybrid architecture, allowing you to run apps on-premises and in multiple clouds.

Let's look at each of these technology's use cases:

- Docker containers:

  - Docker is easy for adopting containers and has good ecosystem tools that help build developer productivity.

  - It is the most popular container runtime and supports the Open Container Initiative image format.

- Kubernetes orchestration:

  - This is the most popular container orchestration platform. It has widespread adoption and is production-ready.

  - Kubernetes is a complex container orchestration platform, but you can run cloud-scale applications on top of it.

  - With the maturity that it has, it has a vast feature set, such as autoscaling, rolling upgrades, support for running stateful apps, and many others.

Cloud-native strategies are often pioneered in software development projects by developers who are convinced there must be a better way. Once the projects gain traction, automation is the next logical step. Teams will formalize the hand-offs and workflows to get predictable outcomes. At some point, these approaches become core to the companies that adopt them, and any disruption will significantly impact their business. They will focus on scale, performance, availability, security, access, and more to ensure that these approaches become part of the business infrastructure. This is where managed services from Oracle make adoption easier, more reliable, and more cost-effective.

The following diagram shows how Oracle managed to position their strategy and help companies get into the modern cloud-native application deployment phase:

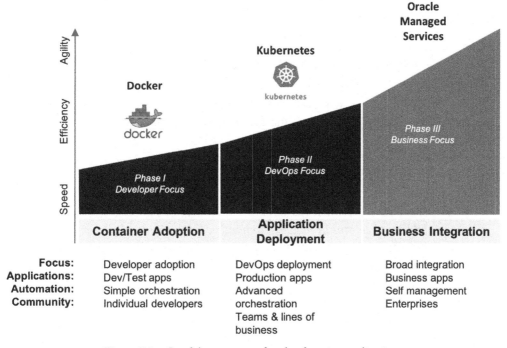

Figure 7.2 – Oracle's strategy to for cloud-native applications

Oracle has taken up a strategy for container-based infrastructure. Let's look at each of its pillars:

- **Complete cloud-native stack**: This strategy is used to help customers deliver tools and services that are complete, integrated, and open:

  - Continuous integration and deployment, container registry, orchestration/ scheduling, management/operations, analytics/introspection

  - Provides an application development platform for serverless and microservices

- **Open source**: This strategy is used to help customers actively participate in community-driven, open source container technologies:

  - Investing in Kubernetes, Docker, Fn, CNCF, DevTools, and DevOps by providing engineering resources, code contributions, and sponsorships

  - Active support from Oracle's portfolio of open source assets (Java and so on)

- **Managed services**: This strategy is different in terms of the implementation's quality, services, and operational excellence:

  - Full, transparent management.

  - Open source compatible.

  - Standards compliant.

  - Deployed to Oracle Cloud Infrastructure.

  - It is a purpose-built managed service for meeting enterprise-grade performance, security, HA, and governance.

But the key question here is, why should business leaders care about cloud-native application development? Well, as per the Cloud Native Computing Foundation at `https://www.cncf.io/wp-content/uploads/2020/08/CNCF-Webinar- _-Delivering-Cloud-Native-Application-and-Infrastructure- Management.pdf`:

> *"Cloud-native technologies empower organizations to build and run scalable applications in modern, dynamic environments such as public, private, and hybrid clouds, as well as containers, service meshes, microservices, immutable infrastructure, and declarative APIs".*

Cloud-native application development helps us independently invest and evolve features according to our business needs. It breaks monolithic applications into resilient, manageable, observable systems. It improves developer productivity, makes high-impact changes frequently at the same time open source technologies make solutions portable across clouds, and avoids lock-in. So, as you can see, you can use cloud-native technologies to break monolithic applications into small container-based distributed applications. This can be seen in the following diagram:

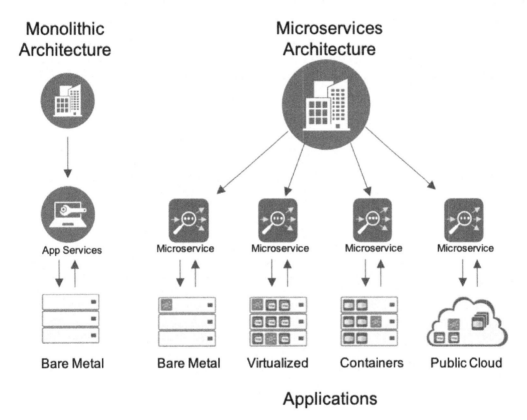

Figure 7.3 – Monolithic architecture for microservices

So far, you've learned about the evolution of OCI and how it provides services that help you with your journey of modern cloud-native application development and deployment. In the next section, we will talk about how OCI provides a free managed service for storing application container images.

Storing application images on the OCI registry

The OCI registry is a highly available Docker v2 container registry service that provides either a private or public service for storing and sharing container images. It is a regional service, which means you have different endpoints for different regions. It is a fully managed service and Oracle doesn't charge you for it. You can use the Docker CLI to push and pull images from the registry, and you can also use Kubernetes to download the images and run them on a fully managed Kubernetes environment.

Developers need to store these container images on a registry to maintain their state. You can use free and open source registries as well, but there are issues with doing this, such as access rights. The OCI registry is fully integrated with **OKE** and runs on the same OCI backend infrastructure. The following diagram shows these two service's integration and the customer's responsibilities:

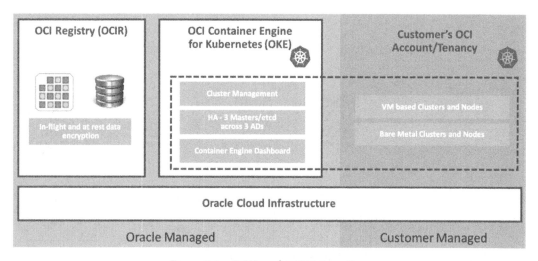

Figure 7.4 – OCIR and OKE integration

The gray shaded area designates the functions that Oracle manages for the customers, including an integrated registry and image storage and the managed Kubernetes. Users *do not* pay for any of Oracle's managed container infrastructure (the gray area). This is the control plane and enables you to configure these services and maintain operations, versions, their availability, and so on. The user pays regular fees for the compute, storage, and networking services that are used in the data plane (the customer managed area), which is where the applications run, data is stored, and so on.

Oracle manages the `etcd` and master nodes of the Kubernetes instance, in a high availability setup for the customer. Upgrading to new versions of Kubernetes will also be supported in the OKE dashboard, within the OCI console. The customer will manage the clusters/worker nodes that have been set up by the managed service for that instance in their own OCI account/tenancy. This is shown as **customer managed** in the preceding diagram.

Let's learn how to create the prerequisites and then create a repository before we push Docker images and pull them after that from the same repository.

Preparing for pushing and pulling images from the registry

To access the OCI registry, you need to know the URL endpoints for every region. As we've already mentioned, OCI registry is a regional service and an endpoint OS defined for each region. The following link states the OCIR endpoints for each region: `https://docs.oracle.com/en-us/iaas/Content/Registry/Concepts/ registryprerequisites.htm`. This list is ever growing as Oracle is consistently adding regions at a rapid pace. So, it is always a good idea to check this portal to see the latest available region and its corresponding OCIR link.

Secondly, you need to generate an auth token so that you can authenticate yourself and access the repository. Follow these steps to generate an auth token and keep it somewhere safe. We will use it to authenticate from Cloud Shell later on:

1. Sign into the Oracle Cloud Infrastructure console.

2. Open the **Profile** menu and click on **User Settings**.

3. Click on **Auth Tokens**.

4. Click on **Generate Token**.

5.   Provide a description and click on **Generate Token**, as shown in the following screenshot:

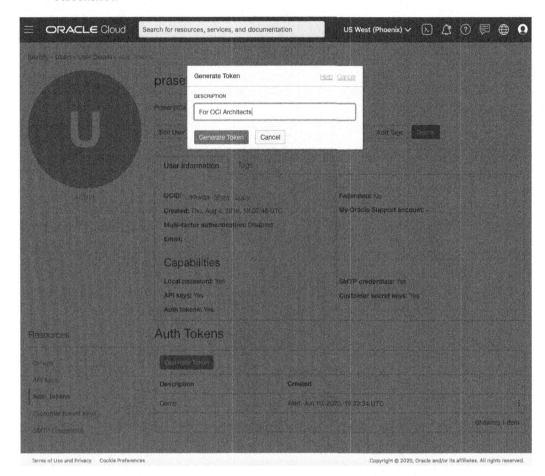

Figure 7.5 – Auth token generation

6.   Once it's generated, click on the **Show** button to check the token and copy it to a safe place, as shown here:

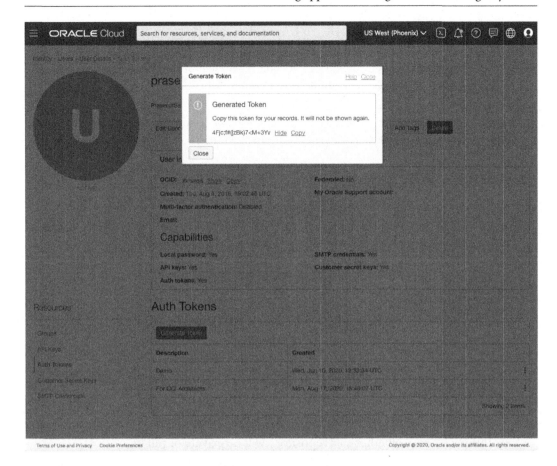

Figure 7.6 – Token value

7. Click on **Close**.

8. Lastly, to use the registry service, the users need to be either a part of the admin group or part of a group that the policy grants the appropriate permissions to, as follows:

    - **Allow group dev-viewers to inspect repositories in tenancy**: This policy defines the ability to see all the repositories in OCI registry that belong to the tenancy.

    - **Allow group dev-managers to manage repositories in tenancy**: This policy defines the ability to perform any operation on any repository in OCIR that belongs to the tenancy (pull an image, push an image, create/delete repositories, and so on). We looked at the policy statement in detail in *Chapter 2, Understanding Identity and Access Management*, so you already know how to write a statement and at what level.

> **Note**
> Repositories are tenancy-level resources, so if you want to control the access of these repositories, then you must create policies at the root compartment. This is because this is the top tier compartment of the tenancy.

In this section, we learned how to access the registry. The token that you just generated is required to access the registry. We'll create a registry in the next section.

Creating a repository

OCIR stores the container images in repositories. You can either create the repository in advance or have it ready to use. However, when you push an image to the OCIR, if there is no existing repository with the name provided, then the OCIR will create a private repository automatically for you.

Let's create a repository:

1. Sign into the Oracle Cloud Infrastructure console.

2. Select the region where you want to create this repository.

3. Click **Create Repository**.

4. Specify the following details for the new repository:

    - **Repository Name**: Provide a repository name of your choice.

    - **Public**: Choose whether this repository will be private or public.

    Click **Submit**. You can see an example of this in the following image:

Figure 7.7 – Creating an OCIR repository

With that, you've learned how to create a repository. Now, we will create a Docker container image and push it to the repository.

Creating a Docker container image

Let's build a Docker image using a sample Python flask application and push it to our OCIR repository. We will use the OCI Cloud Shell to do this:

1. In the top-right corner of the console, open **Cloud Shell**.

2. Run `git clone https://github.com/stretchcloud/flask-rate-limiter-cors-auth`.

3. Go inside the cloned directory by typing `cd flask-rate-limiter-cors-auth/`. You will see a `Dockerfile` inside this directory.

4. Now, build the Docker image by typing `docker build -t flaskapp:latest`. This can be seen in the following screenshot:

Figure 7.8 – Creating a Docker container image

5. Check the Docker image once it's been built by typing `docker images`. Copy the Docker image's ID.

With that, you've created a Docker container. Now, let's push it to the registry.

Pushing and pulling a Docker container image

Once you have the image ready, you can log into OCIR to push this image and then pull it anywhere you like:

1. We need to log into OCIR and to do that enter `docker login <region-key>.ocir.io`. You need to replace the `region-key` according to the OCIR region where you are logging in.

2. It will ask for the username at first and the format for the username is `tenancy-namespace/username`. You need to replace `tenancy-namespace` with your tenancy namespace, and you will get that from the **Tenancy Details** page. If you are using federated identity with Oracle Identity Cloud Service, then you need to use `tenancy-namespace>/oracleidentitycloudservice/username` as your format.

3. When prompted, enter the auth token you copied from the *Preparing for pushing and pulling images from the registry* section.

4. Tag to the image that you're going to push to the OCIR, like so:

   ```
   docker tag image-id target-tag
   ```

   For example, you might enter the following:

   ```
   docker tag 35255459d043 phx.ocir.io/intprasenjits/
   demoproject/flaskapp:latest
   ```

5. If you want to check whether the image has been tagged correctly, run the Docker images and verify that the list of images includes the tag you specified. The following screenshot shows an example of this:

Figure 7.9 – Tagging a Docker image

6. Push the Docker image from the client machine to the OCIR by entering the following:

```
docker push target-tag
```

The following is an example of this:

```
docker push phx.ocir.io/intprasenjits/demoproject/
flaskapp:latest
```

7. From the navigation menu, navigate to **Developer Services** and click on **Container Registry**.

8. Check the image that you pushed and click on the tag. You will see the image's layers, the size of the image, how many times it has been pulled, and so on:

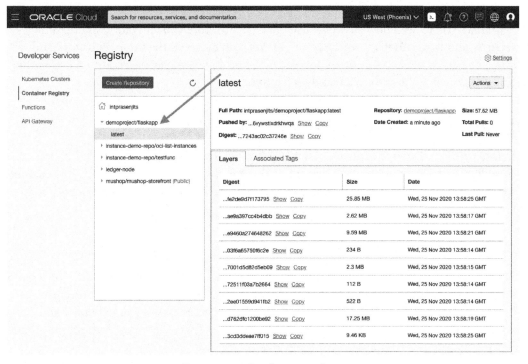

Figure 7.10 – Docker image layer

9. To pull the image, you must use the same Docker CLI. Pull the Docker image from OCIR to the client machine by entering the following:

```
docker pull region-key.ocir.io/tenancy-namespace/repo-
name/image-name:tag
```

The following is an example of this:

```
docker pull phx.ocir.io/intprasenjits/demoproject/
flaskapp:latest
```

10. Once you've pulled this image into your local dev machine, check if you can run this container and access the application endpoint.

Run the container by entering the following:

```
docker run -d -p 5000:5000 phx.ocir.io/intprasenjits/
demoproject/flaskapp
```

Access the application endpoint by entering the following:

```
curl -X GET -H "Content-type: application/json"
http://127.0.0.1:5000/ping
```

With that, you've seen how easy is to use the OCIR to store your private container images securely and then run it anywhere you wish. You can even use the same repository and image to deploy the application on top of OKE. For that, you need to create a secret within Kubernetes using the auth token and go from there.

Deploying microservices on OKE

Before we deep dive into Oracle's managed Kubernetes offering, let's provide a short introduction to Kubernetes itself. Learning about Kubernetes is a huge topic. This chapter will not cover all the aspects of Kubernetes; it will only focus on the key concepts and how OCI's managed Kubernetes service works.

Getting started with Kubernetes

Kubernetes is an open source project that's maintained by a community of developers and was created to solve container orchestration problems. By its very nature, Kubernetes is highly available and forms a single cluster unit. Kubernetes allows you to deploy and run your application in the form of disjoined/distributed software services, without pinning it to run on a specific computer.

You can manage your cluster through a web UI or through a CLI (kubectl). A Kubernetes cluster has two types of resources, as follows:

- A **master** node, which is responsible for managing the state of the cluster and coordinates the jobs within the cluster.

- A worker or **node**, which is responsible for running the scheduled containers (applications).

A Kubernetes worker node is responsible for running the containers on them and they can be either in the form of a virtual machine or even a physical machine. Each worker machine runs a process called a kubelet. This kubelet is responsible for managing nodes and communicating with the Kubernetes master. The following is a diagram of the Kubernetes architecture:

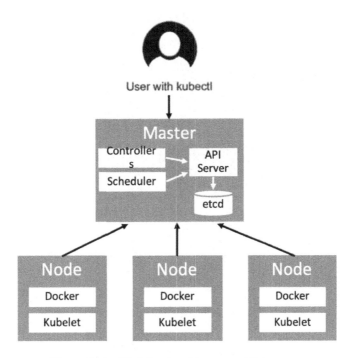

Figure 7.11 – High-level architecture of Kubernetes

You deploy your distributed applications in the form of containers on top of a Kubernetes cluster. You need to create a declarative file in YAML format to deploy your application. Sometimes, you can deploy your application using the command line as well. The advantage of using this declarative method is that you can update the parameters later on, to change how Kubernetes should maintain the state of this application.

When you send this YAML file using the kubectl command line, the Kubernetes master node that runs the API server sends an instruction to the kube scheduler, which schedules the container on an available node.

When you create a deployment, Kubernetes create **pods** to host your application instance.

However, Kubernetes doesn't run the container directly; instead, it creates a wrapper on top of it called a pod. This pod can run one or more containers within it. A pod also shares some key resources with those containers, such as its storage and a unique IP address.

Each pod gets scheduled on a particular node by the kube scheduler and remains running on that node until you terminate or delete it. If your Kubernetes cluster observes a node failure, then identical pods will come up, based on the number of pods to maintain in the deployment YAML.

The following diagram shows the high-level architecture of how pods are tied up to nodes:

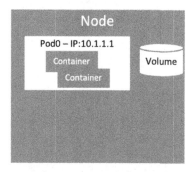

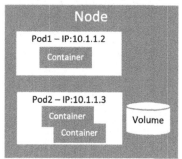

Figure 7.12 – Kubernetes deployment

So, now you know that you can deploy an application on top of a Kubernetes cluster. But how do you access it? By using a Kubernetes service.

A Kubernetes service creates a logical boundary by using a set of pods. This is called a service. Each of these logical boundaries will have a unique IP address assigned to it. Although your pods have IP address, they are not exposed outside the cluster.

Kubernetes services have been designed to receive traffic for the applications that are deployed within them. A pod within the cluster can send the network traffic or another service outside of the cluster can also send network traffic towards the service; for example, from the internet via a load balancer. The following is the architecture diagram of the Kubernetes service:

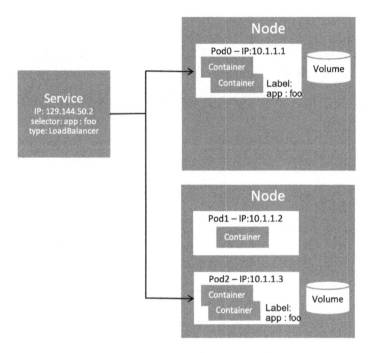

Figure 7.13 – Kubernetes service

Let's take a quick look at the components that make up a Kubernetes cluster:

- **kubectl**: This is a command-line tool that helps you manage Kubernetes resources using REST. You can perform all kinds of CRUD operations against Kubernetes resources.

- **Kubernetes API server**: Commands from kubectl are translated into REST API calls and issued to the API server. Users, other control plane components, and other tools such as CI/CD tools communicate with it.

- **Scheduler**: This works with the API server to schedule pods to the nodes. It provides information about the resources that are available on the nodes and those requested by pods. This is then used to decide which worker node will be selected for deployment.

- **Controller manager**: This is a daemon that watches the state of the cluster and reconciles the current state with the desired state; for example, Kubernetes components replication, keeping track of worker nodes, and handling node failures.

- **etcd store**: This is a simple, reliable, distributed, and consistent **Key Value** (**KV**) store. It persists the state of all REST API objects, how many pods are deployed to each worker node, and so on. Think of it as the `config.xml` domain.

- **Kubelet**: This is a service that's placed on each node that manages containers and is managed by the master. Kubelet keep the communication with the API server and responsible for managing resources on its node. Think of it like the node manager.

- **Docker**: This is the container runtime that runs on each node. It understands the Docker image format and how to run Docker containers.

- **Pod**: This is the smallest deployable unit that can be created, scheduled, and managed. It's a logical collection of containers that belong to an application.

- **Containers**: These are your applications, packaged and run in Docker or another supported container runtime format.

- **Proxy**: It runs on each node, acting as a network proxy and load balancer for a service on a worker node. Client requests that comes through an external load balancer will be redirected to the containers running in a pod through this proxy.

- **Load balancer**: This is an external load balancer that directs traffic to and from the proxy.

The following is a high-level Kubernetes architecture diagram showing all these components:

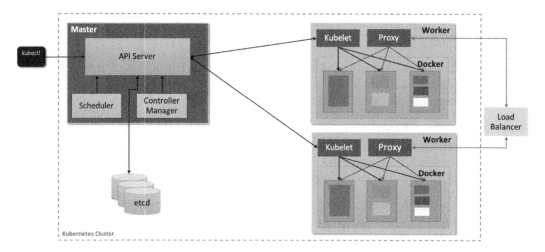

Figure 7.14 – Kubernetes service

So far, we have looked at the basic components and concepts of Kubernetes itself. We'll talk about Oracle's managed Kubernetes service in the next section.

Getting started with Oracle Container Engine for Kubernetes

As we mentioned earlier, **Container Engine for Kubernetes**, also known as **OKE**, is a fully managed Kubernetes service where Oracle will deploy the control plane in a highly available architecture and provide the master nodes free of charge. The customer will only pay for the resources that they are going to consume, such as their compute nodes, storage, load balancer, and so on. The following is the architecture diagram for OKE:

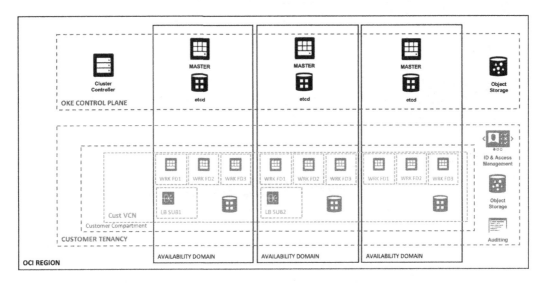

Figure 7.15 – OKE architecture

But what are the use cases for choosing OKE in the first place? Let's take a look.

Lifting and shifting an application to OKE

An Oracle-specific but popular use case for containerization is lift and shift WebLogic. WebLogic consists of WebLogic Application and WebLogic Server. WebLogic works with a database, such as an Oracle database, to serve web requests for, say, a sales portal. The entire WebLogic Application and Server are then containerized and defined in a Dockerfile, without any refactoring. After that, a CI/CD tool such as container pipelines or Jenkins is used to build, test, and push the resulting container image to the Cloud Infrastructure Registry. You can see a workflow of the lift and shift WLS on OKE here:

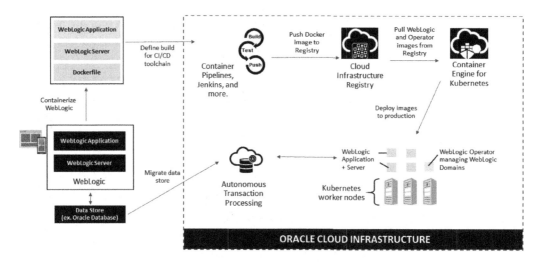

Figure 7.16 – Lifting and shifting WLS on the OKE architecture

This diagram, as well as the WebLogic Operator diagram (source available on GitHub at `https://github.com/oracle/weblogic-kubernetes-operator`), have been pulled from the registry using Oracle Container Engine for Kubernetes. The WebLogic Application and Server, as well as its operator, are then deployed to production on Kubernetes worker nodes. The resulting application is more scalable, available, and performant.

Refactoring an existing application

A general use case for leveraging containers is refactoring existing applications. In order to do this, an existing application, consisting of a user interface, an app server, and data access is rewritten as microservices, with each microservice running in a separate Docker container. The data store is also containerized. Databases such as MySQL, Cassandra, MongoDB, and more are available on the Docker Hub. Typically, you store the code in an **source code management** (**SCM**) system, such as GitHub.

The application and associated build scripts are then pushed into a CI/CD toolchain, such as container pipelines or Jenkins. After building and testing, Docker images are generated, which are then pushed into a private registry such as OCIR. Oracle Container Engine for Kubernetes, an enterprise-grade orchestration system for containers, can then be used to pull these Docker images and deploy the application and data store into production. The use of microservices allows the application to be more agile (code pushed more frequently), efficient, scalable, and easier to debug. The following diagram shows the workflow for refactoring an application and deploying it on OKE:

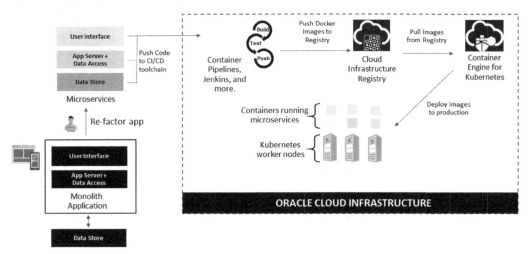

Figure 7.17 – Refactoring an application and deploying it to OKE

So far, you have learned about the characteristics of OKE and how it's used. Now, let's start creating a OKE cluster and then deploy an application and access it over the internet.

Creating an OKE cluster

Deploying an OKE cluster on OCI is really easy. They have two modes: one is a quick create option for most users, and most use cases can be solved using this workflow. But if you have more advanced use cases and you want to define everything on your own, then you can use the custom method that's available. Let's take a look at this:

1. Sign into the OCI console.

2. Click on the **Navigation** menu and go to **Developer Services**. Click on **Kubernetes Clusters**.

3. Click on **Create Cluster**.

4. Select the **Quick Create** option (this is the default option).

5. Click on **Launch Workflow**:

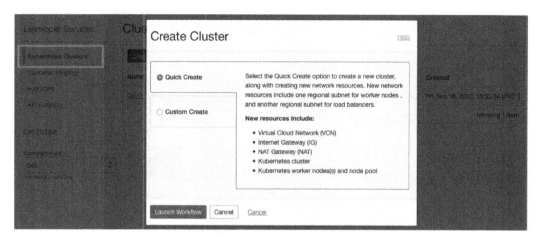

Figure 7.18 – OKE deployment workflow

6. Fill in the following details:

- Provide a name for the cluster.

- Select a compartment where you want to deploy it.

- Select an upstream **Kubernetes version** from the dropdown. By default, OCI will select the latest available version.

- Set the **visibility** type to **Private** or **Public**. For this example, we will create a private node.

- Choose a **shape** for the worker node. You can either choose a bare-metal node or a virtual machine. Both compute types are supported. If you choose the E3 flex type, then you can specify the amount of CPU and memory that you need for your worker node.

- Select your **number of nodes**.

- (Optional) You can choose to specify a **custom boot volume size** as well.

- Click on **Show Advanced Options**, it will show you the **Public SSH Key** field. Paste your public SSH key in there.

- Click on **Next**.

The following is a sample workflow:

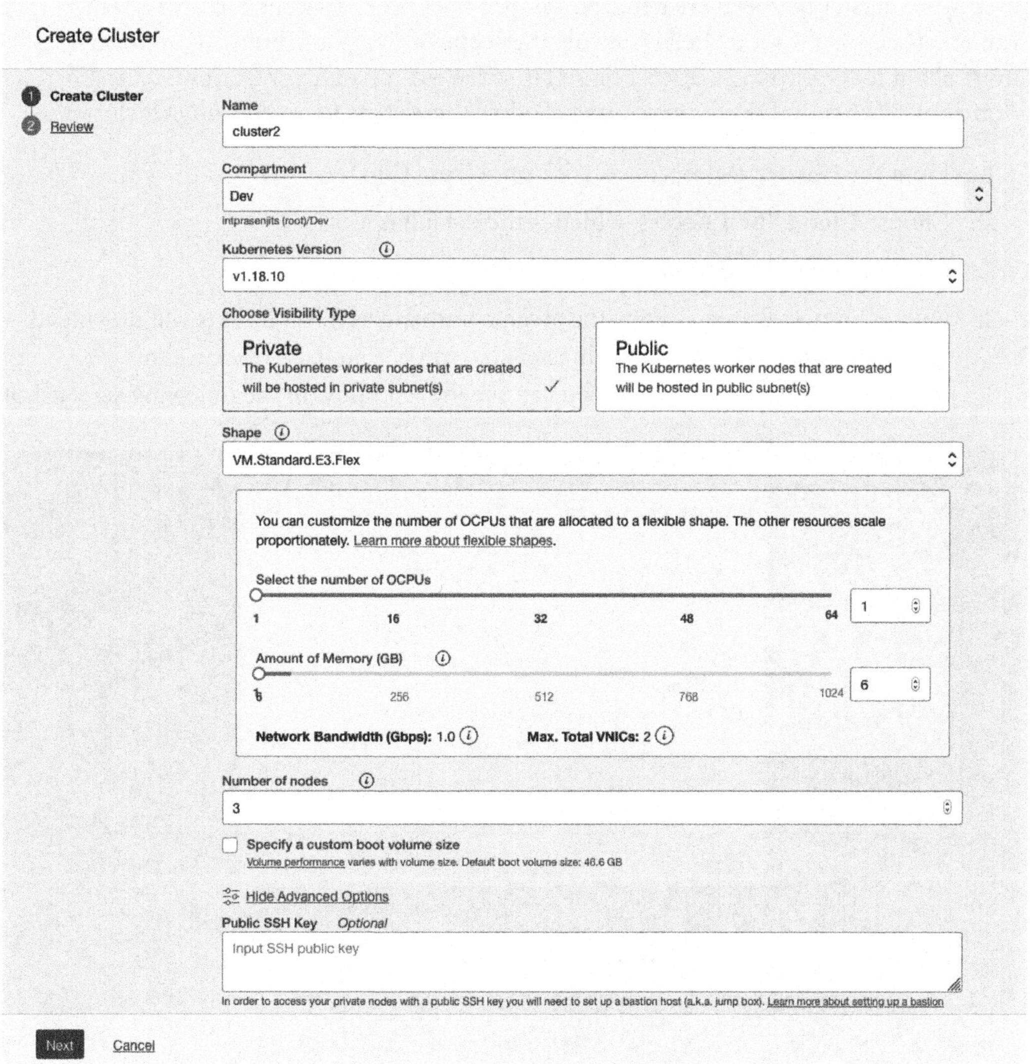

Create Cluster

Create Cluster

1 Create Cluster
2 Review

Name

cluster2

Compartment

Dev

intprasenjits (root)/Dev

Kubernetes Version ⓘ

v1.18.10

Choose Visibility Type

Private		Public
The Kubernetes worker nodes that are created will be hosted in private subnet(s)	✓	The Kubernetes worker nodes that are created will be hosted in public subnet(s)

Shape ⓘ

VM.Standard.E3.Flex

You can customize the number of OCPUs that are allocated to a flexible shape. The other resources scale proportionately. Learn more about flexible shapes.

Select the number of OCPUs

1   16   32   48   64   [1]

Amount of Memory (GB) ⓘ

6   256   512   768   1024   [6]

Network Bandwidth (Gbps): 1.0 ⓘ   **Max. Total VNICs:** 2 ⓘ

Number of nodes ⓘ

3

☐ Specify a custom boot volume size
Volume performance varies with volume size. Default boot volume size: 46.6 GB

⚙ Hide Advanced Options

Public SSH Key *Optional*

Input SSH public key

In order to access your private nodes with a public SSH key you will need to set up a bastion host (a.k.a. jump box). Learn more about setting up a bastion

Next   Cancel

Figure 7.19 – OKE creation options

7. Review your options and click on **Create Cluster**.

Cluster creation will take about 5 minutes. Then, you can go through the next steps to access this cluster from the OCI Cloud Shell.

Accessing an OKE cluster

Once your cluster has been created, you can use the OCI Cloud Shell to access this Kubernetes cluster. Cloud Shell is outside the scope of this book, but you can read more about it at `https://docs.oracle.com/en-us/iaas/Content/API/Concepts/cloudshellintro.htm`. Follow these steps to access an OKE cluster:

1. From the **Cluster Details** page, click on **Access Cluster**.

2. Choose **Cloud Shell Access**, which is the default option.

3. Click **Launch Cloud Shell**.

4. Once Cloud Shell opens, copy the given command and run it. This will download the `kubeconfig` file from the master so that you can use `kubectl` to communicate with the cluster. You can see the workflow in the following screenshot:

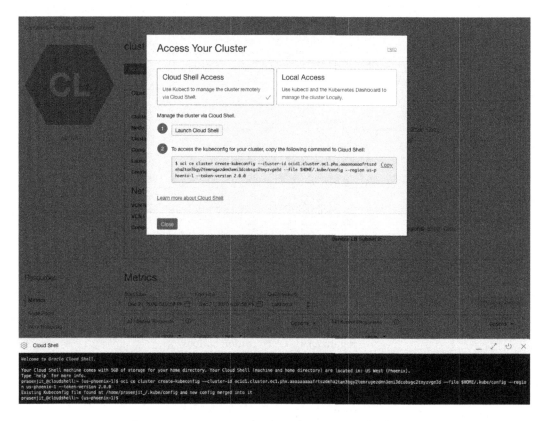

Figure 7.20 – Accessing the OKE cluster using Cloud Shell

5. Type kubectl get nodes -o wide to view the details of the worker nodes of this cluster:

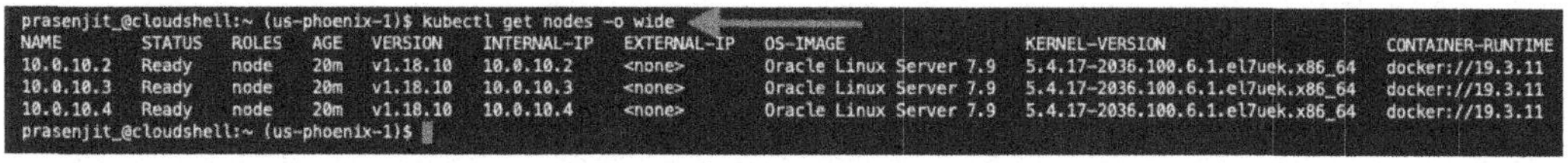

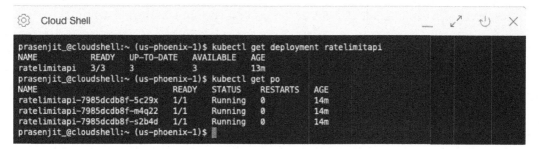

Figure 7.21 – Running kubectl to access the cluster

With that, you have created this cluster and can access it using Cloud Shell. Now, let's move on and deploy a simple web application and try to access it.

Deploying a sample web application on an OKE cluster

You can deploy an application in the same way you can deploy an application on any Kubernetes cluster. Let's take a look:

1. From Cloud Shell, type kubectl apply -f https://raw. githubusercontent.com/stretchcloud/flask-rate-limiter- cors-auth/master/api-deployment.yml to deploy the application.

2. Type kubectl get deployment ratelimitapi to see the status of the deployment.

3. Type kubectl get po to see the status of the pods. It must be in a running state:

```
prasenjit_@cloudshell:~ (us-phoenix-1)$ kubectl get deployment ratelimitapi
NAME           READY   UP-TO-DATE   AVAILABLE   AGE
ratelimitapi   3/3     3            3           13m
prasenjit_@cloudshell:~ (us-phoenix-1)$ kubectl get po
NAME                          READY   STATUS    RESTARTS   AGE
ratelimitapi-7985dcdb8f-5c29x   1/1     Running   0          14m
ratelimitapi-7985dcdb8f-m4q22   1/1     Running   0          14m
ratelimitapi-7985dcdb8f-s2b4d   1/1     Running   0          14m
prasenjit_@cloudshell:~ (us-phoenix-1)$
```

Figure 7.22 – Verifying the deployed microservice

4. So, this application has been deployed, but as we've already mentioned, to access this application, we need to create a Kubernetes service. Type kubectl apply -f https://raw.githubusercontent.com/stretchcloud/flask- rate-limiter-cors-auth/master/api-service.yml to create a Kubernetes service of the LoadBalancer type. In the background, this will deploy an OCI LoadBalancer that's 100 Mbps in size.

5. Type `kubectl get svc` to find out the public IP address of this application. You will need this to access this application over the specified port. In this case, it is `5000`.

6. Pick up the IP address of the service and type `curl -X GET -H "Content-type: application/json" http://<IP-Address>:5000/ping` to access this application, like so:

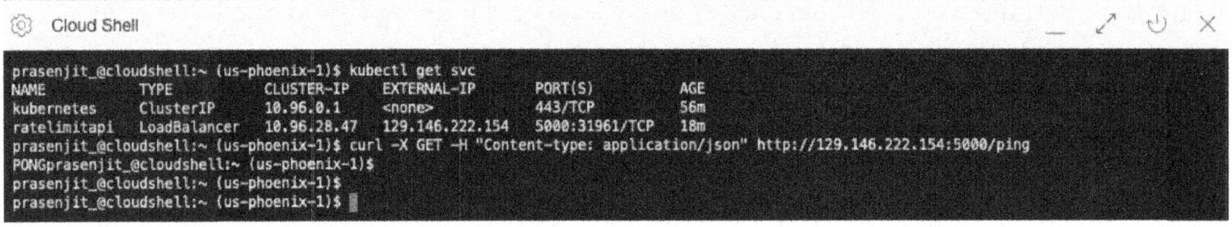

Figure 7.23 – Accessing the Kubernetes service

So far, you have learned how to create an OKE cluster, access it using Cloud Shell, and deploy a sample web application. In the next section, we will talk about how to upgrade the Kubernetes version of the cluster.

Upgrading the Kubernetes version of an OKE cluster

With the fast pace of upstream Kubernetes release, OCI is also keeping up the pace to make those bits available on OKE. If you have a cluster running an old version of Kubernetes, you can upgrade the cluster to the latest version with zero downtime.

Also, you have the choice to either perform an in-place upgrade for the worker node's Kubernetes version or you can choose to do this out-of-place. During the in-place upgrade, you don't need to perform any extra steps. But in the case of out-of-place, you are responsible for creating a new node pool that uses the latest available Kubernetes bits and then eventually delete the old node pool.

Let's upgrade the OKE cluster:

1. First, let upgrade the Kubernetes version of the cluster. To do that, go to the **Cluster List** page, choose the name of the cluster, and you will see a yellow exclamation mark on the **Version** field if an upgrade is available.

2. Click on the actions menu of the cluster where the upgrade is available. Click on **Upgrade Available**, as shown here:

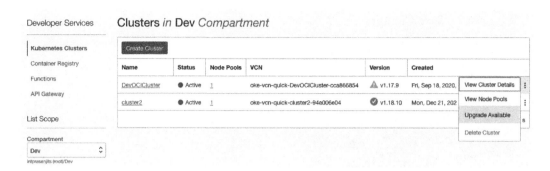

Figure 7.24 – Upgrading the OKE version

3. On the **Upgrade Cluster Master** screen, select the Kubernetes version you want the master to be upgraded to, and then click on **Upgrade**, like so:

Upgrade Cluster Master   Help

Your Kubernetes master node is currently running version v1.17.9.

An upgrade is available. Upgrading your master node will allow you to create new node pools with the upgraded Kubernetes version. Ensure that you have tested that your app is compatible with the new version before upgrading.

Warning: After upgrading a master node, it cannot be downgraded.

Kubernetes Version

v1.18.10	⌃⌄

Upgrade   Cancel

Figure 7.25 – Upgrading the cluster master

This operation will upgrade the master to the version that you choose. Let's upgrade the node's Kubernetes version. We will perform an in-place upgrade in this example:

1. Let's upgrade the Kubernetes version of the node pool. To do that, go to **Cluster** page, select the **Node Pools** tab. Select the node pool to go into the **Node Pool Details** page.

2. Click on **Edit**. Specify the required Kubernetes version from the list in the **Version** field.

3.   Click on **Save Changes**:

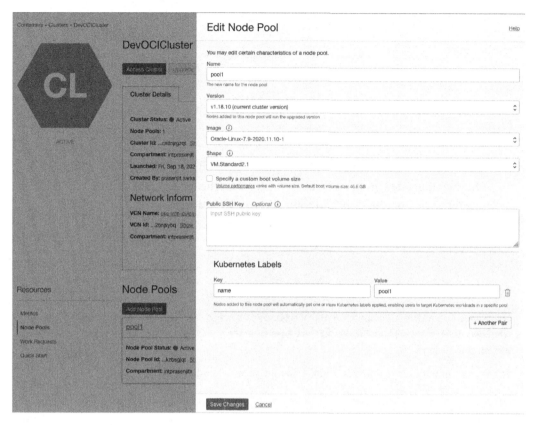

Figure 7.26 – Upgrading the worker nodes

4.   Type `kubectl drain <node_name>`. This will prevent any new pods from starting and at the same time, it will delete the existing pods as well. You are now all set to terminate this instance of worker node and start up a new worker node that has upgraded Kubernetes software version.

5.   From the **Node Pool** page, select the **Node** by going into the **Nodes** tab. It will take you to the **Instances** page.

6.   Select **Terminate** from the **More Actions** menu of the instance that you want to terminate.

7.   Repeat *steps 4* to *6* for all the other worker nodes.

With that, you've seen how quickly and easily the upgrade process of Kubernetes happened for not only on the master but also on the worker nodes without gaining downtime for your application. In the next section, we will discuss using an API gateway as an ingress method for the applications running on OKE.

Exposing microservices using the OCI API gateway

An API gateway is a network attached device, much like **Load Balancer as a Service (LBaaS)**. It is fully managed by Oracle; the customer does not need to manage it. If you want to expose a private application endpoint to the public internet and implement authentication, authorization, **cross-origin resource sharing (CORS)**, rate limiting, routing, and so on, then the API gateway is the answer. Not only do you get the benefits of running an API gateway as an ingress to the application, but you can also get fine-grained monitoring and logging entry points for your code flow via the API that's invoked by a client.

You can create one or more gateways and attach them to a regional subnet, which then processes traffic coming in from the clients and then routes those requests to the defined backend services. You can use the same gateway to serve multiple endpoints. This can be a load balancer, compute instances, or Oracle functions. The following is a diagram of an API gateway:

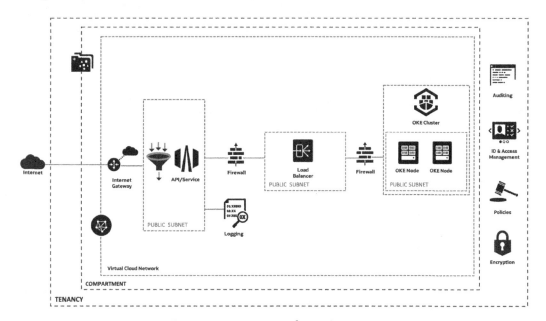

Figure 7.27 – Anatomy of an API gateway

Let's look at the different use cases and modeling for an OCI API gateway.

API gateway within a cloud environment

In this model, APIs are called via the public internet and access backend services running in the cloud. It is fully supported by the OCI security model. It uses **Open Authorization (Oauth)** and JWT to authenticate those API calls. Typical use cases for this are full cloud-native applications, accessing SaaS, and migrating applications to the cloud. The following is the architecture diagram for this use case:

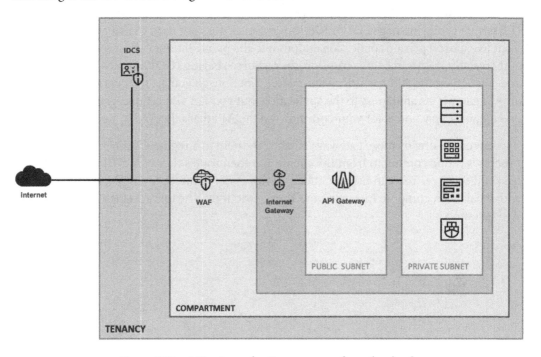

Figure 7.28 – API gateway hosting resources from the cloud

This diagram shows that the API gateway is frontending the resources being hosted within the same cloud environment.

API gateway in a cloud to on-premises model

In this use case, APIs are called via the public internet and access the backend services running on the customer's data center. This model extends the customer DMZ into OCI, thus making use of OCI's security and scalability. A typical use case for this model is to use OCI security and APIGW rate-limiting to protect internal applications. You can use this model to start migrating to the cloud. The following is the architecture diagram for this use case:

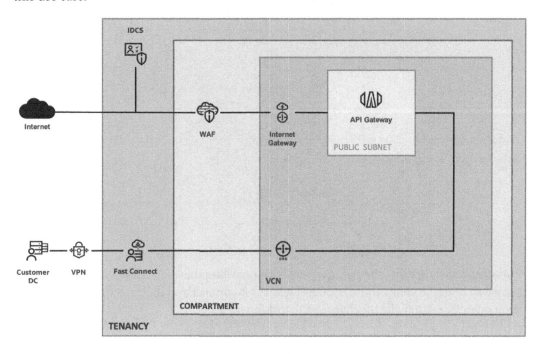

Figure 7.29 – API gateway hosting resources from on-premises

This diagram shows that an API gateway is frontending the application endpoint being hosted in a customer DC. A fast connect connection has been established to connect the customer DC to the cloud.

API gateway in a hybrid model

In this model, APIs are called via the public internet and access the backend services running on OCI and the customer's DC. You can use this model to extend internal applications with new capabilities (for example, microservices). You can also use this to protect external access to internal systems.

The following is an architecture diagram of this use case:

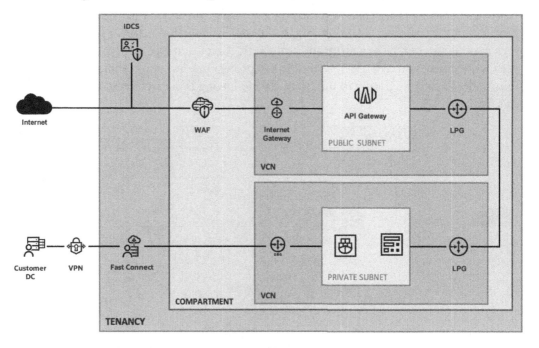

Figure 7.30 – API gateway in a hybrid model

This diagram shows that the API gateway is frontending the application endpoint being hosted in both the cloud and customer DC. A fast connect and local peering gateway has been established to make this hybrid networking possible.

API gateway in a private cloud model

In this model, APIs are called from internal users accessing services in the OCI and internal systems. You can use this model to extend internal applications with new capabilities (for example, microservices), application modernization, data center evacuation, and so on.

The following is an architecture diagram of this use case:

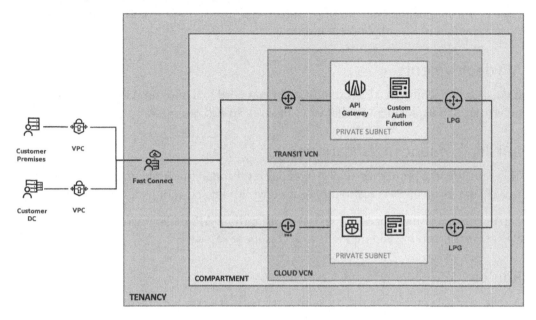

Figure 7.31 – API gateway in a private cloud model

This diagram shows that the API gateway is frontending the application endpoint being hosted in the cloud but is being accessed from the customer DC.

API gateway concepts

At this point, we've provided an overview of the API gateway and its use cases. Let's go through the OCI API gateway concepts that you need to know about before creating an API gateway.

API gateways

Oracle deploys API gateways as virtual appliances, similar to LBaaSes, which are hosted in a regional subnet. API gateways route the incoming requests to the appropriate backend services, which includes a private or public API endpoint. Not only that, OCI API gateway can also route incoming requests to Oracle functions.

APIs

An API is a combination of a set of resources, and the methods that are needed to access those resources (for example, GET and PUT).

API deployments

If you want to deploy an API endpoint, then you need to deploy an API gateway. You need to have an API deployment so that you can serve an API endpoint.

API deployment specifications

This describes the properties of an API endpoint through the deployment specification. An API deployment specification is required while you're creating an API gateway.

You define one or more backend services within those API deployment specifications. You also define the routing and methods to access those services.

Routes

A route is what connects to the backend service using a specified method. You define this routing in your API deployment specification.

Policies

API gateways implement two types of policies. One is called a request policy, while the other is called a response policy:

- The request policy performs a specified action on an incoming request without sending it to the backend. An example of a request policy is limiting the number of incoming requests and enabling CORS support.

- The response policy performs a specified action on a response that has been returned from a backend before but yet to be sent to the caller.

Authentication and authorization policies

The OCI API gateway offers an authentication policy that can be applied to all the routes in the specification, as well as an authorization policy, which is specified and can be applied at the route level.

JWT authentication

With this feature, the API manager can simply configure JWT validation by either manually providing the public verification keys from their authorization server or, alternatively, by configuring the OCI API gateway to pull those keys at runtime.

This will enable them to easily protect access to the APIs that have been deployed on an OCI API gateway. It does this by integrating with any existing JWT-capable identity provider such as Oracle IDCS, Okta, or Auth0.

If a token passes the authentication and authorization policies, the claims are available in the context variables. They can be referenced in the deployment specification; for example, `http://150.136.174.81:3000/users/${request.auth[user_id]}/ todos/${request.path[todoId]}`.

Let's go ahead and create an API gateway and then deploy it so that we can host an application with policies attached to it.

Creating an API gateway

We will use the OCI console to create this gateway. Let's get started:

1. Once you log in to the console, click on the navigation menu and select **Developer Services**, and then click on **API Management**.

2. On the **Gateways** page, click on **Create Gateway**.

3. Provide these values:

   - **Name**: The name of the new API gateway.

   - **Type**: The type of API gateway to create. In this example, we will choose a public gateway.

   - **Compartment**: Where you want to create this gateway.

   - **Custom DNS**: This option lets you determine the TLS certificate (and associated domain name) that the API gateway will use.

   - **VCN**: Which VCN you want to create this gateway in.

   - **Subnet**: Provide a public regional subnet.

4. Click **Create** to create the new API gateway. The following screenshot shows all the aforementioned variables filled in:

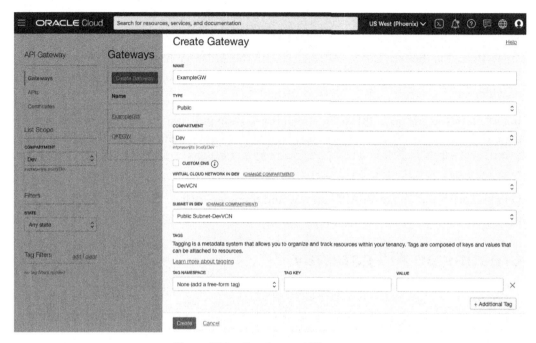

Figure 7.32 – Creating an API gateway

It will take a few minutes to create the new API gateway. Once the gateway is active, you need to create the deployment. Let's do that now.

Creating an API gateway deployment

We will use the OCI console to create this gateway. Let's get started:

1. Once you log in to the OCI console, click on the navigation menu and select **Developer Services** and then select **Gateways**.

2. Select the API Gateway where you want to deploy the API deployment, which will take you to the **Gateway Details** page.

3. Click on the **Deployments** link in the **Resources** list.

4. Click on **Create Deployment**.

5. By default, **From Scratch** is selected.

6. Enter the name of the deployment.

7. Specify a path prefix, such as /v1 or /v2.

8. Choose the compartment where you to deploy this.

9. Specify **Authentication**, **CORS** and **Rate Limiting** policies in the **API Request Policies** section.

10. Select the **Execution Log Level** from the drop-down menu of the **API Logging Policies** section. By default, it is set to **Information**. This can be seen in the following screenshot:

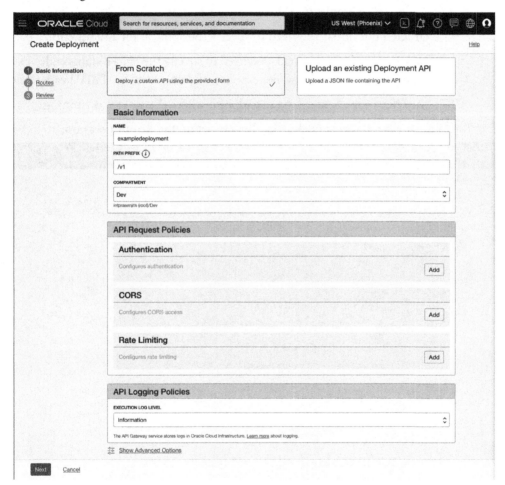

Figure 7.33 – Creating a deployment

11. Click **Next**.

12. In the **Route 1** section, you need to define your first route that maps a path and one or more methods to a backend service:

    - **Path**: A path for API calls that uses the listed methods to the backend service.

- **Methods**: One or more methods accepted by the backend service, separated by commas. In this example, our application handles the GET method, so we specified that method.

- **Type**: The type of the backend service. In this example, we will choose an HTTP endpoint, but you can choose any of the following options:

    - **HTTP**: In this field, you need to specify a URL, timeout details, and whether you want to disable the SSL verification or not.

    - **Oracle Functions**: You need to specify the application and function.

    - **Stock Response**: In this field, you need to specify the HTTP status code, specify the content in the body of the response, and one or more HTTP header fields.

- **URL**: The URL of the actual service endpoint where the service is running.

The following is a screenshot showing how to set up the **Route 1** section:

Figure 7.34 – Defining routes for the deployment

13. Optionally, you can add another route. To do that, click on **Another Route** to enter details for additional routes.

14. Click **Next** to review these details.

15. Click **Create**.

With that, you've just finished creating a deployment that will help you access the application endpoint through an API gateway. Now, let's learn how to access the endpoint.

Accessing the API endpoint through an API gateway

Once your deployment has been created, you just need to get the endpoint from the deployment and access the URL with the path that you set on the deployment. Let's get started:

1. Once you login to the OCI console, click on the navigation menu and click on the **Developer Services** and then select **API Gateway**. It will take you to the **Gateways** page.

2. From there, select the hyperlink of the gateway that has been deployed and it will take you to the **Gateway Details** page.

3. Click on the **Deployments** from the **Resources** list.

4. On the row of your deployment that you have just created, check the **Endpoint** column and click on **Show link**.

5. This will show you the endpoint's URL. Copy this to a web browser of your choice and append the route path that you set in the deployment. In this case, it was set to `/foo`, so the URL will be `https://<Endpoint URL>/foo`. This can be seen in the following screenshot:

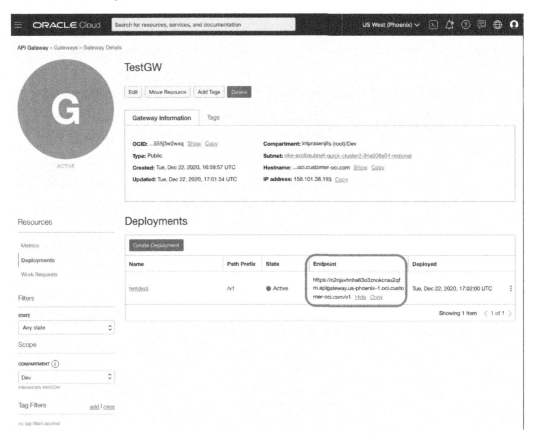

Figure 7.35 – Accessing the API endpoint

With that, you've seen how quickly you can expose an application endpoint based on your choice of topology and also control access to it using authentication, authorization, and request and response policies.

Summary

In this chapter, you learned about the nuances of cloud-native application development, and also why large IT enterprises are adopting more cloud-native approaches for developing their next version of an application or refactoring their old monolithic applications. You also learned about how Oracle is shipping cloud-native services, such as OCIR, OKE, and the API gateway. Throughout this chapter, you have learned how to create a container image and store it in a registry, deploy it on top of a managed Kubernetes service, and then expose that application using an API gateway.

In the next chapter, you will learn how to use a small and fractional compute to satisfy on-demand and serverless computing using the robust Oracle functions service.

8

Running a Serverless Application on Oracle Cloud Infrastructure

Serverless computing is *the next frontier for modern app development!* The serverless framework abstracts the computing resources from the developers so that they don't have to deal with compute or other components to run their code.

But wait – let me tell you a secret: there are still servers involved. Lots of servers and networking gear and storage, too. We just don't want to have to think about them anymore.

In the last two decades, we have shifted our focus from Waterfall model development for a big fat monolithic application and deploying it to a physical server in our on-premises IT, to a DevOps model of delivery for our microservices-based application, running in small containers on the public cloud. This is a big change, not only in terms of technology but also in terms of a quick *go to market* strategy and continuous delivery for new features.

But agility is still not an easy problem to solve. There are various business challenges that we are constantly trying to solve, such as estimating the number of servers in the cloud, paying for idle workloads, and so on. We are also facing growing code and scaling applications, and then our nightmare chasing us in terms of vendor lock-in, dependencies, and so on.

A **Functions as a Service (FaaS)** platform is the beating heart of a serverless architecture. A function is a simple piece of code that does one job well. It takes some input (usually on standard in) and, optionally, writes some output, usually to standard out. We are not talking about functions in the *functional programming* sense here as these functions can have side effects; rather, they are self-contained units of work.

Similar to other OCI services, Oracle Function is also a multi-tenant managed service. Developers just focus on their business logic rather than figuring out how the infrastructure components work together. Oracle Function has been designed to be highly available, scalable, and secure. Developers can also run their code based on cloud events that come from OCI, and they pay only for the resources that were consumed during the execution of their code.

Oracle Function is based on the open source Fn project. This gives us a strong multi-cloud (no lock-in), on-premises, and local development story.

In this chapter, we're going to cover the following main topics:

- Understanding the notion of serverless computing

- Understanding Oracle functions

- Deep diving into Oracle Function

- Understanding the event-based usage of Oracle functions

Understanding the notion of serverless computing

Functions are deployed as a single unit to a FaaS platform. This platform then deals with provisioning the underlying infrastructure, deploying your function code, scaling up and down, resilience and reliability, billing, and security (authentication, authorization, and isolation). It has to do all this blazingly fast, at huge scale and for any language/platform that you wish to use.

The primary focus of a serverless platform is your code. The FaaS platform encourages you to break up your application into small, isolated parts. This is great for developers as small, isolated functions are easier to reason about and manage.

Your FaaS platform will enable your app to scale organically per request, without you having to write any special code to handle it. And not just the gentle seasonal changes in demand that a retail business might experience but also sudden, dramatic surges in demand caused by your app going viral.

With this, we have thickened the plot of what serverless and functions are. Now, we will look at the various distributions of serverless platforms.

Understanding the importance of Oracle Function

Serverless platforms attract and retain application developers by making it extremely easy to consume the underlying resources. Application developers love serverless platforms because they enable them to focus on their own business problems, instead of managing infrastructure. Let's divide these important benefits into different categories:

- **Infrastructure abstraction**: The serverless platform enables application developers to build, deploy, and scale their apps without thinking about the infrastructure underneath. This frees developers to focus on their own business needs by removing a whole set of challenges, such as compute node management, OS management and patching, load balancing traffic, designing apps to scale across multiple nodes and availability domains, and much more.

  The following diagram shows an overview of how functions have evolved over the last two decades, going from bare metal computing environment to running a fraction of the code:

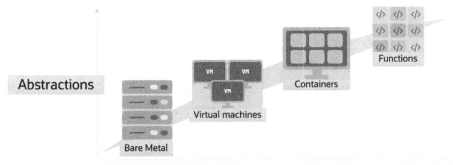

Figure 8.1 – Abstraction of running code in a function

- **Architecture simplification**: Adopting a serverless architecture can greatly simplify application complexity, particularly if the application was already designed in an event-driven fashion.

The following diagram shows an overview of how functions have been instrumental in simplifying the DevOps strategy of computing:

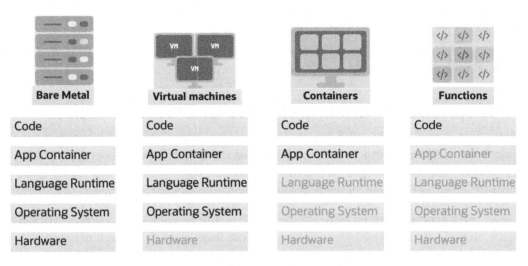

Figure 8.2 – Simplifying DevOps using functions

- **Cost control**: Application developers will only pay for the resources they've consumed, such as CPU cycles, RAM consumed, and I/O. This is billed in sub-second increments, with no costs for idle time.

- **Run anywhere**: Customers want to avoid vendor lock-in by adopting a multi-cloud strategy. Oracle's adoption of Fn as the underlying serverless platform means that their customers can run the exact same code in another cloud, or on-premises, similar to how you can run Oracle functions.

- **High-fidelity local developer experience**: Enable rapid and reliable software engineering by enabling developers to develop and test locally, without the time/cost of deploying to a cloud environment during dev/test cycles.

- **Run arbitrary code**: Run code in any language and any framework.

- **Consistent, isolated, repeatable**: Code runs in the same isolated execution environment every time.

- **Logging and metrics built in**: Oracle functions further simplify the design and operation of an application by providing a pre-defined set of metrics and centralized logging, both of which require no code.

In this section, we discussed the importance of Oracle Function and its architecture, but we haven't discussed why you should use Oracle Function. We'll do that in the next section.

Understanding the use cases of Oracle Function

One of the main use cases of the serverless platform is to be able to run event-driven code based on cloud events; that is, *run a function in response to an event occurring in OCI*.

Integrating Oracle Function into the broader OCI ecosystem provides added value to OCI customers. Oracle Function has been integrated with OCI Event Service to allow customers to trigger their functions in response to events happening in OCI.

An example for this use case is a customer configuring Oracle Function to run a processing function every time a new object arrives in their object store bucket.

Another important use case of Oracle Function is event queue processing; that is, *run a function in response to an item in a queue.*

This use case for Oracle Function is the ability to run a function in response to an item being queued on a queue.

Another use case of running Oracle Function is against a webhook event. With the rapid increase of DevOps tools, it is more common to run code against a webhook event; that, is *run a function in response to a webhook event from an external web service, such as GitHub.*

This use case focuses on the ability to execute a function in response to a webhook. The user of a service can send an outgoing HTTP webhook request to execute functions (for example, GitHub, PagerDuty, and so on).

So far, we have discussed the basics of serverless computing, the importance of it, and why and where you should apply serverless functions. We'll look at how to create and use Oracle functions in the next section.

Creating and using Oracle functions

Oracle's serverless platform is pretty simple and due to its adoption of open source Fn as the base underline platform, it avoids any vendor lock-in as well. It runs in five different steps:

1. Developing a function either locally or on an OCI cloud shell
2. Building and packaging the code using a container
3. Pushing the function image to the OCI registry
4. Configuring how this function will be triggered, either based on HTTP calling or an Event, Stream, or Timer
5. Paying for the code execution time only

The preceding workflow can be seen in the following diagram:

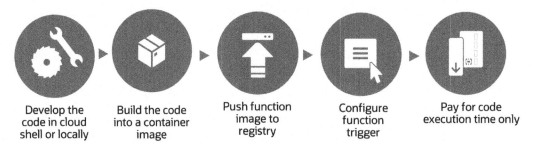

| Develop the code in cloud shell or locally | Build the code into a container image | Push function image to registry | Configure function trigger | Pay for code execution time only |

Figure 8.3 – Life cycle of Oracle Function

Once you've created the function and uploaded the image to the OCIR, you can invoke it in four ways:

- Developers can use the Fn CLI to invoke a function.

- Developers can use OCI SDKs to invoke a function.

- Developers can send a signed HTTP request to the invoking point of a function.

- Developers can use other OCI services to invoke a function as well, such as the OCI Events service.

OCI uses IAM principles such as an IAM policy to verify whether the invoked command entity is entitled to use Oracle functions or not. If there are adequate permissions in place, then the request will be passed to the backend infrastructure that runs the Fn project. The Fn project will use the function definition that a user has written and identify which Docker image it has to pull to run that code. Once it pulls the image from the Docker registry, it compiles the code and runs the container on a dedicated instance that is connected to the particular tenancy.

As this function runs on the subnet that was specified to run, it can read and write to other OCI resources that are connected to the same subnet. It can access other shared OCI resources as well, such as OCI object storage. Since it has long-running functions, OCI can run a function for as long as 5 minutes. But that is something you have to specify in the func.yaml file before deploying the function.

You can either use the OCI logging service and service connector to store the function logs within the OCI itself, or you can send the logs to another centralized log server.

Oracle Function uses Docker containers to run the code inside a dedicated Docker host. However, if the container is idle for some time, then that container will be removed and a new container will be started.

Oracle Function will remove the Docker container once it has finished running the code inside it, but only after a brief period of idle time. However, if a request is received by the Oracle function within the idle time threshold, then Oracle Function will use the same Docker container to run that code again, instead of creating a new one. If there is a parallel request that comes in, then Oracle Function will scale this Docker container to run the same code in parallel.

Using security first measures, Oracle Function has been tightly integrated with OCI **Identity and Access Management (IAM)** principles. This means that to send a call to an OCI API endpoint, you can use an **instance principal**. Let's create a function application that will list the compartments that you have in your tenancy.

In this exercise, you will create a dynamic group, add a policy that must send signed calls to the OCI API endpoint, which is an Oracle Function application, and trigger the function from the Function command line. You will use the OCI Cloud Shell to perform this whole lab.

First, we'll create the dynamic group and then create the policies for the functions. To do so, we need the compartment OCID, which is where we will deploy our function:

1. Sign in to the OCI console.
2. Open the navigation menu, select **Identity**, and then **Compartments**.
3. Find your desired compartment from the list, hover over the cell in the OCID column, and click **Copy** to copy the compartment OCID to your clipboard.
4. Store the compartment OCID as you will use it soon.

Now, let's create the dynamic group:

1. To create a dynamic group, open the navigation menu, select **Identity**, and then **Dynamic Groups**.
2. Click **Create Dynamic Group**.
3. For **Name**, enter `functions-dynamic-group`.
4. For **Description**, enter a group with all the functions in a compartment.

5. To select the functions that belong to the dynamic group, write the following matching rule, which includes all the functions within the compartment you are going to create your application in:

```
All {resource.type = 'fnfunc', resource.compartment.id =
'ocid1.compartment.oc1..example'}
```

> **Note**
>
> Make sure you replace the preceding value with the compartment OCID that you stored earlier.

At this stage, we will define some policies that are required for functions:

1. Under **Governance and Administration**, go to **Identity** and click **Policies**.

2. Choose the root compartment from the compartment menu.

3. Click on **Create Policy**.

4. Provide a name and description.

5. On the **Policy Builder** screen, select **Customize (Advanced)**.

6. Add the following policy statements:

```
Allow group func-pol to use cloud-shell in tenancy
Allow group func-pol to manage repos in tenancy
Allow group func-pol to read objectstorage-namespaces in
tenancy
Allow group func-pol to read metrics in tenancy
Allow group func-pol to manage functions-family in
tenancy
Allow group func-pol to use virtual-network-family in
tenancy
```

7.   Click on **Create**, as shown in the following screenshot:

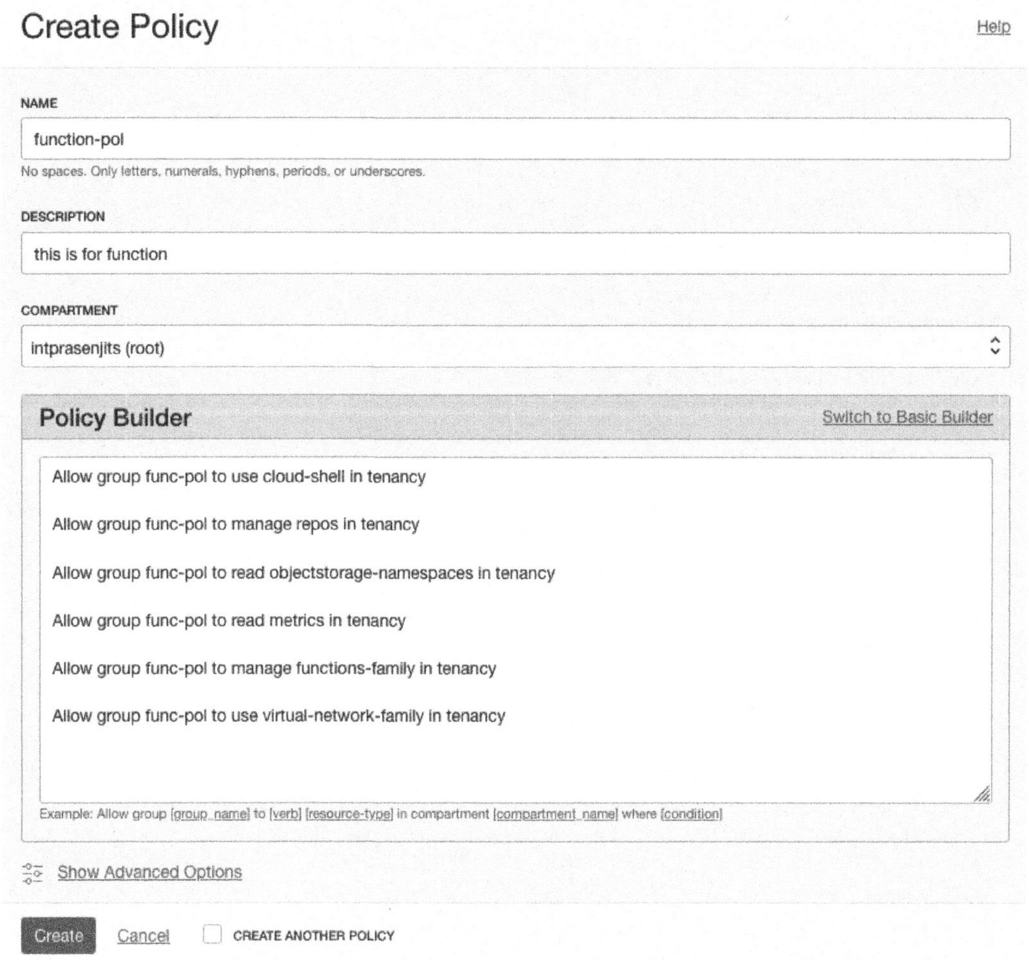

Create Policy

Help

NAME

> function-pol

No spaces. Only letters, numerals, hyphens, periods, or underscores.

DESCRIPTION

> this is for function

COMPARTMENT

> intprasenjits (root)

Policy Builder

Switch to Basic Builder

> Allow group func-pol to use cloud-shell in tenancy
>
> Allow group func-pol to manage repos in tenancy
>
> Allow group func-pol to read objectstorage-namespaces in tenancy
>
> Allow group func-pol to read metrics in tenancy
>
> Allow group func-pol to manage functions-family in tenancy
>
> Allow group func-pol to use virtual-network-family in tenancy

Example: Allow group [group_name] to [verb] [resource-type] in compartment [compartment_name] where [condition]

Show Advanced Options

Create   Cancel   ☐   CREATE ANOTHER POLICY

Figure 8.4 – Policy statement for Oracle Function

You've just created the prerequisites. Now, let's create the actual application:

1.   Under **Solutions and Platform**, go to **Developer Services** and click on **Functions**.

2.   From the compartment dropdown, select the **Compartment** area where you want to create the application.

3.   Click on **Create Application**.

4. Provide a name. Then, select the VCN and subnet where you want to deploy this function.

5. Click on **Create**, as shown in the following screenshot:

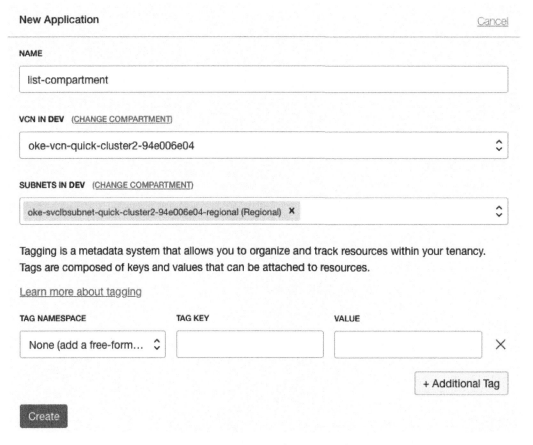

Figure 8.5 – Creating a new function application

Next, we need to launch Cloud Shell:

1. On the **Applications** page, select the application that you have just created.

2. Click on the **Getting Started** link from the **Resources** section.

3. Click on **Cloud Shell Setup**.

4. Click on **Launch Cloud Shell**, as shown in the following screenshot:

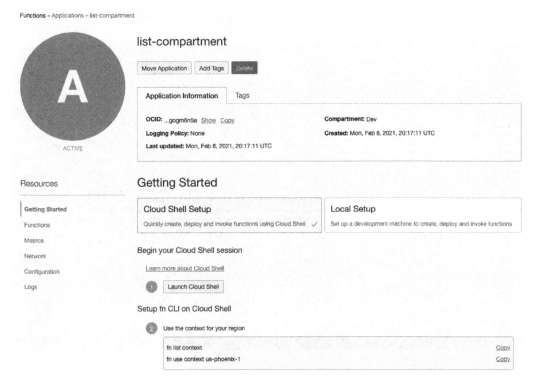

Figure 8.6 – Opening Cloud Shell

5. From this section, run the commands that you can see in the **Setup fn CLI** section of Cloud Shell.

6. These commands are tailor-made for your tenancy, so you can just change some of your parameters, such as your OCI Auth Token, to set up the Cloud Shell environment.

7. Now, we will deploy our application code. Oracle already has some sample code in their GitHub sample code repository for Function, so we will use that.

8. Download the repository by cloning the GitHub repository. To do this, run `git clone https://github.com/oracle/oracle-functions-samples`.

9. Go inside the sample code directory by running `cd oracle-functions-samples/samples/oci-list-compartments-python/`.

10. Run `fn -v deploy -app list-compartment`, as shown in the following screenshot:

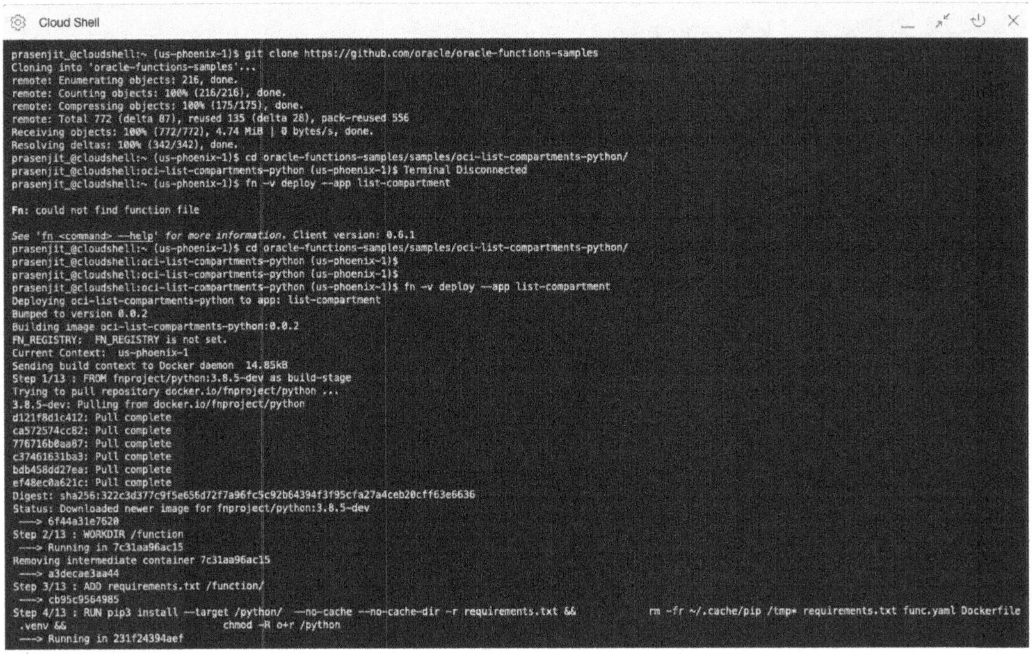

Figure 8.7 – Deploying the function code

11. Once it has been deployed, you can invoke the function by calling it using the same `fn` command line. Run `fn invoke list-compartment oci-list-compartments-python`.

12. This will show you the list of the compartments that you have in your tenancy.

With that, you've learned how to use Oracle functions to run a fraction of your code on demand, as well as how to send signed calls to an OCI API endpoint using an instance principal. In the next section, we will talk about some advanced use cases and deep dive into various Oracle functions.

Deep diving into Oracle functions

We will deep dive into a couple of topics before talking about event-based Oracle Function deployment.

First, let's discuss filesystem access within the Docker container where the function runs:

- Function code running inside the Docker container has read access for all the files and directories within the filesystem.
- Function code only has write access to the /tmp filesystem.

This means that when you write the code and want to perform a file operation, such as downloading a file inside the docker container, you need to make sure that you only download that file to /tmp.

Although this /tmp is writable, it has a size restriction, and it is proportionate to the amount of memory that you allocate to this function. If you allocate 128 MB of memory to the function, then you can get 32 MB of allowed space on your /tmp. For 256 MB of allocated memory, it will be 64 MB, for 512 MB of allocated memory, it will be 128 MB, and for 1,024 MB of allocated memory, you can get 256 MB of allowed space inside /tmp.

Another thing that you have to be careful about is the Docker container permissions when you bring in your own container to run as a function on the OCI. To run your code, Oracle Function creates a container. The container's functionality depends on the Linux permission schema using a **user ID (UID)** and a **group ID (GID)**. So, when you create a container outside of Oracle Function's perimeter and do not provide a USER parameter within the Dockerfile while creating the container, Docker will allow this container to run all the processes as root and add all the default capabilities of a root user. This is a dangerous combination for your security postures.

To mitigate this security flaw, Oracle Function adds a UID and a GID, both named fn and both with an ID of 1000 . As you can imagine, there is no privilege attached to this UID and GID. As a result, if your code depends on the elevated permissions to perform any operation, such as sudo or setuid, then it won't be able to run.

As a best practice for bringing your own container to Oracle Function, you should add the fn UID and GID while creating the container to avoid any other pitfalls. You can see an example of this in the following screenshot, where the RUN parameter is adding this to the end, after running all the commands:

```
FROM oraclelinux:7-slim

RUN  yum -y install oracle-release-el7 oracle-nodejs-release-el7 && \
     yum-config-manager --disable ol7_developer_EPEL && \
     yum -y install oracle-instantclient19.3-basiclite nodejs && \
     rm -rf /var/cache/yum && \
     groupadd --gid 1000 fn && \
     adduser --uid 1000 --gid fn fn

WORKDIR /function
ADD . /function/
RUN npm install

CMD exec node func.js
```

Figure 8.8 – Deploying the function code

Oracle Function uses **Resource Principal** to allow your code to use other OCI resources. Resource Principal works the same as Instance Principal, which we looked at in *Chapter 2, Understanding Identity and Access Management*. You need to create a dynamic group and add the function to it; then, you must write a policy to grant access to other OCI resources.

Within your code, you must call a **resource principal provider**. This uses a **resource principal session token (RPST)**, which gives you permission to access other OCI resources. This token is only valid for the resources that you have granted through the policy.

This token is cached for 15 minutes. This means that if you want to make any changes to the policy, you need to wait 15 minutes before that change will take effect.

Oracle integrates this resource principal provider inside all its SDKs, so use any of the given SDKs to authenticate against OCI API within your function code. However, if you don't use any of the supported SDKs, then you need to create a custom resource principal provider.

The following diagram shows a logical representation of this. Here, a REST token is being provided to the function by RPST, so that it can authenticate itself against other OCI API endpoints:

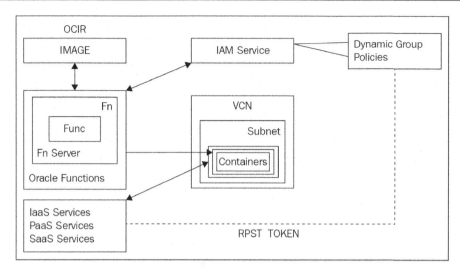

Figure 8.9 – Accessing other OCI resources from Oracle Function

In this section, you have learned about various topics surrounding Oracle Function. In the next section, we will talk about event-driven functions.

Understanding event-based usage of Oracle functions

Oracle functions have been carefully integrated with other OCI services, such as OCI Notification Service, Events Service, API Gateway, Object Storage, Autonomous Database, Key Management System, Compute, VCN, and others. The following diagram shows how Oracle Function can be integrated with other OCI services:

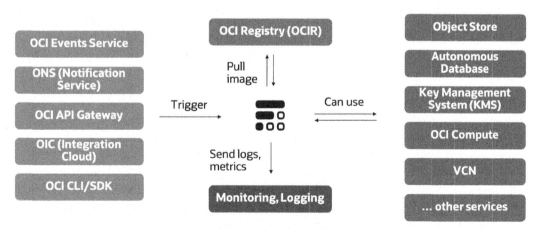

Figure 8.10 – Oracle Function integration with other OCI services

We have been looking at event-driven applications more since the rise of distributed systems. OCI Events Service is real time and uses event alerts and rules to track changes to cloud resources using open standard cloud events. OCI Events Service tracks user-initiated, system, and resource life cycle changes and allows admins to define rules and actions for event types. OCI Events Service can be integrated with OCI Streaming Service, **OCI Notifications Service (ONS)**, and Oracle functions.

Let's look at a classic use case of OCI Events Service and integrating Oracle functions with it. The following diagram shows a high-level overview of this use case:

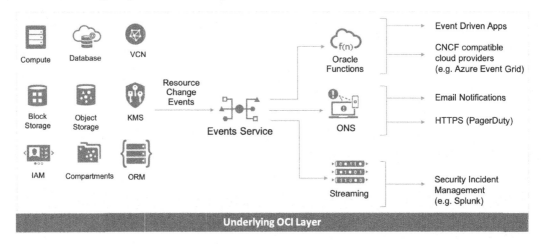

Figure 8.11 – OCI Events Service and Oracle Function integration

In the preceding diagram, you can see that how OCI Events Service allows you to easily respond to **Autonomous Transaction Processing (ATP)** via functions. In this use case, we are creating a new ATP instance, which will generate an event when the instance has been provisioned. This event is processed by Events Service to trigger a function, as well as send a notification. The function uses the data in the event to create database schemas, tables, rows, and other **data definition language (DDL)** constructs. Notifications Service can send event notifications via email and PagerDuty. Let's look at some other common use cases of event-based functions.

You can enforce corporate security policies and governance rules via Events Service and integrate this with Oracle functions. If you want to ensure that all your user-provisioned cloud infrastructure complies with corporate security policies, then define a set of audit functions that validate the configuration of different OCI resources (VM, network, and database). Then, define OCI Events Service rules to trigger audit functions on creation and configuration changes. This deployed audit function will tear down resources that do not meet corporate security policies; for example, if a compute instance has a public IP, then terminate the instance. The following is a logical diagram of how this can be achieved:

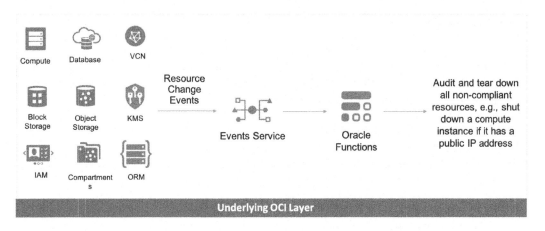

Figure 8.12 – OCI Events Service and Oracle Function integration for enforcing governance rules

Another use case could be ingesting access logs in security incident management. If you want to ensure that all your access and audit logs are sent to a central security incident management system such as Splunk, then define a function to parse the log files and post the log data to the customer's Splunk instance. You also need to define OCI Events Service rules to trigger the function on creation and develop the functions that parse the log file and send data to Splunk. The following diagram shows how this can be achieved:

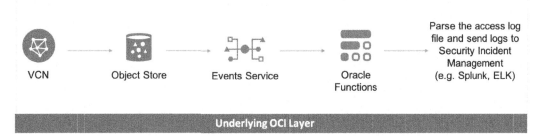

Figure 8.13 – OCI Events Service and Oracle Function integration for sending access
logs to security incident management systems

With that, you've seen how Oracle functions can be integrated with OCI Events Service and how they make a perfect pair for event-driven applications.

Summary

In this chapter, you have learned about the nuances of serverless applications, their use cases, and why serverless platforms are getting popular among enterprises. To reiterate, it is a simple piece of code that does one job. It takes some input (usually on standard in) and, optionally, writes some output, usually to standard out.

You also learned how Oracle has adopted the open source `fn` project to break free from the cloud lock-in of serverless applications. You also looked at the advanced concepts surrounding Oracle functions and how they can be taken further with the integration of OCI Events Service.

In the next chapter, you will learn how to use Terraform and Ansible code to maintain your OCI Infrastructure as Code.

9
Managing Infrastructure as Code on Oracle Cloud Infrastructure

Infrastructure as code (IaC) is a term used to reference the ability to turn a script or a template into functioning infrastructure resources. Some tools such as ad hoc scripts require you to specify all necessary commands in an appropriate sequence in order to create the resources for those scripts. In this scenario, the user would be responsible for managing dependencies and the sequence of all command executions. In addition, they would need to create a similar script to remove all the resources.

Configuration management tools provide both IaC and **configuration as code (CaC)** capabilities. This often allows for a somewhat limited set of infrastructure provisioning capabilities, while yielding significant configuration management capabilities. The concept of idempotency is also important, as tools such as Chef and Puppet will enforce the defined configuration, reverting potentially unwanted manual changes.

Docker, Packer, and Vagrant are all server templating tools. These are gaining popularity as an alternative to Bootstrap and Config tools, and work around snapshotting and delivering templated systems. These tools help in creating immutable infrastructure. Immutable infrastructure states that once you deploy a server, you don't change it. Changes should be via destroy and create operations rather than reconfiguring. Netflix has done a lot around this with **continuous integration** (**CI**), Bakery, Aminator, and Spinnaker. Everything Netflix deploys goes through CI, gets baked into an **Amazon Machine Image** (**AMI**) cloud image, and goes through a test loop. Any changes require a destroy operation and redeployment of the infrastructure. No time is spent curating an image once it has been deployed.

Infrastructure and provisioning tools' or orchestrators' jobs are not only to create servers, but almost anything on a cloud infrastructure, such as databases, networking configurations, and load balancers. Besides Terraform, CloudFormation and OpenStack Heat are typical examples of infrastructure automation tools. These tools can provision servers and do some configuration management, but are mainly there to provision resources that a given infrastructure provider provides.

In this chapter, we're going to cover the following main topics:

- Understanding the need for IaC
- Understanding the use cases of **Oracle Resource Manager** (**ORM**)
- Learning to generate IaC from an existing setup
- Learning to integrate ORM with **source code management** (**SCM**)

IaC has taken center stage in the DevOps realm. Using IaC, you treat your infrastructure the same way as you would your application code. As an example, you will check your IaC code into version control, you will write tests for it, and then you'll make sure that it doesn't diverge from what you have across multiple environments.

By the end of this chapter, you will get to know not only the basics of IaC and Terraform, but also the Managed Service offering of Terraform on **Oracle Cloud Infrastructure** (**OCI**) and how you can integrate it with a source code repository, generate code from an existing deployed infrastructure, and so on.

Understanding the need for IaC

IaC automates infrastructure deployment and updates with software. It enables agile development and DevOps. Terraform is an open source engine that processes IaC written in **HashiCorp Configuration Language (HCL)**.

So, let's take a look at why you need IaC. Developers or DevOps engineers use a fast and reusable process to deploy and update an infrastructure. Thus, it is clear that infrastructure should be automatically provisioned and managed from code, not manually. That's why you use IaC.

In IaC, you define the end state of an infrastructure and let tools manage it for you. IaC is literally a self-documenting infrastructure, which is consistent and achieves repeatable results. It increases efficiency while reducing risk. Here, you can see a high-level diagram of how you can write code to define the end state of an infrastructure and let a tool such as Terraform handle that for you:

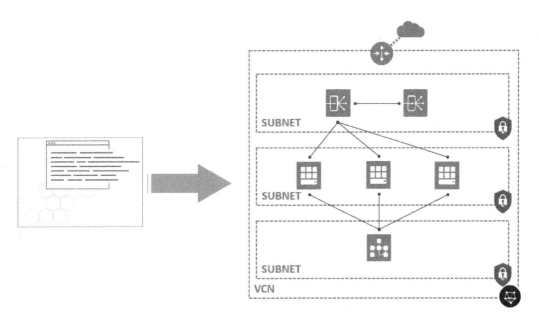

Figure 9.1 – Use case of IaC

Terraform is the front runner in the DevOps toolchain. It can build and change an infrastructure very efficiently and manage this infrastructure state as code using versions as well. Terraform has a rich built-in provider support that you can use to deploy infrastructure on a variety of platforms. Terraform has become a part of the cloud orchestration tools that handle the infrastructure and application life cycle.

IaC's goal is to create and manage cloud infrastructure and deployments predictably and repeatably. It makes use of templates and automation for just about everything. You can see the benefits of using IaC in the following diagram:

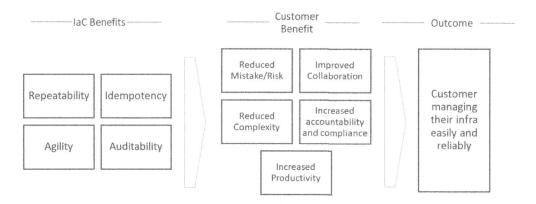

Figure 9.2 – Benefits of IaC

As part of your automation tools, Terraform can be integrated with configuration management tools such as Chef, Puppet, and Ansible.

Let's look at couple of tools from HashiCorp, along with their purpose. HashiCorp builds and maintains a variety of cloud operations tools, and their goal is *"Any application on any infrastructure."* This means that using these tools, you can define and deploy any application on any cloud.

For provisioning, they built **Vagrant**, which is a popular tool for automating development environments whereby you can define the environments as a template. By way of an example, install **Linux, Apache, MySQL, PHP/Perl/Python (LAMP)** and dependencies, set permissions, enable logging, create a database, create users and permissions, and then fire up something to work on—for example, WordPress—and do all of this with a `vagrant up` command.

Packer is a very useful tool for custom creation of operating system images. One way is to use configuration and deployment tools such as Chef, Puppet, Ansible, and SaltStack, and another way is to continually bake ready-to-go images that require minimal or no Bootstrap configuration.

For security, HashiCorp built **Vault**. This is capable of storing keys, certificates, passwords, and other sensitive information. Vault is a **Go** application with a **REpresentational state transfer command-line interface (REST CLI)** that you can use to store secrets.

For running distributed containers, they created **Nomad**, which is a cluster management system for distributed, highly available, data center-aware container schedulers. Nomad *only provides* cluster management and scheduling.

While other orchestration tools provide much more than just cluster management and scheduling, Nomad keeps it simple with a single binary for clients and servers. It is often compared to Kubernetes, but only focuses on scheduling (jobs and tasks).

For the storing of key values, HashiCorp created **Consul**. Consul's mission statement is to automatically know and control what applications and infrastructure are doing at any given time and detect failures, deal with new servers, and update configurations, database names, bucket names, and so on.

So, we have learned about the use cases and benefits of using IaC. Let's learn about the use cases of Oracle's managed IaC service.

Understanding the use cases of ORM

Oracle provides a managed service of Terraform called **ORM**, which manages infrastructure using HashiCorp Terraform. It uses templates to define configurations, and you can reuse those templates as needed. It's a free service and you need to pay only for infrastructure, not for service. ORM is deeply integrated with OCI services, such as identity, security, metering, monitoring, and tagging.

Oracle built this ORM service on unmodified open source software, meaning there is no lock-in and you get simple migrations from or to any private and third-party clouds. Here, you can see a high-level diagram of the ORM stack. This workflow depicts how you can use ORM to deploy a web application to different environments on OCI:

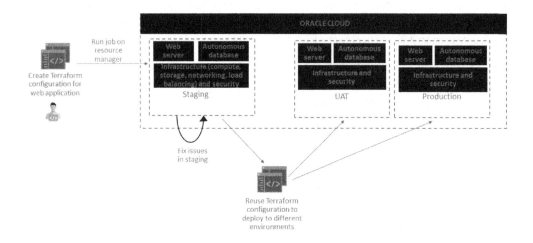

Figure 9.3 – Use case of IaC

Here are the benefits of using ORM:

- As with Terraform, you can use ORM to unlock infrastructure automation capabilities that can help you to standardize your infrastructure, and you can easily replicate your environments into multiple replicas.

- ORM is deeply integrated with the OCI platform, and as a developer, you can leverage the OCI **application programming interface** (**API**) catalog.

- Built on top of Terraform's principal, you can use ORM to share and manage infrastructure configurations as well as Terraform state files across multiple teams and platforms, improving collaboration.

- You don't need to install the Terraform executable on your local developer workstation to invoke the infrastructure creation. You can use the ORM **user interface** (**UI**) to just invoke the code that you have written, or you can use it to push the code to GitHub and GitLab as well. Both of them are integrated with the ORM stack.

- ORM is a free service whereby you only pay for the resources that you create and consume.

So, you have learned about the various different use cases of ORM, why ORM is important, and where you can apply it. Let's now look at the components that make up this service.

ORM components

ORM is nothing but Terraform-as-a-service for OCI resources. You need to write your own code that will be used to create an OCI infrastructure. This is called a **Terraform file**. Then, you need to adjust the variables, and that's it. You can use ORM to start building stacks and executing jobs.

In ORM, a stack represents a set of OCI resources you want to create in a compartment. Each stack holds the Terraform configuration files, which are .tf files where you specify the resources you want to create using ORM.

Once you upload the configuration files, you run a job to create a stack. In ORM, a job is an action on a stack. ORM provides three jobs, and they are **plan**, **apply**, and **destroy**.

You can see a high-level diagram of life cycle operations on the ORM stack in the following diagram:

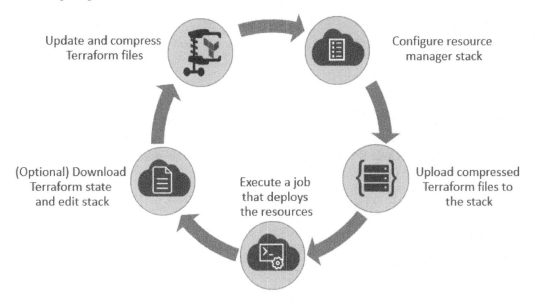

Figure 9.4 – Cycle of ORM components

A plan job, when run on an uploaded stack, parses the Terraform configuration file and creates an execution plan. You can check the logs to see which resources are being added or destroyed.

If you feel that the intended job is just the way you have designed it to be, then you need to apply the job. Once you perform an apply job, then only the stack gets fully provisioned.

Essential information about the state of your resource's configuration is maintained in a state file, which is a **JavaScript Object Notation (JSON)** file. It is ORM's job to create this state file and maintain it. It's stored internally in the OCI object store, and you can download this file.

ORM supports state locking on a stack when you apply a job. This is done by only allowing one job at a time to run on a given stack. You can see the stages of ORM jobs in the following diagram:

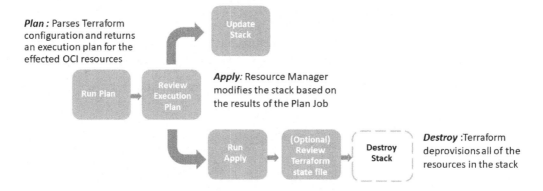

Figure 9.5 – ORM workflow stages

Let's create a sample ORM stack and see how easily you can use ORM to deploy your infrastructure. For this task, you need to have a .zip file of the Terraform code. We have supplied sample code that will create an Oracle container engine for a Kubernetes cluster on OCI using ORM. You need to download the sample code from this link: `https://github.com/stretchcloud/oke-terraform-ci-cd/blob/master/OKE-TF.zip`. Then, follow these next steps:

1. Sign in to the OCI console.

2. Open the navigation menu, select **Resource Manager**, and then **Stacks**.

3. Click on **Create Stack**.

4. Select **My Configuration (default)**, and then select **.Zip file**.

5. Upload the .zip file that you downloaded from the link provided earlier. You can see a sample screenshot here:

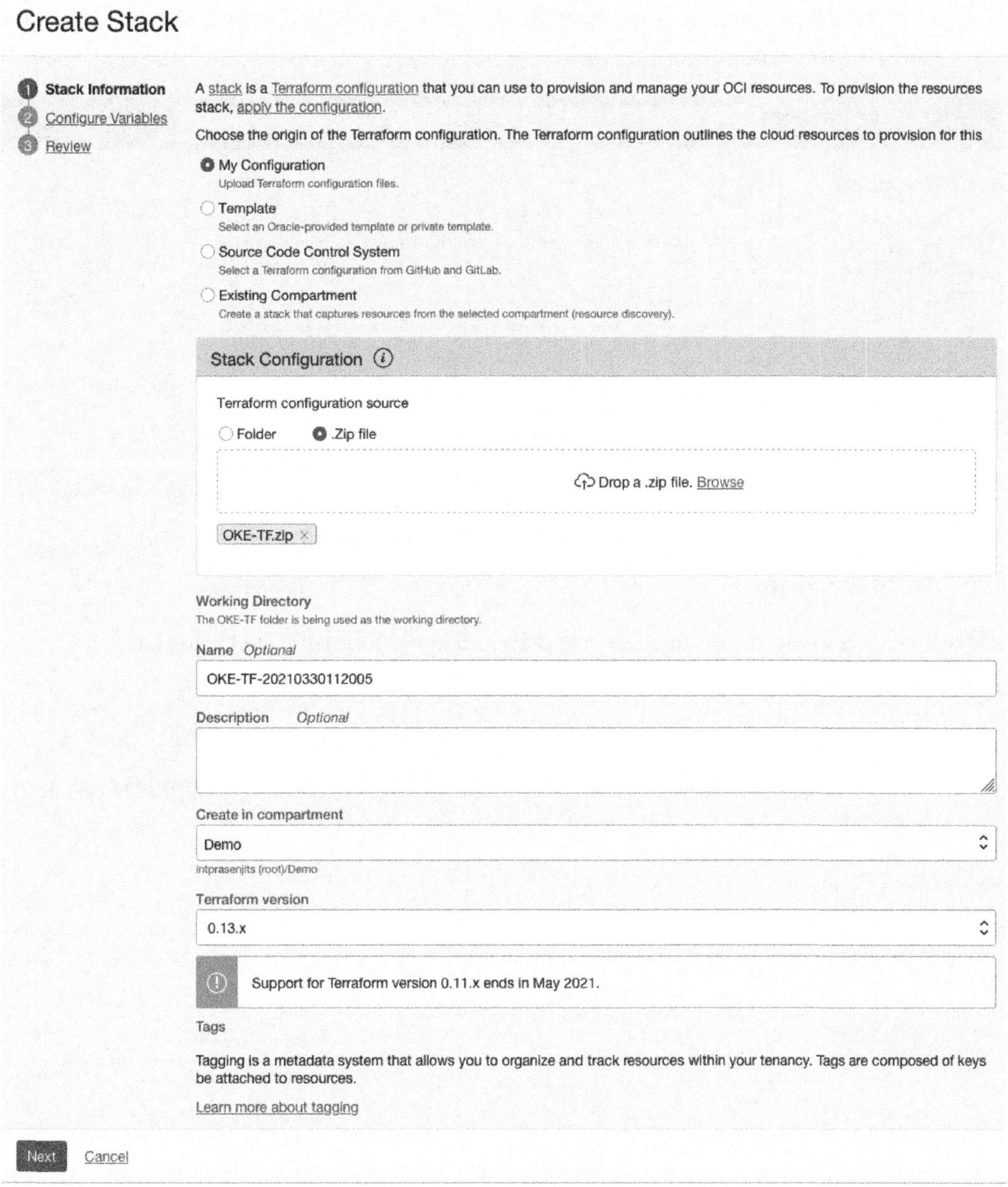

Create Stack

1 **Stack Information**

2 Configure Variables

3 Review

A stack is a Terraform configuration that you can use to provision and manage your OCI resources. To provision the resources stack, apply the configuration.

Choose the origin of the Terraform configuration. The Terraform configuration outlines the cloud resources to provision for this

● **My Configuration**
  Upload Terraform configuration files.

○ **Template**
  Select an Oracle-provided template or private template.

○ **Source Code Control System**
  Select a Terraform configuration from GitHub and GitLab.

○ **Existing Compartment**
  Create a stack that captures resources from the selected compartment (resource discovery).

Stack Configuration ⓘ

Terraform configuration source

○ Folder   ● .Zip file

> ↷ Drop a .zip file. Browse

OKE-TF.zip ×

Working Directory
The OKE-TF folder is being used as the working directory.

Name *Optional*

OKE-TF-20210330112005

Description   *Optional*

Create in compartment

Demo	⌄

intprasenjits (root)/Demo

Terraform version

0.13.x	⌄

ⓘ	Support for Terraform version 0.11.x ends in May 2021.

Tags

Tagging is a metadata system that allows you to organize and track resources within your tenancy. Tags are composed of keys be attached to resources.

Learn more about tagging

Next   Cancel

Figure 9.6 – Creating an ORM stack

6. Click on **Next**.

7. In the **Configure Variables** page, it will automatically pop in the **Oracle Cloud ID (OCID)** compartment and region based on your selection.

8. Provide a node pool **Secure Shell (SSH)** public key and click on **Next**. You can see a sample screenshot here:

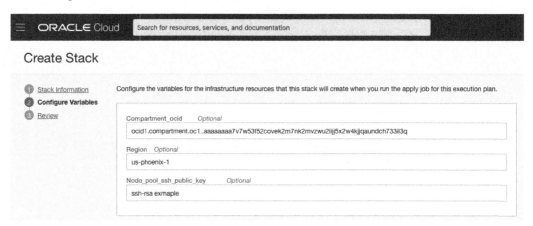

Figure 9.7 – Configuring variables for an ORM stack

9. Click on **Create**.

Once a stack is created, you need to run plan and apply jobs on it. Let's do that now, as follows:

1. From the **Stack Details** screen, select **Jobs** in the **Resources** section.

2. Click on **Terraform Actions** and then select **Plan**. You can see a sample screenshot here:

Figure 9.8 – Plan job for an ORM stack

3. Provide a name for the plan job (optional) and click on **Plan**.

4. Once the plan job is finished, you will see the output of it and will be able to verify how many resources are going to be created. You can see a sample screenshot here:

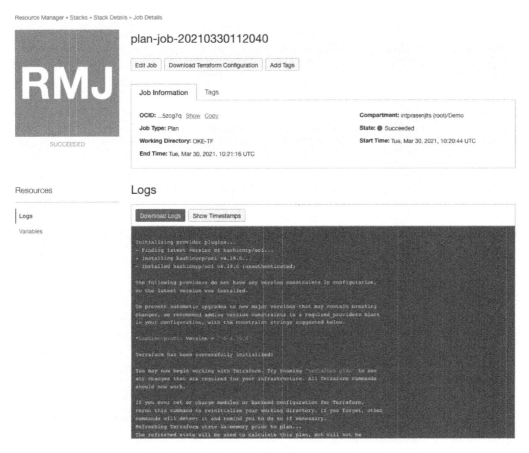

Figure 9.9 – Plan job output for an ORM stack

Once the plan job is finished running, you need to run an apply job to finally create the infrastructure. Let's do that now, as follows:

1. From the **Stack Details** screen, select **Jobs** in the **Resources** section.

2. Click on **Terraform Actions** and select **Apply**, which will take you to the following screen:

Figure 9.10 – Apply job for an ORM stack

3. Choose the default option and click on **Apply**.

4. Once the apply job is finished, you will see the output of it. You can see a sample screenshot here:

Figure 9.11 – Apply job output for an ORM stack

So, you can see how easy it is to create an infrastructure using ORM on OCI. At this point, you can check the associated resources and also download the Terraform state if you want to.

5. From the **Apply** job screen, select **Associated Resources** in the **Resources** section.

6. Here, you will see the resources that have been created. You can see a sample screenshot here:

Resources	Associated Resources			
	Name	**Type**	**Attributes**	**Time Created**
Logs				
Variables	Default DHCP Options for oke-vcn	oci_core_default_dhcp_options	9 attributes Show Copy	Tue, Mar 30, 2021, 10:24:09 UTC
Associated Resources	OCI-Dev-Cluster	oci_containerengine_cluster	14 attributes Show Copy	-
Outputs	oke-igw	oci_core_internet_gateway	10 attributes Show Copy	Tue, Mar 30, 2021, 10:24:09 UTC
View State	oke-routetable	oci_core_default_route_table	9 attributes Show Copy	Tue, Mar 30, 2021, 10:24:09 UTC
	oke-seclist	oci_core_security_list	11 attributes Show Copy	Tue, Mar 30, 2021, 10:24:10 UTC
	oke-subnet-regional	oci_core_subnet	22 attributes Show Copy	Tue, Mar 30, 2021, 10:24:10 UTC
	oke-svclbseclist	oci_core_default_security_list	10 attributes Show Copy	Tue, Mar 30, 2021, 10:24:09 UTC
	oke-svclbsubnet-regional	oci_core_subnet	22 attributes Show Copy	Tue, Mar 30, 2021, 10:24:13 UTC
	oke-vcn	oci_core_vcn	18 attributes Show Copy	Tue, Mar 30, 2021, 10:24:09 UTC
	pool1	oci_containerengine_node_pool	19 attributes Show Copy	-
			Showing 10 Associated Resources	< 1 of 1 >

Figure 9.12 – Associated resources created by an ORM stack

If you want to destroy the infrastructure that you have just created, run a destroy job now.

7. From the **Stack Details** screen, select **Jobs** in the **Resources** section.

8. Click on **Terraform Actions** and select **Destroy**.

9.   Provide a name (optional) and select **Destroy**. You can see a sample screenshot here:

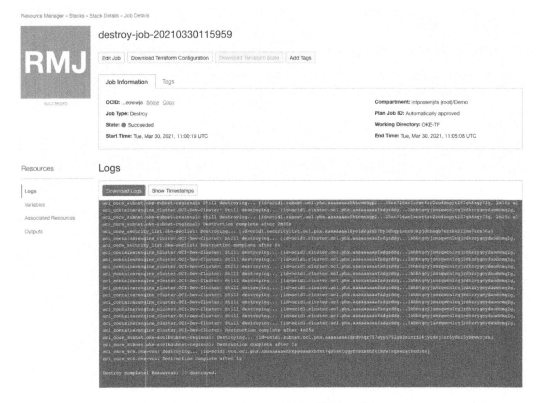

Figure 9.13 – Destroying an ORM stack

Up to now, you have learned how to create an ORM stack and apply jobs to create your infrastructure on OCI. You have also learned how to destroy resources. In the next section, we will discuss the benefits of using ORM to create sample Terraform code from an existing compartment and its associated infrastructure.

Learning to generate IaC from an existing setup

Terraform **Resource Discovery** has been created to help you to discover deployed resources within a compartment and then export all of them to Terraform configuration and state files.

The goal of this feature is to generate Terraform configurations for an OCI customer's compartment. The idea is that a customer infrastructure that has been created in one compartment (mainly via the console) can be replicated in other compartments and/or tenancies.

The generated resource configurations should be able to duplicate the user infrastructure across compartments, tenancies, and regions.

This will solve the pain points of customers when they start creating resources using a console but, at a later stage, think of moving to code-based infrastructure deployment, and will help them to significantly reduce the learning curve of writing HCL from scratch.

To discover resources using ORM, you need to go through the **Create Stack** workflow, as follows:

1. Sign in to the OCI console.
2. Open the navigation menu, select **Resource Manager**, and then **Stacks**.
3. Click on **Create Stack**.
4. Choose **Existing Compartment**.
5. Under the **Stack Configuration** section, select the compartment from where you want to discover resources.
6. Choose a region where you want to discover the resources from.

7. You can either select **All** from **Terraform Provider Services** or select a particular type of resource by choosing **Selected** and selecting an option from the **Services** dropdown. Examples of these services include `apigateway`, `auto_scaling`, `availability_domain`, `containerengine`, core, database, functions, and `load_balancer`, to name a few. You can see a sample screenshot here:

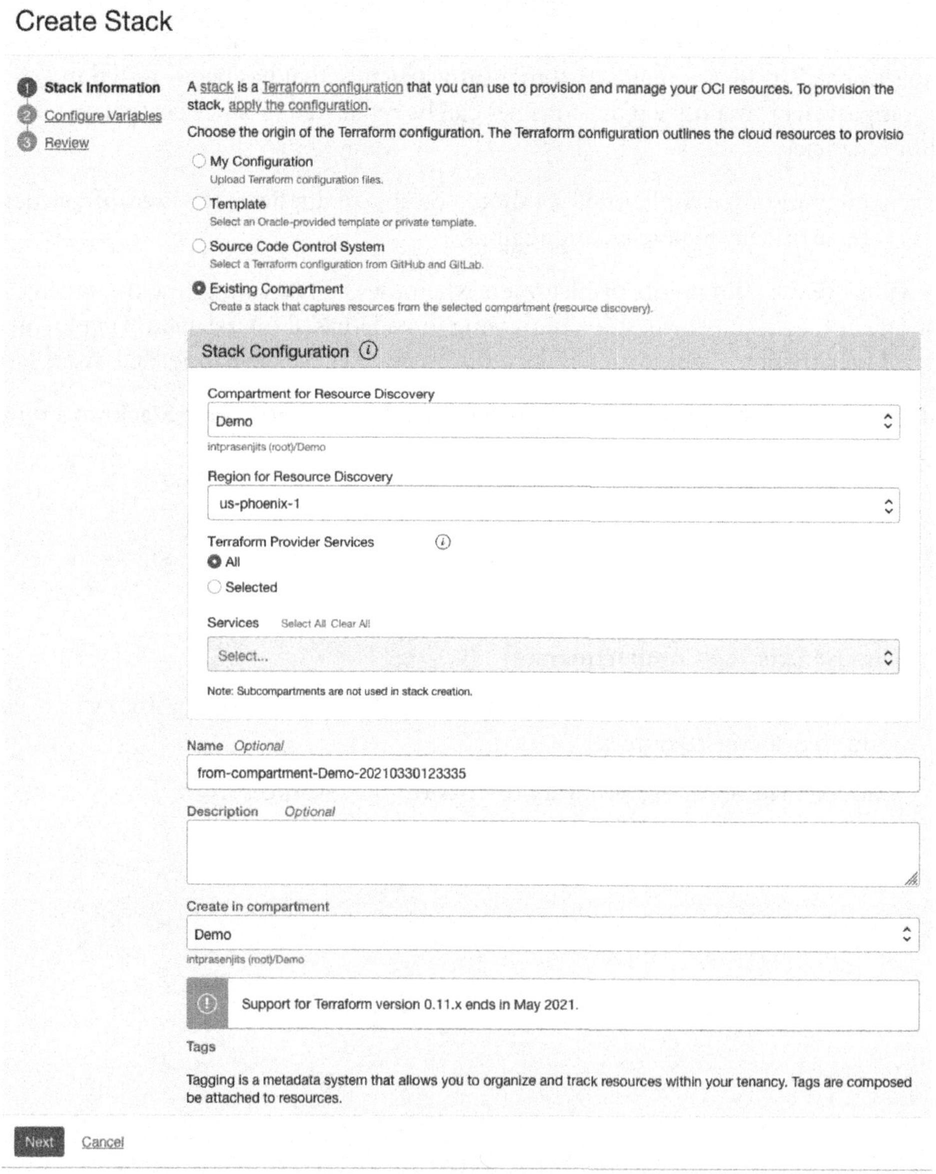

Figure 9.14 – Discovering resources using ORM

8. Click on **Next**.

9. Click on **Next**.

10. Click on **Create**.

11. Once the job is finished, you can download the **Terraform Configuration File (.zip)** from the **Stack Details** page. You can see a sample screenshot here:

Figure 9.15 – Downloading a Terraform configuration file using Resource Discovery

So, you see how easy it is to adopt IaC by using ORM and its **Resource Discovery** service. In the next section, we will show you how to use an SCM system such as GitHub to integrate the code check-in and discover resources on the ORM stack to create an infrastructure.

Learning to integrate ORM with SCM

In a DevOps world, keeping a source Terraform configuration file on a local laptop is highly unlikely. All service teams typically store their Terraform code in an SCM tool such as GitHub or GitLab.

ORM provides a way to integrate two of the most popular SCM providers within ORM so that you can use SCM to store the Terraform configuration files to create an infrastructure. Those providers are GitHub and GitLab.

In this section, we will show you how to configure an SCM provider and then how to use it to create an infrastructure. Follow these next steps:

1. Sign in to the OCI console.

2. Open the navigation menu, select **Resource Manager**, and then **Configuration Source Providers**.

3. Click on **Create Configuration Source Provider**.

4. Provide a name for the provider.

5. Select **GitHub** for the **Type** option.

6. Provide the **Server URL**. As we are using free GitHub user accounts, we are using `https://github.com`.

7. If you do not have a **personal access token (PAT)**, then go to `https://docs.github.com/en/github/authenticating-to-github/creating-a-personal-access-token` to create a PAT for your GitHub account. You can see a sample screenshot here:

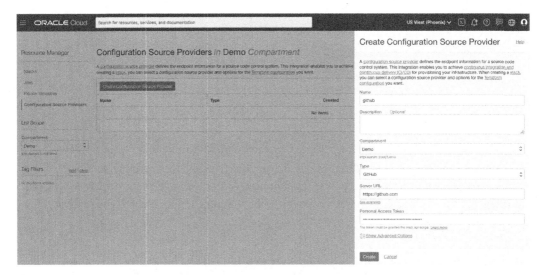

Figure 9.16 – Creating a configuration provider

8. Paste the token into the **Personal Access Token** field and click on **Create**.

Once the configuration provider is created, you can create a stack from the code that is present in any one of the repositories that you created. Let's go through these steps now, as follows:

1. From the **Resource Manager** screen, select **Stacks**.

2. Click on **Create Stack**.

3. Select **Source Code Control System**.

4. Choose an option from the **Configuration Source Provider** dropdown.

5. Select the **Repository** and **Branch** where you kept your code. You can see a sample screenshot here:

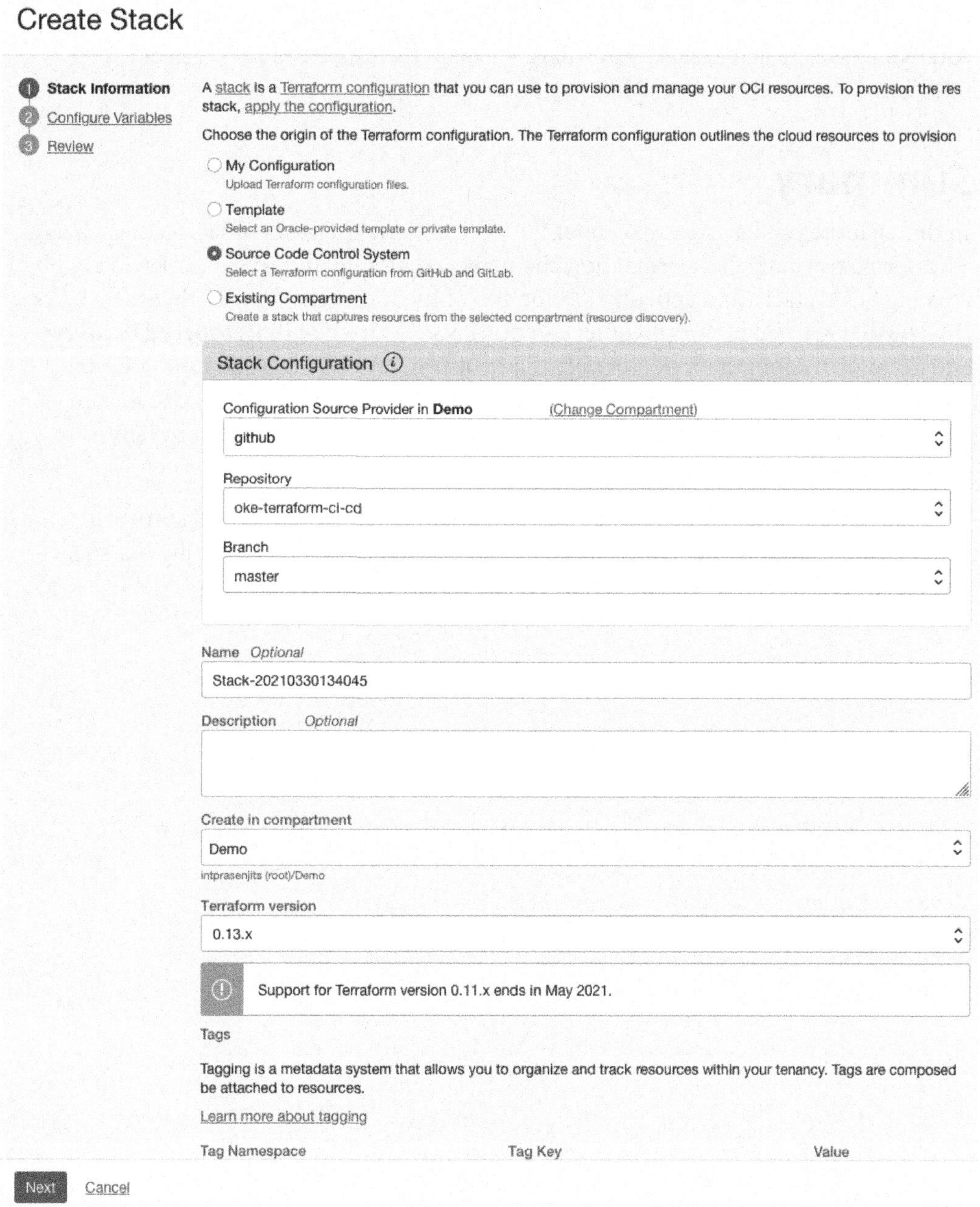

Create Stack

1 **Stack Information**
2 Configure Variables
3 Review

A stack is a Terraform configuration that you can use to provision and manage your OCI resources. To provision the res stack, apply the configuration.

Choose the origin of the Terraform configuration. The Terraform configuration outlines the cloud resources to provision

○ My Configuration
  Upload Terraform configuration files.

○ Template
  Select an Oracle-provided template or private template.

◉ Source Code Control System
  Select a Terraform configuration from GitHub and GitLab.

○ Existing Compartment
  Create a stack that captures resources from the selected compartment (resource discovery).

Stack Configuration ⓘ

Configuration Source Provider in **Demo**   (Change Compartment)

github	↕

Repository

oke-terraform-ci-cd	↕

Branch

master	↕

Name *Optional*

Stack-20210330134045

Description   *Optional*

Create in compartment

Demo	↕

intprasenjits (root)/Demo

Terraform version

0.13.x	↕

ⓘ   Support for Terraform version 0.11.x ends in May 2021.

Tags

Tagging is a metadata system that allows you to organize and track resources within your tenancy. Tags are composed be attached to resources.

Learn more about tagging

Tag Namespace	Tag Key	Value

Next   Cancel

Figure 9.17 – Creating a stack from SCM

6. Click on **Next** and if there is any variable, provide the value of it in this page and click on **Next**.

7. Click on **Create** to create this stack.

After you have created a stack, you will go through the usual steps to create an infrastructure, which involves planning and applying jobs to this stack.

Summary

In this chapter, you have learned about the need and the use cases of IaC tools such as Terraform. You have also learned how the managed Terraform service works on OCI by creating ORM stacks and applying jobs on top of them (in other words, the stacks). You have further learned how a customer can quickly get started with **Resource Discovery** and Terraform configuration. Not only that, but you have also learned how you can use development tools such as SCM to check in your code and use that code to spin up infrastructure. This is required for adopting a DevOps culture within the software development life cycle.

In the next chapter, you will see how you can use the OCI CLI, API, and **software development kit (SDK)** to automate processes that you have been carrying out so far using the console.

10
Interacting with Oracle Cloud Infrastructure Using the CLI/API/SDK

There are many ways to access **Oracle Cloud Infrastructure** (**OCI**). Although OCI has a console where you can create resources, it also offers an **Application Programming Interface** (**API**)-first approach. Using the OCI APIs you can do almost everything that you can do from the Console itself. The OCI APIs are nothing but **REpresentational State Transfer** (**REST**) API calls over **HyperText Transfer Protocol Secure** (**HTTPS**). But that is not all. If you want to use a **Software Development Kit** (**SDK**), you can do so to access all OCI APIs, with SDKs for Java, Ruby, Python, Golang, and .NET.

Apart from the REST API and the Console, you also have the option to invoke the CLI to perform the same operation. To invoke the OCI CLI, you have the option to either locally install the CLI binary or you can use OCI Cloud Shell to do the same thing. The benefit of using the OCI CLI from Cloud Shell is that you don't need to use security credentials to send the API calls to the OCI API backend.

Apart from the OCI Console, REST API, SDKs, and CLI, you can also control and provision resources on OCI using Oracle Resource Manager, which uses Terraform at the backend and not only that, you can also use Ansible. With Ansible, not only can you provision infrastructure resources; it also gives you the ability to deploy and update software assets.

In this chapter, we will walk you through how to use the CLI, covering both how you install it onto your local workstation and how to use it from OCI Cloud Shell. We will also see how to use SDKs to send API calls to the OCI backend, as well as how to use a REST API client to send the same calls to create or update resources.

In this chapter, we're going to cover the following main topics:

- Using the OCI CLI to interact with OCI resources
- Using OCI SDKs to automate OCI operations
- Using the OCI API to send REST calls for managing OCI

Using the OCI CLI to interact with OCI resources

At the beginning of this chapter, we discussed how you can use other tools to access and create resources on OCI. Here's a quick recap of the fundamentals to show you the different methods to access OCI to create, update, and delete resources. You can see a logical diagram of how these tools are connected to OCI:

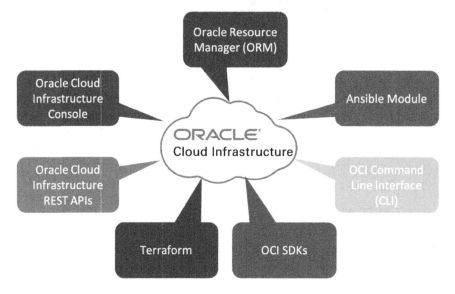

Figure 10.1 – Access methods for OCI

The OCI CLI is a small program that you can either run on a standalone workstation of your choice or you can use OCI Cloud Shell to run the same binary. As stated earlier, the CLI is the easiest way to automate tasks that you can do from the Console.

Let's look at the OCI CLI to see how you can use it to create, update, and delete resources. To install and use the OCI CLI on your local workstation, you need these on the OCI side:

- An OCI account
- A user with the desired permissions
- A key pair for signing API requests with the public key uploaded to OCI

We will use an OCI Linux instance to install the OCI CLI and configure it with permissions to send the calls.

Let's create a standard OCI compute instance:

1. Sign in to the OCI Console.
2. Open the navigation menu, select **Compute**, and then select **Instances**.
3. Click **Create Instance**.
4. Provide a **Name** and select a **Compartment** where you want to deploy it.
5. In the **Availability Domain** section of the **Configure placement and hardware** section, choose where you want to place the availability domain. Additionally, you can click on the **Choose a Fault Domain for this Instance** checkbox and select a **Fault Domain** from the drop-down menu.
6. Select an **Image** for the operating system that you want to deploy. We will talk about the different types of images in the next section. By default, it will be the latest **Oracle Linux** image.

7. In the **Shape** section, by default, the **VM.Standard.E3.Flex** shape type will be selected, which has a 1-core OCPU, 16 GB memory, and 1 Gbps network bandwidth shape. Click on **Change Shape** if you want to change it to a different one. You can either select another type of standard shape or use the slider to change the allocated OCPU and memory for this default instance type. You can see an example of this in the following screenshot:

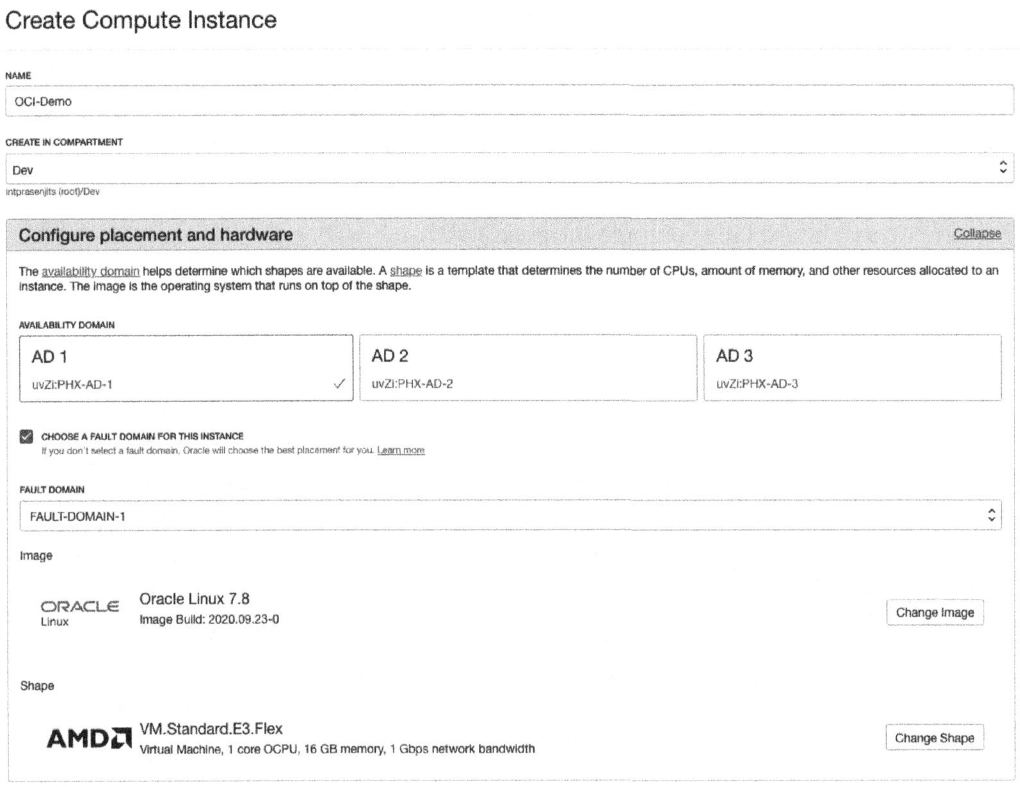

Figure 10.2 – Create Compute Instance wizard

8. In the **Configure networking** section, choose the **Virtual Cloud Network (VCN)** and the subnet that you want to connect this instance to.

9. Select the **Assign a Public IP Address** radio button to have access to this instance over the public internet.

10. Select **Generate SSH Key Pair** if you're unsure of how to generate an SSH key pair to access this instance.

11. Click on **Save Private Key** and **Save Public Key** so that you can use these keys to connect to this instance. You can use these keys to provision other instances in the future. You can see an example of this in the following screenshot:

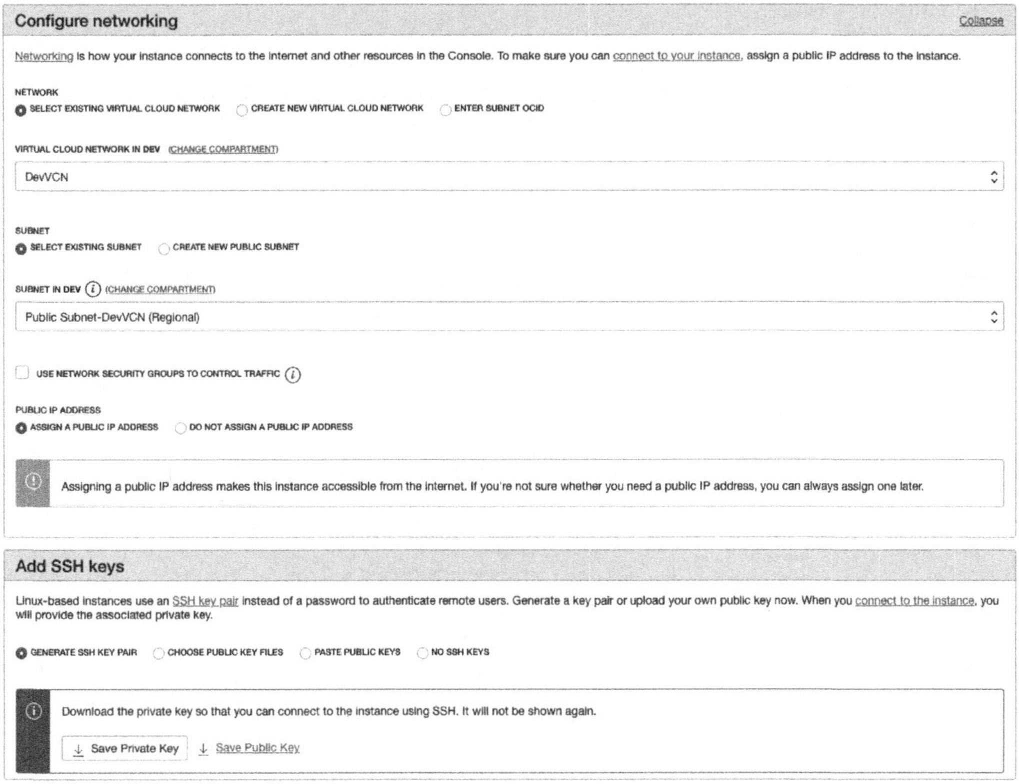

Figure 10.3 – Create Compute Instance wizard – Configure networking section

12. Optionally, you can choose **Specify a custom Boot Volume size**. While creating this instance, you can choose the default boot volume size of this instance or a custom boot volume size up to 32 TB.

If you are provisioning a Linux image-based instance, then you must set your custom boot volume size so that it's more than its default volume size, which is 50 GB. If you want to create an instance based on Windows operating system images, then the same rule applies; that is, you must set the custom boot volume size so that it's more than the default boot volume size, which is 256 GB.

The reason behind setting up this default boot volume size is so that you have enough space for Windows patches and a pagefile.

13. Optionally, you can specify **Use in-transit encryption**. In-transit encryption allows you to encrypt the volume when it's being created.

14. Optionally, you can specify **Encrypt this volume with a key that you manage**.

15. Click on **Create**.

16. Once it is in the **Running** state, you must copy the instance's public IP address and connect to it. An example of this can be seen in the following screenshot:

Figure 10.4 – Instance details

As the instance is up and running now, let's log in to it using an SSH terminal of your choice. You need to specify the SSH key to log in to the instance. Run the following command if you're using a macOS or Linux Terminal:

```
$ ssh -i /path-to-the-ssh-private-key opc@<Public-IP-Address>
```

Once you log in to the instance, you then install the OCI CLI binary. Let's run the installer script:

```
$ bash -c "$(curl -L https://raw.githubusercontent.com/oracle/
oci-cli/master/scripts/install/install.sh)"
```

You need to respond to the installation script prompts. You can see an example of the process in the following screenshot:

Figure 10.5 – The OCI CLI install script running

Before you can actually use the OCI CLI, you need to set up a config file that will hold information about your tenancy. Run the following command:

```
$ oci setup config
```

Follow the prompt and provide details, that is, your user OCID and tenancy OCID, and generate an API signing RSA key pair if you do not have one already. You can see some sample output in the following screenshot:

```
[opc@oci-cli ~]$ oci setup config
    This command provides a walkthrough of creating a valid CLI config file.

    The following links explain where to find the information required by this
    script:

    User API Signing Key, OCID and Tenancy OCID:

        https://docs.cloud.oracle.com/Content/API/Concepts/apisigningkey.htm#Other

    Region:

        https://docs.cloud.oracle.com/Content/General/Concepts/regions.htm

    General config documentation:

        https://docs.cloud.oracle.com/Content/API/Concepts/sdkconfig.htm

Enter a location for your config [/home/opc/.oci/config]:
Enter a user OCID: ocid1.user.oc1..aaaaaaaa4a17gtyucaw7jyzk73aldx7qhfpy476ccd6ru6vywstixdrkhwqa
Enter a tenancy OCID: ocid1.tenancy.oc1..aaaaaaaaqmq5gmfb7vyqn7smwvyk7orckdtwa5wf3f2xqe2i34zygqqa6bha
Enter a region by index or name(e.g.
1: ap-chiyoda-1, 2: ap-chuncheon-1, 3: ap-hyderabad-1, 4: ap-melbourne-1, 5: ap-mumbai-1,
6: ap-osaka-1, 7: ap-seoul-1, 8: ap-sydney-1, 9: ap-tokyo-1, 10: ca-montreal-1,
11: ca-toronto-1, 12: eu-amsterdam-1, 13: eu-frankfurt-1, 14: eu-zurich-1, 15: me-dubai-1,
16: me-jeddah-1, 17: sa-santiago-1, 18: sa-saopaulo-1, 19: sa-vinhedo-1, 20: uk-cardiff-1,
21: uk-gov-cardiff-1, 22: uk-gov-london-1, 23: uk-london-1, 24: us-ashburn-1, 25: us-gov-ashburn-1,
26: us-gov-chicago-1, 27: us-gov-phoenix-1, 28: us-langley-1, 29: us-luke-1, 30: us-phoenix-1,
31: us-sanjose-1): us-phoenix-1
Do you want to generate a new API Signing RSA key pair? (If you decline you will be asked to supply the path to an existing key.) [Y/n]: Y
Enter a directory for your keys to be created [/home/opc/.oci]:
Enter a name for your key [oci_api_key]:
Public key written to: /home/opc/.oci/oci_api_key_public.pem
Enter a passphrase for your private key (empty for no passphrase):
Private key written to: /home/opc/.oci/oci_api_key.pem
Fingerprint: 1d:ff:db:ab:85:70:6c:e4:fb:5a:74:96:11:61:00:7f
Config written to /home/opc/.oci/config


    If you haven't already uploaded your API Signing public key through the
    console, follow the instructions on the page linked below in the section
    'How to upload the public key':

        https://docs.cloud.oracle.com/Content/API/Concepts/apisigningkey.htm#How2


[opc@oci-cli ~]$ 
```

Figure 10.6 – The OCI CLI config file creation

You need to upload the public API signing key to your tenancy so that you can be authenticated for sending OCI CLI calls. Let's upload the public API key to the OCI Console and then try to send a sample OCI CLI command to verify:

1. Sign in to the OCI Console.

2. From the right corner, select **Profile**, and then select **User Settings**.

3. Go to the **API Keys** section.

4. Click on **Add API Key**.

5. Choose **Paste Public Key** and paste the content of the `oci_api_key_public.pem` file from the Linux instance.

Now run a sample command to check the object storage namespace of your tenancy. To do that, run the following command:

```
$ oci os ns get
{
  "data": "intprasenjits"
}
```

This validates that the OCI CLI setup is complete. Let's use the CLI to create and remove some resources.

The basic syntax of OCI is as follows:

```
$ oci <service> <type> <action> <options>
```

If you want to list the compartments, then run the following command:

```
$ oci iam compartment list -c <tenancy-ocid>
```

You can see some sample output in the following screenshot:

```
[opc@oci-cli ~]$ oci iam compartment list -c ocid1.tenancy.oc1..aaaaaaaaqmq5gmfb7vyqn7smwvyk7orckdtwa5wf3f2xqe2i34zygqqa6bha
{
  "data": [
    {
      "compartment-id": "ocid1.tenancy.oc1..aaaaaaaaqmq5gmfb7vyqn7smwvyk7orckdtwa5wf3f2xqe2i34zygqqa6bha",
      "defined-tags": {},
      "description": "This is the main compartment",
      "freeform-tags": {},
      "id": "ocid1.compartment.oc1..aaaaaaaa7v7w53f52covek2m7nk2mvzwu2lijj5x2w4kjjqaundch733il3q",
      "inactive-status": null,
      "is-accessible": null,
      "lifecycle-state": "ACTIVE",
      "name": "Demo",
      "time-created": "2021-01-20T09:44:57.466000+00:00"
    },
    {
      "compartment-id": "ocid1.tenancy.oc1..aaaaaaaaqmq5gmfb7vyqn7smwvyk7orckdtwa5wf3f2xqe2i34zygqqa6bha",
      "defined-tags": {
        "OracleInternalReserved": {
          "ServiceType": "Other"
        }
      },
      "description": "Dev Comp",
      "freeform-tags": {},
      "id": "ocid1.compartment.oc1..aaaaaaaabifl33rrjfy7qckktu3jkbq7b5jaf47lxcgk226igq6vcox6qj5a",
      "inactive-status": null,
      "is-accessible": null,
      "lifecycle-state": "ACTIVE",
      "name": "Dev",
      "time-created": "2020-08-06T17:50:11.213000+00:00"
    },
    {
      "compartment-id": "ocid1.tenancy.oc1..aaaaaaaaqmq5gmfb7vyqn7smwvyk7orckdtwa5wf3f2xqe2i34zygqqa6bha",
      "defined-tags": {},
      "description": "For Dyn Demo and Test",
      "freeform-tags": {},
      "id": "ocid1.compartment.oc1..aaaaaaaa4tmuc26fodp6qiyytaimvbxw4si2aldgjmj2cox4yaujh33skglq",
      "inactive-status": null,
      "is-accessible": null,
      "lifecycle-state": "ACTIVE",
      "name": "Dyn",
      "time-created": "2017-09-14T14:04:42.893000+00:00"
    },
    {
      "compartment-id": "ocid1.tenancy.oc1..aaaaaaaaqmq5gmfb7vyqn7smwvyk7orckdtwa5wf3f2xqe2i34zygqqa6bha",
      "defined-tags": {},
      "description": "Test",
      "freeform-tags": {},
      "id": "ocid1.compartment.oc1..aaaaaaaaazxqpuis6bihjyr5eueflge53yksuroheizm6wbuczajqacamma",
      "inactive-status": null,
      "is-accessible": null,
      "lifecycle-state": "ACTIVE",
      "name": "FirstTuesday",
      "time-created": "2017-02-07T13:00:30.325000+00:00"
    },
    {
      "compartment-id": "ocid1.tenancy.oc1..aaaaaaaaqmq5gmfb7vyqn7smwvyk7orckdtwa5wf3f2xqe2i34zygqqa6bha",
      "defined-tags": {},
      "description": "PoC",
      "freeform-tags": {},
      "id": "ocid1.compartment.oc1..aaaaaaaa5q2efwl7wzugahn4fy5c4hxzf6vcywg4i2tainvaquz5d56iybwq",
      "inactive-status": null,
      "is-accessible": null,
      "lifecycle-state": "ACTIVE",
      "name": "Golang",
      "time-created": "2017-05-24T09:33:28.939000+00:00"
    },
    {
      "compartment-id": "ocid1.tenancy.oc1..aaaaaaaaqmq5gmfb7vyqn7smwvyk7orckdtwa5wf3f2xqe2i34zygqqa6bha",
      "defined-tags": {},
      "description": "This is the Mgmt Comp for Managing Management Resources",
      "freeform-tags": {},
      "id": "ocid1.compartment.oc1..aaaaaaaadron74mugrb4csyzy3k64dbc5k27zggqd2kzh2rvrughn7m5vvkq",
      "inactive-status": null,
      "is-accessible": null,
      "lifecycle-state": "ACTIVE",
      "name": "Management",
      "time-created": "2017-10-19T16:01:38.956000+00:00"
    },
    {
      "compartment-id": "ocid1.tenancy.oc1..aaaaaaaaqmq5gmfb7vyqn7smwvyk7orckdtwa5wf3f2xqe2i34zygqqa6bha",
      "defined-tags": {},
      "description": "This is for all OSS Testing",
      "freeform-tags": {},
      "id": "ocid1.compartment.oc1..aaaaaaaarcnhae2ua5d52woc4wnvhifsqa6obv3rq7o3ftkmyul5d52qlrua",
      "inactive-status": null,
```

Figure 10.7 – The OCI CLI compartment list output

> **Note**
>
> Make sure you replace the `<tenancy-ocid>` with the tenancy OCID of your tenancy.

Let's create an object storage bucket in a given compartment using the OCI CLI. Run the following command:

```
oci os bucket create --name testbucket --compartment-id
<compartment-ocid>
```

You can see some sample output in the following screenshot:

```
[opc@oci-cli ~]$ oci os bucket create --name testbucket --compartment-id ocid1.compartment.oc1..aaaaaaaa7v7w53f52covek2m7nk2mvzwu2lijj6x2w4kjjqaundch733il3q
{
  "data": {
    "approximate-count": null,
    "approximate-size": null,
    "auto-tiering": null,
    "compartment-id": "ocid1.compartment.oc1..aaaaaaaa7v7w53f52covek2m7nk2mvzwu2lijj6x2w4kjjqaundch733il3q",
    "created-by": "ocid1.user.oc1..aaaaaaaa4al7gtyucaw7jyzk73aldx7qhfpy476ccd6ru6vywstixdrkhwqa",
    "defined-tags": {},
    "etag": "8d1b3f90-f95c-4b4a-8682-92c80e43bb4b",
    "freeform-tags": {},
    "id": "ocid1.bucket.oc1.phx.aaaaaaaadmcp6je5zbay6hbffjq2ghiutmo2lmnfltxxgeztuhuputxw6kha",
    "is-read-only": false,
    "kms-key-id": null,
    "metadata": {},
    "name": "testbucket",
    "namespace": "intprasenjits",
    "object-events-enabled": false,
    "object-lifecycle-policy-etag": null,
    "public-access-type": "NoPublicAccess",
    "replication-enabled": false,
    "storage-tier": "Standard",
    "time-created": "2021-06-05T09:12:25.522000+00:00",
    "versioning": "Disabled"
  },
  "etag": "8d1b3f90-f95c-4b4a-8682-92c80e43bb4b"
}
[opc@oci-cli ~]$
```

Figure 10.8 – Creating an object storage bucket

So, you can see how easy and interactive it is using the OCI CLI to create, update, or delete resources. OCI allows its customers to use the OCI CLI not only from the local workstation but by using its Cloud Shell as well.

OCI Cloud Shell is a terminal that is accessible from the Oracle Cloud Console. OCI doesn't charge its users to use this but there is a monthly tenancy limit. You can get a Linux shell prompt where the OCI CLI is installed and configured using your tenancy session credentials. So, you need to generate separate keys and configure the OCI CLI to authenticate itself.

Cloud Shell provides the following:

- An ephemeral virtual host that you use for the Linux shell. This host has the latest version of the OCI CLI installed and configured along with other useful tools, including Terraform, Ansible, and Docker.

- You will get 5 GB of storage in your home directory. You can store any useful files here, such as code or scripts.

Let's use OCI Cloud Shell to delete the object storage bucket that you have just created using the OCI CLI from the local workstation:

1. Sign in to the OCI Console.

2. From the right corner, select **Cloud Shell**, as shown in the following screenshot:

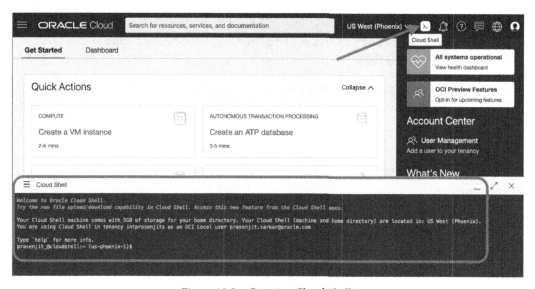

Figure 10.9 – Opening Cloud Shell

3. Let's run the following command to delete the object storage bucket that you have created:

```
$ oci os bucket delete --bucket-name testbucket
Are you sure you want to delete this resource? [y/N]: y
```

So, you see that OCI has a tiny little console that gives us the ability to run important tools, such as the OCI CLI, Terraform, Ansible, Docker, Python, Go, and Java.

In the next section, we will show you how to use the OCI SDKs to do the same job, but by writing code using the SDK.

Using OCI SDKs to automate OCI operations

OCI provides several SDKs to develop custom solutions. You can use SDKs for building and deploying applications on OCI, and not only that, but you can also integrate those applications with OCI services as well. You can use the OCI SDK to develop applications for a specific platform, such as Java, Python, Go, Ruby, TypeScript and JavaScript, and .NET.

OCI provides code samples for each language and for each specific API call. So, it is very easy for you to consume these samples, as well as referring to the rich documentation to help you build something for your organization. OCI has open sourced these SDKs, so you can contribute to them as well.

The SDKs available are the following:

Figure 10.10 – Supported SDKs for OCI

Let's install and configure the Python SDK to list some of the OCI resources:

1. Log in using SSH to the OCI instance that you have created in the *Using the OCI CLI to interact with OCI resources* section. We will use the following topology to run the Python code:

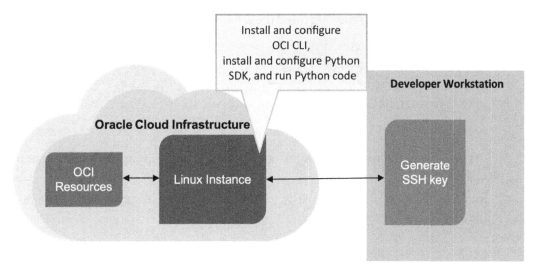

Figure 10.11 – SDK topology

2.   Run the following command to install the OCI SDK:

```
$ python3.6 -m pip install oci
```

You can see a sample output of the command in the following screenshot:

```
                                    prassark — opc@oci-cli:~ — ssh -i Desktop/ssh-keys/id_rsa opc@129.146.167.152 — 294×88
[opc@oci-cli ~]$ python3.6 -m pip install oci
Defaulting to user installation because normal site-packages is not writeable
Requirement already satisfied: oci in /usr/lib/python3.6/site-packages (2.28.0)
Requirement already satisfied: certifi in /usr/lib/python3.6/site-packages (from oci) (2018.10.15)
Requirement already satisfied: configparser==4.0.2 in /usr/lib/python3.6/site-packages (from oci) (4.0.2)
Collecting cryptography==3.2.1
  Downloading cryptography-3.2.1-cp35-abi3-manylinux2010_x86_64.whl (2.6 MB)
     |████████████████████████████████| 2.6 MB 19.3 MB/s
Collecting pyOpenSSL<=19.1.0,>=17.5.0
  Downloading pyOpenSSL-19.1.0-py2.py3-none-any.whl (53 kB)
     |████████████████████████████████| 53 kB 3.9 MB/s
Collecting python-dateutil<3.0.0,>=2.5.3
  Downloading python_dateutil-2.8.1-py2.py3-none-any.whl (227 kB)
     |████████████████████████████████| 227 kB 54.8 MB/s
Requirement already satisfied: pytz>=2016.10 in /usr/lib/python3.6/site-packages (from oci) (2016.10)
Collecting six>=1.4.1
  Downloading six-1.16.0-py2.py3-none-any.whl (11 kB)
Requirement already satisfied: cffi!=1.11.3,>=1.8 in /usr/local/lib64/python3.6/site-packages (from cryptography==3.2.1->oci) (1.14.5)
Requirement already satisfied: pycparser in /usr/lib/python3.6/site-packages (from cffi!=1.11.3,>=1.8->cryptography==3.2.1->oci) (2.14)
Installing collected packages: six, cryptography, python-dateutil, pyOpenSSL
Successfully installed cryptography-3.2.1 pyOpenSSL-19.1.0 python-dateutil-2.8.1 six-1.16.0
[opc@oci-cli ~]$
```

Figure 10.12 – Installing the OCI SDK

3.   At this point, you are ready write your first Python code to do any operations that you want using the SDK.

4.   Create a file by running vi user.py. Paste the following code and save the file by pressing *Esc* and then type :wq! and press *Enter*:

```
import oci
config = oci.config.from_file()
identity = oci.identity.IdentityClient (config)
user = identity.get_user(config["user"]).data
print(user)
```

5.   Let's run the program and check the output and then we will explain what it does in each line.

6.   Run it by typing python3 user.py. You can see a sample output of the code in the following screenshot:

```
[opc@oci-cli ~]$ python3.6 user.py
{
  "capabilities": {
    "can_use_api_keys": true,
    "can_use_auth_tokens": true,
    "can_use_console_password": true,
    "can_use_customer_secret_keys": true,
    "can_use_o_auth2_client_credentials": true,
    "can_use_smtp_credentials": true
  },
  "compartment_id": "ocid1.tenancy.oc1..aaaaaaaaqmq5gmfb7vyqn7smwvyk7orckdtwa5wf3f2xqe2i34zygqqa6bha",
  "defined_tags": {},
  "description": "PrasenjitSarkar",
  "email": null,
  "email_verified": false,
  "external_identifier": null,
  "freeform_tags": {},
  "id": "ocid1.user.oc1..aaaaaaaa4al7gtyucaw7jyzk73aldx7qhfpy476ccd6ru6vywstixdrkhwqa",
  "identity_provider_id": null,
  "inactive_status": null,
  "is_mfa_activated": false,
  "last_successful_login_time": "2021-06-05T10:44:42.400000+00:00",
  "lifecycle_state": "ACTIVE",
  "name": "prasenjit.sarkar@oracle.com",
  "previous_successful_login_time": null,
  "time_created": "2016-08-04T19:02:48.925000+00:00"
}
[opc@oci-cli ~]$
[opc@oci-cli ~]$
```

Figure 10.13 – Running Python code using the OCI SDK

So, you can see that the code fetches details about the current user and its details.

Let's explain what the code does in each line:

- The import statements are used to import the required packages that are used later in the program:

```
import oci
```

- To set up the config, by default OCI CLI refers to the ~/.oci/config file from the following line of code. This is what you set up while configuring the OCI CLI:

```
config = oci.config.from_file()
```

- When the communication of OCI is set up, the following API code creates a service client to OCI. Refer to https://oracle-cloud-infrastructure-python-sdk.readthedocs.io/en/latest/api/landing.html for more OCI APIs:

```
identity = oci.identity.IdentityClient (config)
```

- The following line of code uses a service client to get the current user with all its details:

```
user = identity.get_user(config["user"]).data
```

- The following line of code prints the current user details to the terminal after execution of the code:

```
print(user)
```

So, you see that OCI provides not only a CLI for interaction, but also lets you use your choice of programming language to automate the management of OCI resources. You can choose between Python, Java, Ruby, Go, .NET, TypeScript, and JavaScript to automate things.

In the next section, we will dive deep into the actual REST API implementation and will see how you can use a simple shell script to send REST API calls to the OCI API endpoint.

Using the OCI API to send REST calls for managing OCI

OCI has taken an API-first strategy, which means that before they develop their UIs, they develop the API that will interact with the backend resources. The OCI APIs are typical REST APIs, meaning they use the standard HTTPS requests and responses.

Every OCI service has its own API endpoint. To check the current endpoint related to the specific region you want to send the call to, refer to `https://docs.oracle.com/en-us/iaas/api/`.

OCI maintains its own API versioning as well. If you look carefully at the endpoint, then you will find the desired API version from the base path of the API endpoint. For example, as of now, most of the APIs are versioned as 20160918.

Here's an example for a GET request to list users in the Phoenix region:

```
GET https://identity.us-phoenix1.oraclecloud.com/20160918/users
```

For tighter security, all OCI API requests must be signed for authentication purposes. For more details on the signature generation for API signing, refer to the following link, as Oracle may change the version of the signature in the future: `https://docs.oracle.com/en-us/iaas/Content/API/Concepts/signingrequests.htm`.

Let's use a bash script to send a REST API call to list the VCNs in a given compartment:

1. Log in using SSH to the OCI instance that you created in the *Using the OCI CLI to interact with OCI resources* section. We will use the following topology to run the Python code.

2. Type vi vcns.sh and paste the following code. Change the values of the tenancy ID, user OCID, fingerprint, and compartment OCID:

```bash
#!/bin/bash
######################### Fill these in with your values
#########################
#OCID of the tenancy calls are being made in to
tenancy_ocid="ocid1.tenancy.oc1..<unique-id>"
# OCID of the user making the rest call
user_ocid="ocid1.user.oc1..<unique-id>"
# path to the private PEM format key for this user
privateKeyPath="/home/opc/.oci/oci_api_key.pem"
# fingerprint of the private key for this user
fingerprint="1d:ff:……"
# The REST api you want to call, with any required
paramters.
rest_api="/20160918/vcns?compartmentId=ocid1.compartment.
ocl..<unique-id>"
# The host you want to make the call against
host="iaas.us-phoenix-1.oraclecloud.com"
###################################################################
#############################

date=`date -u "+%a, %d %h %Y %H:%M:%S GMT"`
date_header="date: $date"
host_header="host: $host"
request_target="(request-target): get $rest_api"
# note the order of items. The order in the signing_
string matches the order in the headers
signing_string="$request_target\n$date_header\n$host_
header"
headers="(request-target) date host"
echo "=====================================================
=================================="
```

```
printf '%b' "signing string is $signing_string \n"

signature=`printf '%b' "$signing_string" | openssl dgst
-sha256 -sign $privateKeyPath | openssl enc -e -base64 |
tr -d '\n'`

printf '%b' "Signed Request is  \n$signature\n"


echo "==================================================
====================================================="

set -x
curl -v -X GET -sS https://$host$rest_api -H
"date: $date" -H "Authorization: Signature
version=\"1\",keyId=\"$tenancy_ocid/$user_ocid/$fingerpri
nt\",algorithm=\"rsa-sha256\",headers=\"$headers\",signat
ure=\"$signature\""
```

3. Save the file by pressing *Esc*, then type wq! and press *Enter*.

4. Change the permission of this file and provide execute permission by typing chmod
    +x vcns.sh and press *Enter*.

5. Run the script and observe the output. You will see output like that shown in the
    following screenshot, which shows the standard **200 OK** HTTP response and then
    the details of the VCNs in the provided compartment:

Figure 10.14 – Running a shell script to list the VCNs using the OCI REST API

Let's explain what this script does on each line:

1. First of all, the first four lines are standard, and these variables will hold your tenancy-specific information. So, provide your tenancy OCID, user OCID, private key path, and fingerprint.

2. This line holds the API version and path-specific information. In this case, it holds the path to list the VCNs in a given compartment. You need to change the compartment OCID to your specific details:

    ```
    rest_api="/20160918/vcns?compartmentId=ocid1.compartment.
    ocl..<unique-id>"
    ```

3. This line holds the API endpoint. Every service has its own API endpoint. To find out your specific API endpoint, refer to https://docs.oracle.com/en-us/iaas/api/:

    ```
    host="iaas.us-phoenix-1.oraclecloud.com"
    ```

4. The following code section defines the headers that you need to create the signing string. You need to define these headers in an appropriate format that will be used in conjunction with your signing string. Headers are dependent on your request type (that is, GET or PUT).

    For a GET request, you need the request target, host, and date:

    ```
    date=`date -u "+%a, %d %h %Y %H:%M:%S GMT"`
    date_header="date: $date"
    host_header="host: $host"
    request_target="(request-target): get $rest_api"


    # Note the order of items. The order in the signing_
    string matches the order in the headers.


    signing_string="$request_target\n$date_header\n$host_
    header"
    headers="(request-target) date host"
    ```

5. The next code block is the signature generation, created from your signing string:

```
echo "=====================================================
=====================================================" 
printf '%b' "signing string is $signing_string \n"
signature=`printf '%b' "$signing_string" | openssl dgst
-sha256 -sign $privateKeyPath | openssl enc -e -base64 |
tr -d '\n'`
printf '%b' "Signed Request is  \n$signature\n"
```

6. The last section is the actual use of the signature and all of the other details that you set and send to the API endpoint to list the VCNs:

```
curl -v -X GET -sS https://$host$rest_api -H
"date: $date" -H "Authorization: Signature
version=\"1\",keyId=\"$tenancy_ocid/$user_ocid/$fingerpri
nt\",algorithm=\"rsa-sha256\",headers=\"$headers\",signat
ure=\"$signature\""
```

Let's break it down piece by piece:

1. The first part is as follows:

```
curl -v -X GET -sS
```

The -v option is to generate verbose output. -X GET is to request a GET operation. The -sS is for silent mode, but still shows errors.

2. Let's look at the second part, as follows:

```
https://$host$rest_api
```

The first section is the endpoint that you stored in the variable, and the second part is the API version stored in the variable as well.

3. For all types of requests, that is, for GET, DELETE, PUT, or POST, you need the date header. You need this date in the correct HTTP header format. You have already computed this:

```
-H "date: $date"
```

4. The entire header is then passed in the `Authorization` header. You can see that as follows:

```
-H "Authorization: Signature version=\"1\"
```

If you look closely, you will notice that the first header field is `Signature version`. The OCI documentation says it is version 1 at the time of writing.

5. Next, you need to pass `keyId`, which we have taken as input into the variable. `keyId` is required for all request types. The syntax is `keyId="<TENANCY-OCID>/<USER-OCID>/<KEY-FINGERPRINT>"`:

```
keyId=\"$tenancy_ocid/$user_ocid/$fingerprint\"
```

6. Next, you need to pass the signing algorithm, which must be `rsa-sha256`:

```
algorithm=\"rsa-sha256\"
```

7. Lastly, put down the header and the signature that you generated earlier in the code:

```
headers=\"$headers\",signature=\"$signature\""
```

So, you can see how you can use a simple bash script to send OCI REST API requests to manage OCI resources.

Summary

In this chapter, you learned the various way of managing resources in OCI other than using the Console. OCI's API-first strategy is excellent in that all the other developer tools can utilize its benefits and produce various other ways to interact with resources such as the OCI CLI, Cloud Shell, SDKs, and REST API. You learned how to use the OCI CLI to create and delete resources not only from your local workstation, but also using Cloud Shell. The various programming languages on offer give you the ability to choose your preferred option and automate operations using code. Finally, the REST API offers an intuitive, easy, robust and at the same time secure way of interacting with the API endpoint.

In the next chapter, you will see how you can use a VMware solution and craft a hybrid cloud solution.

11
Building a Hybrid Cloud on Oracle Cloud Infrastructure using Oracle Cloud VMware Solution

Oracle and VMware jointly developed a fully certified and supported **software-defined data center solution** (**SDDC**) known as **Oracle Cloud VMware Solution** (**OCVS**). This solution leverages the underlying **Oracle Cloud Infrastructure** (**OCI**) to host a highly available VMware SDDC, allowing seamless migration of all on-premises VMware workloads to OCVS.

OCVS is a fully secure VMware SDDC that's comprised of OCI resources and VMware software and licenses. The base configuration of the OCVS includes three OCI bare-metal compute hosts (3x BM.DenseIO2.52 instances) to achieve high availability, along with other OCI products such as OCI **virtual cloud network** (**VCN**). The OCVS is highly scalable, starts with three hosts, and can scale up to 64 hosts in a single OCVS cluster. The base OCVS configuration comes with 156 OPCU, 2,304 GB of physical memory, and 153 TB of **Non-Volatile Memory Express** (**NVMe**)-based raw storage. The OCVS includes VMware software such as vSphere, vSAN, NSX-T, and vCenter Server. The vSAN converged storage technology ensures the availability of data and replicates data across all the bare-metal hosts that are used for the OCVS cluster.

OCVS is the only VMware SDDC on the public cloud that provides L2 network capabilities. It allows the applications that depend on L2 networking to run on the public cloud.

Unlike other cloud provider's VMware SDDC solutions, the OCVS is fully secured and controlled by the customer, and it can be customized based on the customer's needs. OCVS is also well integrated with other OCI services through the OCI VCN, configured with a different gateway to communicate with the other network and OCI services.

In this chapter, we're going to cover the following main topics:

- Understanding the solution overview of the OCVS solution
- Deploying an OCVS cluster
- Accessing an OCVS cluster
- Connecting an OCVS cluster to the internet

Understanding the solution overview of the OCVS solution

In this section, we will illustrate the basics of how OCVS is designed and deployed in OCI and its integration with other OCI services running natively, as well as other Oracle PaaS solutions.

OCVS is designed as per the VMware validated design guidelines, and the architecture uses from 3 to 64 BM.DenseIO2.52 nodes to provide full VMware SDDC capabilities.

The OCVS architecture shown in the following diagram illustrates how each component of the VMware SDDC stack is configured and deployed on an OCI compute BM instance.

The OCVS architecture can be divided into three key components: network (VMware NSX-T), compute (VMware vSphere), and storage (VMware vSAN). This section will describe the different components that are used for the VMware SDDC stack in OCI:

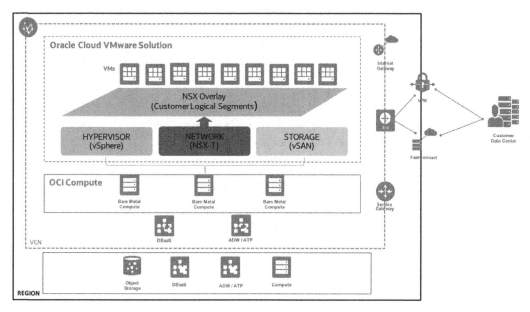

Figure 11.1 – OCVS solution integration within OCI

There are some restrictions as to what you can do on top of OCVS, and they are as follows:

- Customers cannot bring their own VMware licenses.
- The vSAN layer in OCVS will use local NVMe drives.
- The OCVS cluster will boot its ESXi image off a remote **Internet Small Computer Systems Interface (iSCSI)** boot volume.
- The smallest cluster a customer can provision contains three hosts.
- The largest cluster a customer can provision contains 64 hosts.
- **Border Gateway Protocol (BGP)** is not supported in the environment and all routing with the external networks (outside overlay) will be done using static routes.
- Following the initial bring-up, hosts can be added to an OCVS using the provisioning service. The customers are responsible for adding/removing these new nodes to/from the VMware cluster.

Now, let's dive into each of the solution components of OCVS.

Virtual cloud network (VCN)

One of the key components or resources of OCI is VCN, and this is the foundational component for OCVS as well. VCN carries out the connection point for all the topologies that OCVS provides, such as connecting on-premises data centers, connecting OCI resources, connecting to the internet, and connecting to the Oracle services network. You can think of it as an on-premises traditional network that provides switching, routing, and firewall capabilities. This VCN is spanned across an OCI region that provides a single IPv4 space.

Different properties and components comprise a VCN, such as subnets, VLANs, route tables, security lists, gateways, and **network security groups** (**NSGs**). The next one on the component list is ESXi hosts. Let's take a look at them.

Compute – VMware vSphere (ESXi)

This is the fundamental layer of the solution and provides an OCI BM DenseIO instance to run VMware vSphere Hypervisor. VMware ESXi is an enterprise-class Type-1 hypervisor for running virtual computers known as **virtual machines** (**VMs**). VMware ESXi, when deployed on a BM instance, provides a strong foundation for the entire SDDC stack. At the time of writing, only the BM.DenseIO.2.52 OCI shape is supported to run the VMware SDDC on OCI.

The VMware vSphere cluster in OCVS offers a three-node ESXi cluster that delivers 156 OCPUs and 2.25 TB of memory. This can be scaled up to 64 nodes in a cluster. The high availability of the ESXi host's BM instances is taken care of by OCI. In the following diagram, you can see the placement of the ESXi host (OCI instances) and how the solution components of OCVS sit on top of it:

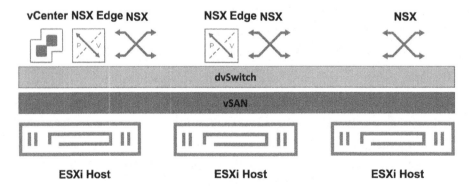

Figure 11.2 – OCVS solution logical diagram

At this stage, we are ready to look at various VMware components. Within these, the main component for all layer 2 networking is NSX. Let's look at what this is.

Networking – VMware NSX-T

The network is another important function of the architecture. The BM instance that's hosting VMware ESXi is deployed in an OCI VCN and its subnets to provide core networking underlay capabilities, in addition to security lists and route tables. The VMware NSX-T is a separate product suite from VMware that's deployed as part of the OCVS, which effectively provides agile, software-defined networking capabilities.

The OCVS BM instance that's used for the SDDC stack is backed by 2x25 Gbps network bandwidth and supports 52 **virtual Network Interface Cards (vNICs)** in total (26 per physical NIC), ensuring high throughput, low latency, and a fully redundant network.

Three different management components are deployed as part of NSX-T called NSX Manager, NSX Controller, and NSX Edge. All these components reside in a vSphere cluster, running as VMs on top of ESXi hosts backed by an OCI BM instance. The high availability of the software NSX components depends on the availability of the ESXi host and VMware vSphere cluster's native HA/DRS functionality. The high availability of NSX's underlay networking depends on OCI VCN. The OCI VCN regional subnet provides a greater extension to SDDC cluster scale-out operations. In the following diagram, you can see what the physical architecture of an ESXi instance looks like when it is deployed as part of an OCVS solution:

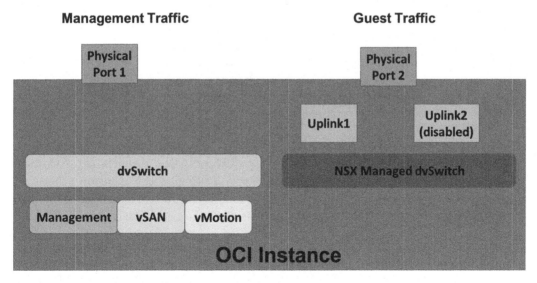

Figure 11.3 – OCVS solution logical diagram

After networking, you need to know about the storage solution that comes with OCVS. Let's take a look at the VMware vSAN solution.

Storage – VMware vSAN

vSAN has been chosen as the storage platform for OCVS to provide a hyper-converged, enterprise-class, and software-defined storage. vSAN was built to take advantage of cheap servers since they have locally attached flash disks.

The OCVS includes VMware vSAN storage technology, which provides a single shared datastore (vSAN Datastore) for compute and management workloads (VMs). The OCVS solution provides high-performance storage that has low latency and is built using the NVMe disks from the DenseIO instances. In the following diagram, you can see a logical representation of the vSAN all-flash construct:

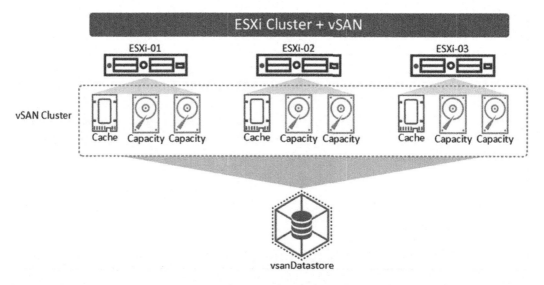

Figure 11.4 – OCVS solution logical diagram

vSAN implements a concept known as fault domains. This term is different from OCI Fault Domain and is referred to in the context of vSAN only. The idea behind the vSAN fault domain is to group the hosts that participate in creating a vSAN datastore. This is a logical grouping, not physical. Using the fault domain construct, vSAN maintains multiple replicas of the same storage objects so that in case of a failure, just one replica is affected.

vSAN storage policies are used to decide on the high availability of individual VMs. Different failures to tolerate policies can be configured with OCVS to decide on the number of failures to tolerate. These storage policies will be configured by OCVS tenants.

OCVS does not support stretched clusters for DR scenarios.

Deploying OCVS

OCVS is deployed as per VMware's recommended best practices; all VMware components are highly distributed across different fault domains within a given OCI region's AD.

To get started with OCVS, a user will need to create a VCN or use an existing VCN to deploy an OCVS cluster.

If you plan to use an existing VCN, Oracle recommends using a VCN that has a /23 or larger IP address CIDR available for running a VMware cluster.

As a part of VMware provisioning, the provisioning cluster will create the following network segments for various VMware functionalities. These disparate network segments ensure that the appropriate traffic segregation is provided:

Network Name	Purpose
Provisioning/Management	An ESXi management interface (vmk0) resides on this subnet.
vSphere	This VLAN is used for managing vSphere components (vCenter, NSXT, and NSX Edge).
vMotion	This VLAN is used for vMotion (VMware migration tool) of the management and customer workload components.
vSAN	This VLAN is used for vSAN (VMware storage) data traffic.
NSX VTEP	This VLAN is used for data plane traffic between ESXi hosts.
NSX Edge VTEP	This VLAN is used for data plane traffic between the ESXi host and NSX Edge.
NSX Edge Uplink 1	This is the VLAN that is being used for network communication between the VMware SDDC cluster and other OCI resources.
NSX Edge Uplink 2	This VLAN is used for future use to deploy public-facing applications to the VMware SDDC.
Replication Network	This VLAN is used for virtual machine cold migration or if you want to do cloning or snapshot migration of your workload VMs.
HCX (optional)	This VLAN is used for HCX network flows.

So far, you have been provided with an overview of the OCVS solution and the components that comprise it. In the next section, we'll deploy an OCVS cluster.

Deploying an OCVS cluster

Deploying an OCVS cluster is done in two parts. First, we must deploy the cluster, and then, we must deploy a Windows host on the same VCN to access the cluster. First, let's learn how to deploy a cluster:

1. Sign into the OCI console.
2. Open the navigation menu, select **Hybrid**, and then **VMware Solution**.
3. Click on **Create SDDC**.
4. Provide an **SDDC Name**.

5. Select which compartment you want to place this cluster on.

6. You can **Enable HCX (default option)**. **Hybrid Cloud Extension** (HCX) hides the complexity of moving applications between on-premise and OCI. It is a plugin that will be installed once you select it. However, you cannot add HCX once you've created the SDDC.

7. If you've selected HCX, then you must select the appropriate license type as well. The **Advanced HCX** license is suitable for a smaller number of workload migrations, whereas **Enterprise License** is suitable for a higher number of application migrations.

8. Select **vSphere version**. At the time of writing, OCI allows you to deploy vSphere 7.0 update 2, 6.7 update 3, and 6.5 update 3.

9. Choose **Pricing Interval Commitment**. In OCI, there are four different types of commits. You can see some sample output in the following screenshot:

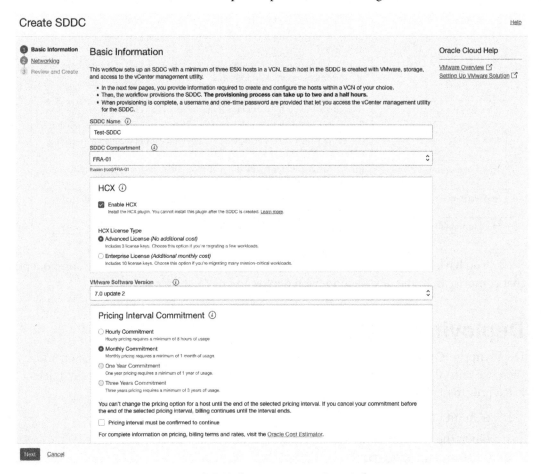

Figure 11.5 – OCVS cluster creation – Basic Information

10. Select the number of ESXi nodes that you want to deploy. The minimum number of nodes is 3.

11. Provide a **name prefix**.

12. Provide an **SSH key**. You will need this to SSH to the ESXi node, in case you want to do some troubleshooting.

13. Choose **Availability Domain** from the drop-down menu and click on **Next**. The following screenshot shows some sample output:

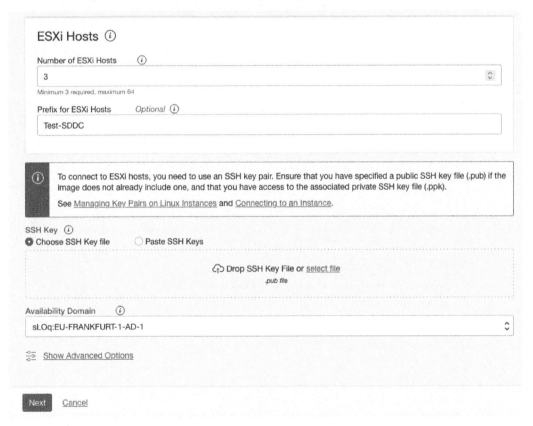

Figure 11.6 – OCVS cluster creation – Basic Information continued

14. The **Networking selection** section is crucial for OCVS cluster deployment. First of all, choose a VCN that will host this SDDC cluster. As a rule of thumb, you need to have at least a /21 subnet for this VCN if you are deploying vSphere 7.x, or a /22 subnet for this VCN if you are going to deploy vSphere 6.x.

OCI will chunk the VCN subnet into multiple /25 segments for the logical segment, which you learned about in the *Deploying OCVS* section. For vSphere 7.x, OCI will create nine segments, while for vSphere 6.x, OCI will create seven segments.

OCI recommends that you let the workflow create the new subnet and VLANs. However, you can use your existing subnet and VLANs if you have pre-created those.

15. In the **SDDC Networks** section, provide a /22 since we have chosen vSphere 6.7. Once you've typed in the subnet, it will validate on the fly. If the provided subnet is available, then you will see **This CIDR block is available**.

16. You will notice that the workflow is also looking for a **NAT gateway** since we selected HCX on the first screen. If there is an existing gateway connected to the same VCN, then the workflow will use it; otherwise, it will create one. This NAT gateway is required for HCX license activation, updates, and internet connectivity. You can see an example output in the following screenshot:

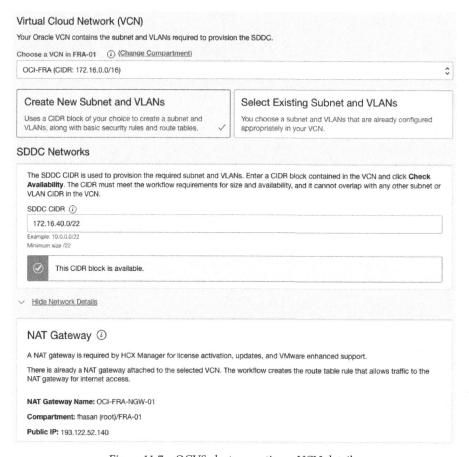

Figure 11.7 – OCVS cluster creation – VCN details

17. At this point, you will see that OCI has populated the **Subnet** and **VLANs** information.

    The last thing that you need to provide (although it is optional) is the logical network segment that the workload will be connected to using an NSX logical switch. A minimum of /30 is required. You can see an example output in the following screenshot:

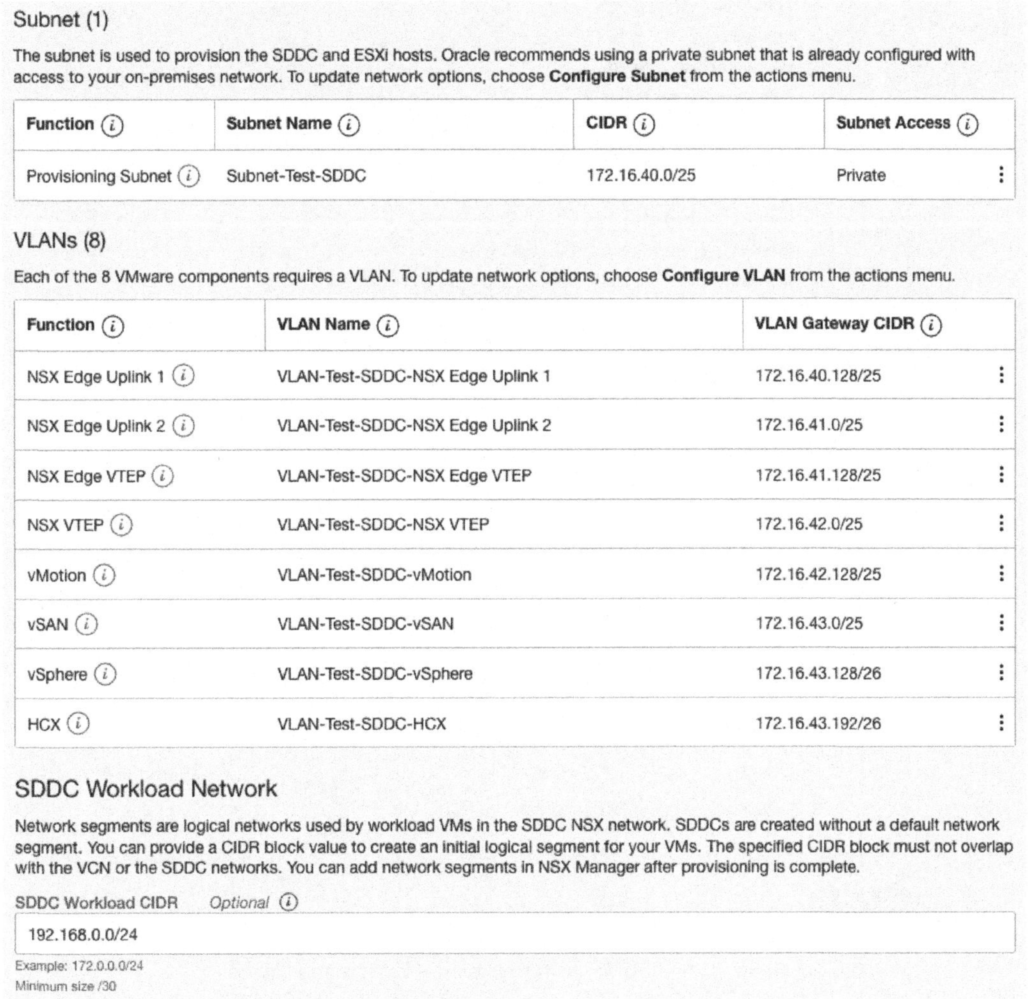

Subnet (1)

The subnet is used to provision the SDDC and ESXi hosts. Oracle recommends using a private subnet that is already configured with access to your on-premises network. To update network options, choose **Configure Subnet** from the actions menu.

Function ⓘ	Subnet Name ⓘ	CIDR ⓘ	Subnet Access ⓘ	
Provisioning Subnet ⓘ	Subnet-Test-SDDC	172.16.40.0/25	Private	⋮

VLANs (8)

Each of the 8 VMware components requires a VLAN. To update network options, choose **Configure VLAN** from the actions menu.

Function ⓘ	VLAN Name ⓘ	VLAN Gateway CIDR ⓘ	
NSX Edge Uplink 1 ⓘ	VLAN-Test-SDDC-NSX Edge Uplink 1	172.16.40.128/25	⋮
NSX Edge Uplink 2 ⓘ	VLAN-Test-SDDC-NSX Edge Uplink 2	172.16.41.0/25	⋮
NSX Edge VTEP ⓘ	VLAN-Test-SDDC-NSX Edge VTEP	172.16.41.128/25	⋮
NSX VTEP ⓘ	VLAN-Test-SDDC-NSX VTEP	172.16.42.0/25	⋮
vMotion ⓘ	VLAN-Test-SDDC-vMotion	172.16.42.128/25	⋮
vSAN ⓘ	VLAN-Test-SDDC-vSAN	172.16.43.0/25	⋮
vSphere ⓘ	VLAN-Test-SDDC-vSphere	172.16.43.128/26	⋮
HCX ⓘ	VLAN-Test-SDDC-HCX	172.16.43.192/26	⋮

SDDC Workload Network

Network segments are logical networks used by workload VMs in the SDDC NSX network. SDDCs are created without a default network segment. You can provide a CIDR block value to create an initial logical segment for your VMs. The specified CIDR block must not overlap with the VCN or the SDDC networks. You can add network segments in NSX Manager after provisioning is complete.

SDDC Workload CIDR   Optional ⓘ

192.168.0.0/24

Example: 172.0.0.0/24
Minimum size /30

Figure 11.8 – OCVS cluster creation – Subnet and VLAN details

18. Click on **Next**.

19. Review and edit this information from this screen if you need to.

20. Click on **Create SDDC**. This should look as follows:

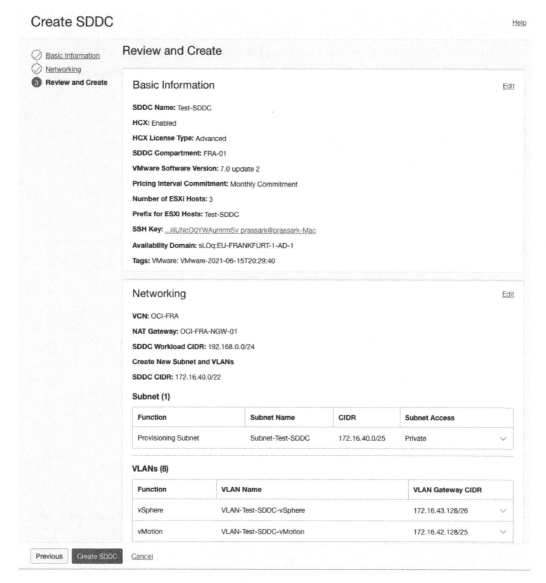

Figure 11.9 – OCVS cluster creation – Review and Create

21. It takes a considerable amount of time to finish deploying the SDDC cluster. Once done, you can go to the **Software-Defined Data Center Details** screen and check the status of this. You can also use this page to get the vCenter and NSX Manager login information, as well as the URL.

So far, you have learned how to create a cluster. You may have noticed that OCI has provided a neat workflow for hiding a lot of the complexity surrounding it. In the next section, we will show you how to access the SDDC cluster. You will also learn how to access vCenter Server and NSX Manager.

Accessing an OCVS cluster

Accessing an OCVS cluster requires a Windows host on the same subnet where you deployed the SDDC cluster. Let's create one and then use it to connect to the OCVS cluster.

Let's create a standard OCI compute instance:

1. Sign into the OCI console.

2. Open the navigation menu, select **Compute**, and then select **Instances**.

3. Click **Create Instance**.

4. Provide a **Name** and select a **Compartment** where you want to deploy it.

5. In the **Availability Domain** section of the **Configure placement and hardware** section, choose where you want to place the AD. Additionally, you can click on the **Choose a Fault Domain for this Instance** checkbox and select a **Fault Domain** from the drop-down menu.

6. Select **Windows** from the **Image** page. Click on **Select Image**.

7. In the **Shape** section, by default, the **VM.Standard.E4.Flex** shape type will be selected, which has 1 core OCPU, 16 GB memory, and 1 Gbps network bandwidth shape. You can see an example of this in the following screenshot:

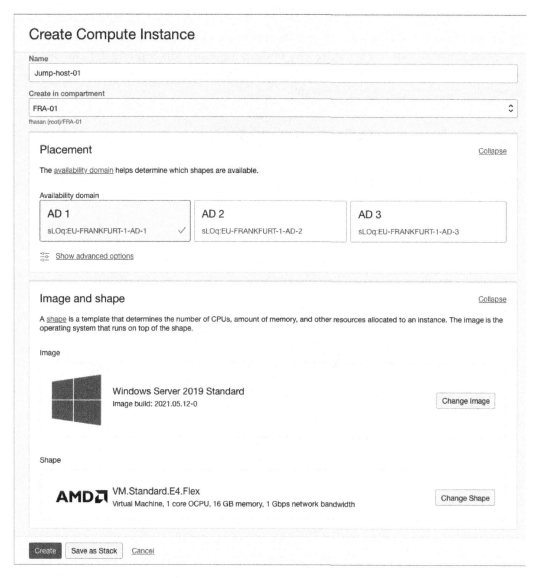

Figure 11.10 – Instance image selection

8. In the **Configure Networking** section, choose the VCN and the subnet that you want to connect this instance to.

9. Select the **Assign a Public IP Address** radio button so that you have access to this instance over the public internet. You can see an example of this in the following screenshot:

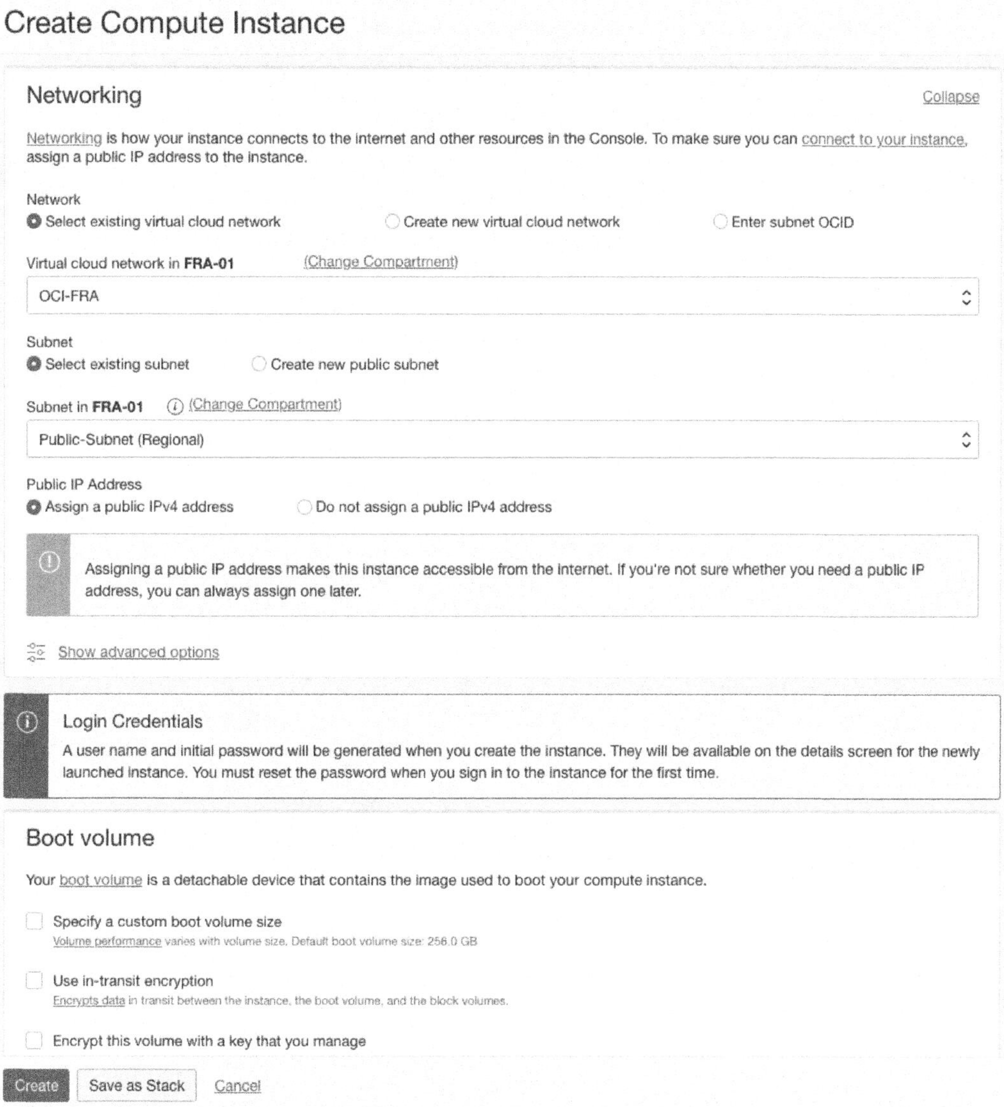

Create Compute Instance

Networking   Collapse

Networking is how your instance connects to the internet and other resources in the Console. To make sure you can connect to your instance, assign a public IP address to the instance.

Network
● Select existing virtual cloud network   ○ Create new virtual cloud network   ○ Enter subnet OCID

Virtual cloud network in **FRA-01**   (Change Compartment)

OCI-FRA	⌄

Subnet
● Select existing subnet   ○ Create new public subnet

Subnet in **FRA-01**   (i) (Change Compartment)

Public-Subnet (Regional)	⌄

Public IP Address
● Assign a public IPv4 address   ○ Do not assign a public IPv4 address

> (!) Assigning a public IP address makes this instance accessible from the internet. If you're not sure whether you need a public IP address, you can always assign one later.

≡ Show advanced options

> (i) **Login Credentials**
> A user name and initial password will be generated when you create the instance. They will be available on the details screen for the newly launched instance. You must reset the password when you sign in to the instance for the first time.

Boot volume

Your boot volume is a detachable device that contains the image used to boot your compute instance.

☐ Specify a custom boot volume size
Volume performance varies with volume size. Default boot volume size: 256.0 GB

☐ Use in-transit encryption
Encrypts data in transit between the instance, the boot volume, and the block volumes.

☐ Encrypt this volume with a key that you manage

[Create] [Save as Stack] Cancel

Figure 11.11 – Create Compute Instance wizard – Networking section

10. Optionally, you can **Specify a custom boot volume size**. While creating this instance, you can choose the default boot volume size of this instance or a custom boot volume size up to 32 TB.

If you are provisioning a Linux image-based instance, then you must set your custom boot volume size so that it's more than its default volume size, which is 50 GB. If you want to create an instance based on Windows operating system images, then the same rule applies; that is, you must set the custom boot volume size so that it's more than the default boot volume size, which is 256 GB.

The reason behind setting up this default boot volume size is so that you have enough space for Windows patches and a page file.

11. Optionally, you can specify **Use in-transit encryption**. In-transit encryption allows you to encrypt the volume when it's being created.

12. Optionally, you can specify **Encrypt this volume with a key that you manage**.

13. Click on **Create**.

14. Once it is in a **Running** state, you must copy the instance's public IP address and connect to it. You will get the initial password from this page as well. An example of this can be seen in the following screenshot:

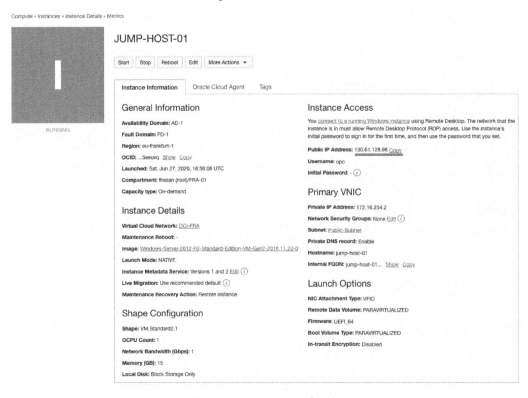

Figure 11.12 – Instance details

15. When you get the instance up and running, use your favorite RDP client to log into it.

16. Once you've logged into the Windows host, you need to open a browser and paste the URL of the vCenter Server that you saved from the SDDC details page. You will have also saved the initial credentials for both vCenter and NSX Manager.

17. Paste in your **vCenter Server URL** and press *Enter*.

18. Click on **Launch vSphere Client (HTML5)**, as shown in the following screenshot:

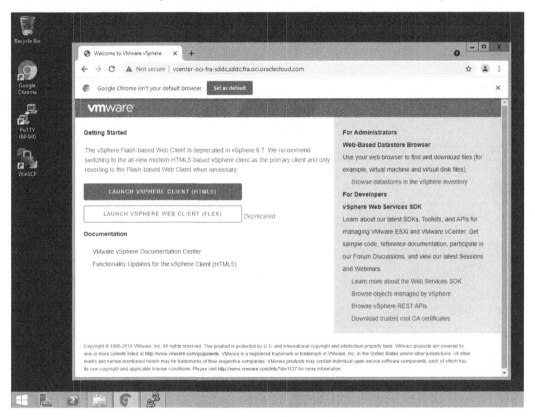

Figure 11.13 – vSphere client

19. Provide the necessary credentials and click **Login**.

20. You will be logged into vCenter Server, as shown in the following screenshot:

Figure 11.14 – vCenter Server

21. Follow the same procedure for NSX Manager as well. When you log into NSX Manager, you will see the following screen:

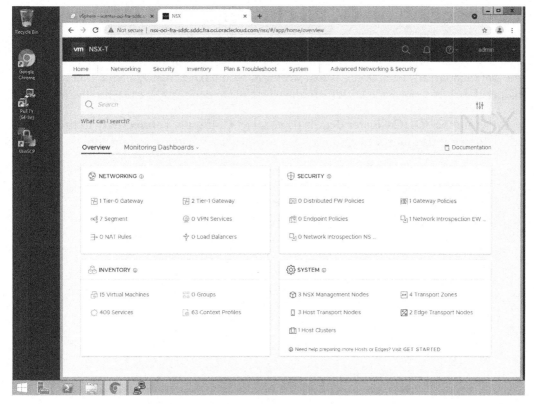

Figure 11.15 – NSX manager

In this section, you learned how to access an SDDC cluster by deploying a Windows host onto the same VCN. In the next section, we will show you how to connect your SDDC to the internet using the workflow that OCI provides.

Connecting an OCVS cluster to the internet

Connecting an OCVS cluster to the internet is very straightforward and can be done using a simple workflow. If you selected the HCX option while deploying the cluster, then half of the work has already been done, as that workflow would have created a NAT Gateway, if one hadn't already been provided. Let's run the workflow to connect the cluster to the internet:

1. From the **SDDC Cluster details** page, select **Configure connectivity to the internet through NAT gateway**, as shown in the following screenshot:

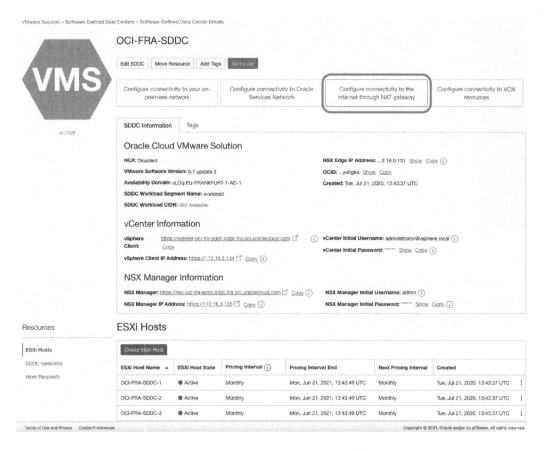

Figure 11.16 – Internet connectivity workflow

2. Since a NAT gateway has already been provided, this workflow will use it.

3. It will add a route rule to the Route Table entry for the NSD Edge Uplink 1 VLAN subnet. Basically, it will allow all the internal traffic to go out but via the NAT gateway.

4. It will also add an allow any-any egress rule to the NSX Edge uplink VLAN's network security group, as shown in the following screenshot:

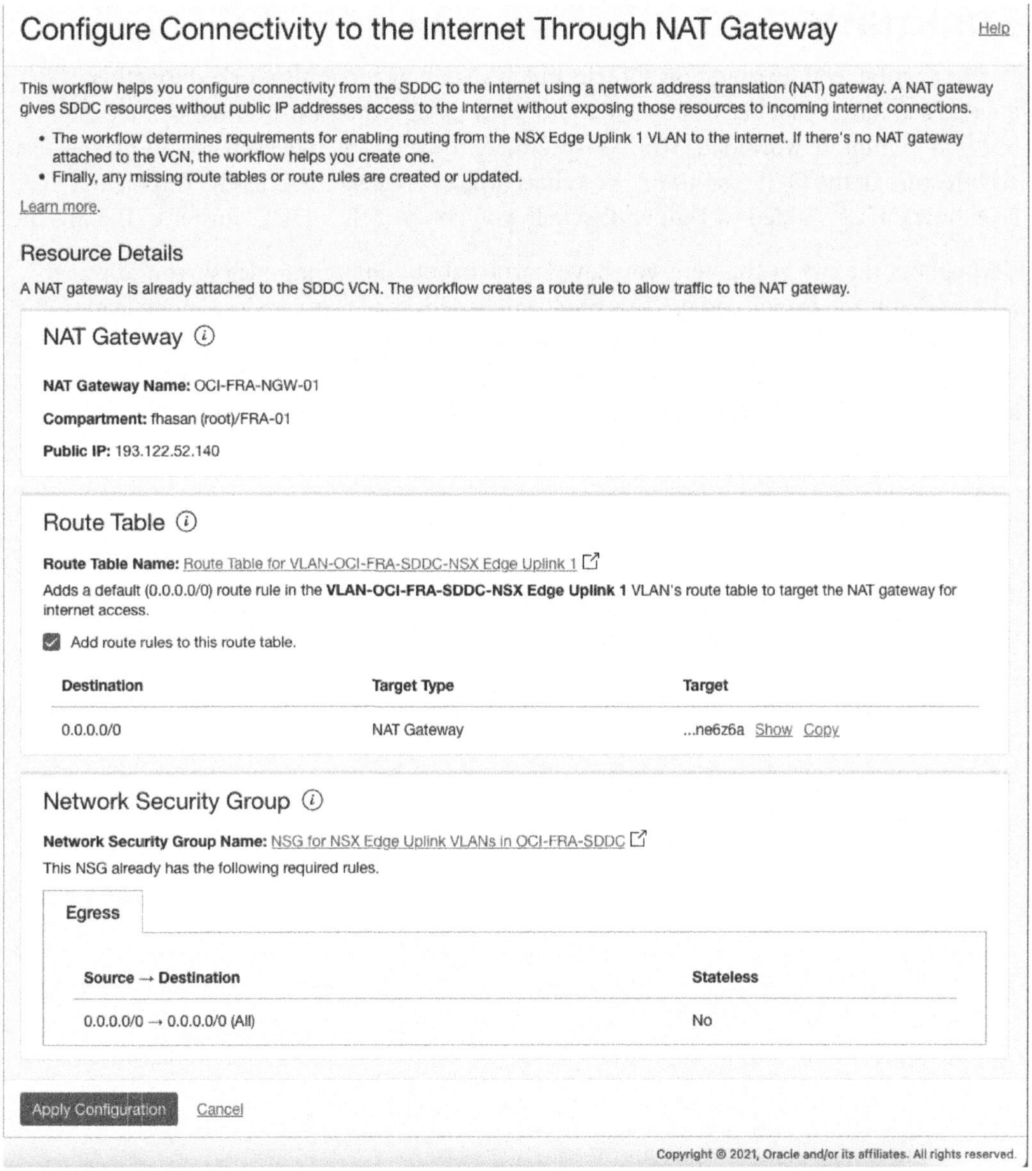

Configure Connectivity to the Internet Through NAT Gateway   Help

This workflow helps you configure connectivity from the SDDC to the internet using a network address translation (NAT) gateway. A NAT gateway gives SDDC resources without public IP addresses access to the internet without exposing those resources to incoming internet connections.

- The workflow determines requirements for enabling routing from the NSX Edge Uplink 1 VLAN to the internet. If there's no NAT gateway attached to the VCN, the workflow helps you create one.
- Finally, any missing route tables or route rules are created or updated.

Learn more.

Resource Details

A NAT gateway is already attached to the SDDC VCN. The workflow creates a route rule to allow traffic to the NAT gateway.

NAT Gateway ⓘ

NAT Gateway Name: OCI-FRA-NGW-01

Compartment: fhasan (root)/FRA-01

Public IP: 193.122.52.140

Route Table ⓘ

Route Table Name: Route Table for VLAN-OCI-FRA-SDDC-NSX Edge Uplink 1 ☐

Adds a default (0.0.0.0/0) route rule in the **VLAN-OCI-FRA-SDDC-NSX Edge Uplink 1** VLAN's route table to target the NAT gateway for internet access.

☑ Add route rules to this route table.

Destination	Target Type	Target
0.0.0.0/0	NAT Gateway	...ne6z6a Show Copy

Network Security Group ⓘ

Network Security Group Name: NSG for NSX Edge Uplink VLANs in OCI-FRA-SDDC ☐

This NSG already has the following required rules.

Egress

Source → Destination	Stateless
0.0.0.0/0 → 0.0.0.0/0 (All)	No

Apply Configuration   Cancel

Figure 11.17 – The Configure Connectivity to the Internet Through NAT Gateway page

5. Click on **Apply Configuration**.

6. Click on **Close**.

Your SDDC cluster now has access to the internet, which means you can use the HCX plugin to activate licenses and more!

Summary

In this chapter, you learned how Oracle and VMware have jointly worked together and created a solution that customers use to not only extend their on-premises data centers, but also to migrate workloads from on-premises to OCI. You have learned about the basic architecture of the OCVS solution, as well as how to create and access it. You have also seen how OCI-provided workflows can help you connect the SDDC cluster to the internet.

Throughout the last 11 chapters, you have learned about different topics surrounding OCI, and we thank you for joining us. This book will benefit you if you are looking to learn Oracle Cloud from an Architect's perspective and can easily uplift your career as an Oracle Cloud Architect. This book will also certainly help you prepare for your Oracle Cloud certifications, such as Oracle Cloud Infrastructure Architect Associate or Architect Professional.

Packt>

Other Books You May Enjoy

If you enjoyed this book, you may be interested in these other books by Packt:

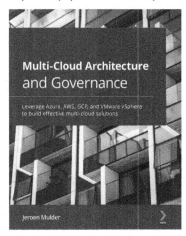

Multi-Cloud Architecture and Governance

Jeroen Mulder

ISBN: 978-1-80020-319-8

- Get to grips with the core functions of multiple cloud platforms

- Deploy, automate, and secure different cloud solutions

- Design network strategy and get to grips with identity and access management for multi-cloud

- Design a landing zone spanning multiple cloud platforms

- Use automation, monitoring, and management tools for multi-cloud

- Understand multi-cloud management with the principles of BaseOps, FinOps, SecOps, and DevOps

- Define multi-cloud security policies and use cloud security tools

- Test, integrate, deploy, and release using multi-cloud CI/CD pipelines

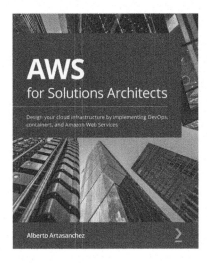

AWS for Solutions Architects

Alberto Artasanchez

ISBN: 978-1-78953-923-3

- Rationalize the selection of AWS as the right cloud provider for your organization
- Choose the most appropriate service from AWS for a particular use case or project
- Implement change and operations management
- Find out the right resource type and size to balance performance and efficiency
- Discover how to mitigate risk and enforce security, authentication, and authorization
- Identify common business scenarios and select the right reference architectures for them

Packt is searching for authors like you

If you're interested in becoming an author for Packt, please visit `authors.packtpub.com` and apply today. We have worked with thousands of developers and tech professionals, just like you, to help them share their insight with the global tech community. You can make a general application, apply for a specific hot topic that we are recruiting an author for, or submit your own idea.

Share Your Thoughts

Now you've finished *Oracle Cloud Infrastructure for Solutions Architects*, we'd love to hear your thoughts! Scan the QR code below to go straight to the Amazon review page for this book and share your feedback or leave a review on the site that you purchased it from.

https://packt.link/r/1800566468

Your review is important to us and the tech community and will help us make sure we're delivering excellent quality content.

Index

A

V

W

Made in United States
North Haven, CT
25 October 2022

25923044R00187